LET'S GET IT ON!

The Making of MMA
and Its Ultimate Referee

LET'S GET IT ON!

The Making of MMA and Its Ultimate Referee

"BIG" JOHN McCARTHY

with Loretta Hunt

MEDALLION
P R E S S

Medallion Press, Inc.

Printed in USA

Published 2011 by Medallion Press, Inc.

The MEDALLION PRESS LOGO
is a registered trademark of Medallion Press, Inc.

Copyright © 2011 by John McCarthy with Loretta Hunt
Cover design by James Tampa
Cover photography by Eric Curtis
Back cover fighters: Alan Shook, David Weber
Edited by Emily Steele
Interior photos courtesy of John McCarthy and Loretta Hunt

Ultimate Fighting Championship®, the titles and trade names of all Ultimate Fighting Championship televised and live programming, talent names, images, likenesses, slogans, and moves, and all Ultimate Fighting Championship logos and registered trademarks are the property of Ultimate Fighting Championship.

Images on color insert #2, page 2 courtesy of MAD # 348 © 1996 E.C. Publications, Inc. Used with Permission.

Typeset in Adobe Garamond Pro
Printed in the United States of America

Cataloging-in-Publication Data is on file with the Library of Congress.

10 9 8 7 6 5 4 3 2 1
First Edition

DEDICATION

To my dad, who always has been and always will be my hero. You have shown me from the beginning what a real man is and have lived your life with honor, integrity, and humility. You are a force of nature.

To my mom, who was always there for me while I was growing up. You patched me up and got me back into whatever I was doing at the time. You were at not only every game I played but just about every practice too. Thank you for everything. I love you.

To my children, Ron, Britney, and John. I know I was far from perfect, but I was always trying. I am sorry that I sometimes missed things I should have been at because of MMA. I made some bad choices, and I apologize.

To Rorion and Royce. Thank you for what you did. You inspired me and made me a believer. Your father, Helio, is the creator of MMA, and you both are responsible for putting it on the map.

To Bob Meyrowitz. Thank you for believing in MMA and me. You kept the sport alive when everyone was trying to kill it. Everyone who loves MMA owes you a thanks.

To Lorenzo, Frank, and Dana. Thank you for saving the sport of MMA. When you came in, things were looking rather bleak. I know it did not turn around overnight, but through your hard work and vision, you made it happen.

Last and certainly not least, I have to talk about Elaine. Thanks would not nearly cover what you have meant to me and how you have made my life complete. You have been there since the beginning and have put up with all of the craziness that has surrounded my life. I could not have asked for a greater partner in life. You have made the ride special, and I will always love you.

I am the last of a dying breed. I talk, walk, dress, and act the way I want in a world where few others do. I will tell you the truth, even if you don't like it. Many of you don't like me, are even afraid of me because I tell it like it is and you don't like to hear it. I am always there for my friends and will tell them the truth even if they don't like it, because that is what a friend does. Strength and Honor is my bloodline. I take the lead, back my friends, and will stand with them no matter if it is an army standing in front of us. I will fight until the end. Death before Dishonor is our motto. I am a man of Honor.

—Nick Castiglia, for his sensei Pat Cooligan

CONTENTS

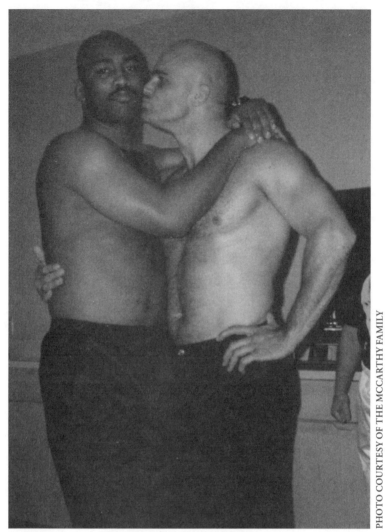

Bas having a "moment" with Maurice Smith

Bas is pointing out who's number one. Really.

FOREWORD

I really like the book *The Alchemist* by Paulo Coelho. In that book, the author talks about omens: things or people that you meet for a reason and that, if you listen, will help you to find what you want in life.

John McCarthy has crossed paths with many omens in his lifetime and often *listened*.

His first omen was his father, a tough, no-nonsense Los Angeles police officer and Medal of Valor winner credited with originating the modern-day Special Weapons and Tactics (SWAT) program still used to this day. Both his mom and dad loved sports, and his father once told John that if a sport had no contact, he wouldn't consider it a sport. I love that advice.

Following in his father's footsteps, John was always interested in learning how to keep himself and his fellow officers safe. He was ahead of his time, because when everybody still believed that stand-up fighting, like karate, tae kwon do, boxing, or Thai boxing, was the most effective type of martial art, John already knew he could take guys down and simply sit on them. Then it was pretty much over for them.

So when, after the Los Angeles Riots, the LAPD was looking for the best ways to subdue a person, they invited a plethora (I had to use this word, being "El Guapo" and all) of martial artists to the table. When John challenged some of the teachings of the other instructors in real-life police settings, he grabbed the attention of Rorion, who invited John to train at the Gracie Academy. You see? Rorion Gracie was John's omen that day because that was the person who, a year later, started the UFC.

Rorion saw in John the qualities that we all see. John was imposing because he was big and strong but, most important, he had great insight and knowledge of skills and was a decision maker. After UFC 1, Rorion asked John if he wanted to referee at UFC 2, a show John wanted to fight in himself. Nobody knows all this stuff that happened when MMA became important, but guess who was right there from the beginning? That's right: John!

A month and a half before the UFC held its first show on November 12, 1993, I started fighting in Japan for the organization Pancrase. What I did was called free fighting, while the UFC called its fighting No Holds Barred. We had rules and were wearing shoes plus shin protection, but it was fighting. And since I was right there when it all started, I always thought I knew a lot about what happened in MMA from its birth. After reading this book, I guess I was wrong.

For instance, I thought the phrase "intelligently defending oneself" was something made up in the last ten years with all of the newer rules. Nope. John came up with that after UFC 2, as he did many of the sport's rules still used to this day. (Sound familiar?) There are so many more cool facts that I jotted down to share with you here, but I realized I'd ruin all of the surprises!

I also always believed I was so cool for coming up with a good way to explain to the nonbelievers that MMA is not a violent sport. I always said MMA is a combination of four Olympic sports and while Olympians train solely for *one* sport, a mixed martial artist has to know them all. It turns out that John was years ahead of me, telling that same story, because he's the one who actually made it up. I probably just heard it from him and stole it.

Reading the book, I was shocked to see the similarities John and I had growing up. We were both kids who got bullied early on in life, were called "four eyes," had asthma, and because of that were in the water a lot. We both loved sports, watched the same movie that changed our lives, like to push things to the limit, and like to make things perfect. Heck, even our daughters were born on the exact same day and year! When I read about all these similarities, I even began to wonder if I was an omen for John in writing this foreword, or is he the omen for me?

Because we have so much in common, it's not surprising to me now that we all clicked when I met John and Elaine for the first time at UFC Japan in 1997. We've been friends ever since, and I've always had and still have, of course, great respect for John. If you need somebody to be there for you, that's John. I actually asked him one time for advice in the middle of a fight because I got worried about something. Thank God he gave me good advice! (You will read what I mean later.)

I'm not the only one who respects John. I know the fans, promoters, managers, cornermen, cutmen, athletic commissions, and most important, *all of the fighters*, respect him tremendously as well.

Luckily for us fighters, John's omens directed him to the cage, where he's kept us safe for nearly twenty years. I know I always felt safe when John was in the cage with me. I think you should have that feeling with every referee.

And when the godfather of mixed martial arts, Helio Gracie, tells you, and I quote, "Everything that I have done with jiu-jitsu, you have done with the sport. You are the best there ever was or ever will be. I am proud of who you are and what you have done," you know you really are the best at what you do.

Godspeed, John, up to your next omen. "Let's get it on!"

—Bas Rutten

P.S. I might not have come up with the "four Olympic sports" explanation, but I *did* come up with the word "Livershot." Party on!

Christmas with my mom and sister: probably the only picture where I can say I look kind of cute

Fishing with my best friend, Chris Lingwall, who caught a cool sting-ray while I got a lousy crab

SON OF THE GUN

Tiger father begets tiger son.

—Chinese proverb

His eyes tell me he's had enough. Not his midsection, bruised and tenderized by a round of short, sobering body shots and unmerciful knees. Not his legs, discolored and swollen from a steady attack of low kicks from his opponent. Not his broken nose or forehead, sliced open and dripping red from a perfectly placed elbow shot.

It's his eyes. I look into the fighter's eyes, and they tell me he's scared. He doesn't know how to get out of this predicament, but he continues because that's what a fighter does.

It's in this moment that I know the fight is over. I know he won't come back. This is when what I do counts most.

I am a mixed martial arts referee. The first of my kind in the United States, I started with the Ultimate Fighting Championship in 1994. Before MMA was even considered a sport, back when it was called No Holds Barred and Ultimate Fighting, I officiated the fights. A one-off pay-per-view spectacle evolved over eighteen years into something followed and cherished by millions of die-hard fans worldwide, and I'm lucky to be able to say I was a part of it.

In its simplest definition, mixed martial arts is the execution of multiple combat sports' disciplines with the goal of knocking out, submitting, or outscoring an opponent before he does it to you. Fighters jab like boxers, kick like kickboxers, throw knees and elbows like muay Thai stylists, take down opponents like wrestlers, and contort and trap appendages in chokes and holds like jiu-jitsu practitioners. They can perform one or all of these elements in a matter of seconds to win, which makes the sport excitingly unpredictable. A bout can stay on the feet or go to the mat or even dabble in a little of both, wherever the greater athlete or tactician chooses to take it.

There are no guarantees in MMA other than that no two fights ever look the same. An experienced champion can get knocked out by an underdog's single punch. An overwhelming favorite can make a mistake, and his opponent will capitalize.

For me, MMA is competition. There's nothing like witnessing two well-trained fighters engaged in battle. There's an artistry to it. Like a choreographed ballet, when it's done right, with two well-matched partners, it's beautiful. It's poetry in motion, and I can't take my eyes off it. It's my sport.

Some people don't understand MMA. They say it's dangerous, brutal, and barbaric. They don't understand the motivation because they personally fear the thought of being in a fight, the rush of adrenaline that will make them shake uncontrollably, the possibility of pain or being dominated with no way to end it.

My job is to stop the competition at just the right moment, in that split second when a fighter becomes overwhelmed and can no longer protect himself. It can happen in the blink of an eye, with one punch, kick, tug, or squeeze. Sometimes I've called a fight right on the money. Other times I've missed that crucial moment, the one that decides whether a fighter will walk out of the cage on his own accord.

Thankfully, my life prepared me for these moments. I grew up around violence and made not one but two careers out of controlling it.

As a twenty-two-year LAPD veteran, I've stared down the barrel of a gun thinking my next move could either save or destroy a life. In situations like these, I've learned to think quickly. I push aside the nerves and distractions and just act.

It's the same in mixed martial arts. Making fast, clean decisions is paramount, and not everyone is cut out for that. It takes a certain temperament, an ability to stay focused in pressure-filled situations.

How did I learn this? I think it has everything to do with Ron McCarthy, my dad, the man who made me who I am. Ever since I can remember, he's been my idol. Through my young eyes, he was my Incredible Hulk, Bruce Lee, Spider-Man, and "Smokin'" Joe Frazier all rolled into one. He's the most fearless man I know, and he taught me how to go after life and live on my own terms.

That's how he did it from the hardest of beginnings. He was born in Oregon in 1937 and raised in Winslow, Arizona. Far from the quaint scene of Americana described in the Eagles song "Take It Easy," the dust bowl town greets visitors with a big "Welcome to Winslow" sign and then, after what feels like five feet, sends them off with a "Thank You for Visiting." Apparently those famous lyrics didn't apply to my dad either. His childhood was far from easy.

His father, my grandfather Joseph McCarthy, had a wife and

five kids, whom he gave up to be with the woman who gave birth to his son, my dad. Supposedly she was very beautiful and had a penchant for marrying rich men, which my grandfather, the owner of a small-town car dealership, certainly was not. She soon left my grandfather, who returned to his wife and five kids with his two-year-old in tow.

Be it by accident or suicide, my grandfather killed himself, I'm told, while cleaning a gun that went off and shot him in the stomach.

My grandfather's wife cared for my dad until his biological mother came back for him when he was two and a half. The McCarthy family tried to stop the separation, and afterward they searched for him for years.

When my dad was four years old, his mother abandoned him in a local orphanage and nuns raised him for the next few years, until his maternal grandmother took him in to her Arizona home. He lived with her until he was eleven, when his grandmother died.

His mother returned to take him to Oregon, where she was getting remarried. Along with a new father, he now also had a new older stepbrother, Jack, who would hold him down and spit in his face or throw darts into his back.

My dad, miserable in his new home, ran away at age thirteen to manage on his own in Arizona, living in a boxcar in a local railroad yard and working at a gas station. He wouldn't see his mother for the next fifteen years.

To this day, I've never met my grandmother. I don't even know her name and have never asked for it. The last time I heard, she'd been married something like seventeen times. I wouldn't recognize her if I bumped into her on the street.

On his own, my dad couldn't work to support himself and

go to school at the same time, so he dropped out until he met the Lacey family. When a classmate named Terry Lacey told his dad, Tom, about my dad's predicament, Tom allowed my dad to live with them on two conditions: my dad had to keep going to school and get good grades, and he had to play sports. The Lacey family's generosity allowed my dad the opportunity to go back for his junior and senior years.

Though he was wiry, my dad was nimble and could play football positions usually reserved for the bigger guys, including defensive end and noseguard. He'd prove himself on the basketball court as well. In both football and basketball, he earned all-state honors.

While Tom's son, Terry, was an all-state quarterback and earned a scholarship to Notre Dame, my dad won a scholarship to a local college. I suspect my dad was afraid he wasn't good enough to go to college, however, because he didn't follow through with it. After graduation, he moved right out of the Lacey's house. Maybe his overwhelming sense of independence got the better of him.

Hard as nails and not afraid to prove it, my dad decided to enlist with the Marines. When he arrived at the row of recruiting offices, an officer said, "Could you come back tomorrow to sign the paperwork?"

My dad agreed and, having nowhere else to go, slept on a park bench outside all night.

The next morning, a Navy recruiter greeted him. When he learned what my dad was doing, he said, "The Marines representative isn't coming in today."

Eyes bleary and stomach rumbling, my dad signed with the Navy instead. The Marines recruiter walked in shortly after with a stunned look on his face.

The military led my dad to my mom, Charlotte Gold, whom he met while he was stationed in Long Beach, California. Two years later, they married. My sister, Sheri, was born a year and a half after that. On October 12, 1962, I came into the world.

For the first few years of my life, my family settled in Lakewood, California. My father served in the Navy four years and then worked for the local gas company while he tested for a position with the Los Angeles Police Department.

Not only did he get a spot with the LAPD, but he went on to build one of the most distinguished careers in law enforcement. As he rose to the rank of sergeant II over the next twenty-five years, he earned the Medal of Valor for his actions in the 1974 shoot-out with the Symbionese Liberation Army; originated the modern-day Special Weapons and Tactics (SWAT) Unit; protected dignitaries and Presidents Ford, Carter, Reagan, and Bush Sr.; and oversaw the terrorist-related precautions and response team during the 1984 Summer Olympics in Los Angeles.

Given so little in life, my dad accomplished much more than many ever do. Having to fight for everything, he learned to protect himself and to make decisions on his own. Right or wrong, my dad learned early on that fighting was a way to establish himself. He let people know he wasn't somebody to be messed with, and word traveled fast. Violence was a means to get what he needed or to keep what he had, and I can understand his attraction to it.

One of the most impressive things to me about my dad is that he never complained about his childhood. In fact, he's told me many times it was good for him. He doesn't dwell on the past. As I've grown into an adult, with a wife and three children of my own, I've learned to understand the patience and wisdom it takes to not allow past hardships to seep into your everyday life. Despite the difficult relationships he endured in his childhood, my dad was always affectionate toward his kids, giving hugs and kisses and telling us he loved us.

He's also always been strict and opinionated. In his mind, there's right and there's wrong. If you're on the right side, no matter what you do, you're okay in his book. If you're on the wrong side, though, you're wrong.

I grew up under this system, and I don't think it was necessarily bad. In fact, as usually happens in families, many of my dad's principles became my own. Just ask my wife and kids: I can be set in my ways. I'm as bullheaded as a Minotaur and as stubborn as an ass most of the rest of the time. I have a deep sense of justice, so it's no wonder I eventually followed in my dad's footsteps and became a police officer.

I learned early from my dad that if somebody did something to me, I didn't cry or whine about it; I did something back. When I turned three, my parents bought me a shiny gold bike with training wheels. Wanting to be like all the big kids on my block, I asked my parents to take the training wheels off. My mom spent the day watching me crash, and by sunset I could ride that bike.

When my dad came home from work, he pulled his Volkswagen into the driveway. When he saw I could balance myself on the bike, he was so excited he nearly leapt out of the car while it was still moving.

Things took a turn when Chris, the six-year-old bully on our block, came by. Like any kid, when he saw me pedaling my bike, he wanted to ride it. When no one else was around, he pushed me off and slid onto the vinyl seat, then glided away as if that golden beauty had been his all along.

Wiping the tears from my cheeks, I walked into the garage, where my dad was tidying up the shelves. Between frantic breaths and gulps, I pleaded my case.

Now remember, my dad wasn't the type to say, "Let's go talk to his mommy and daddy." No, he told me plainly, "Go hurt him, and he won't take the bike again." Grabbing a yellow Wiffle Ball bat, he led me outside and told me what to do.

Following his instructions, I crouched behind the cool cinder-block wall, bat at the ready in my tiny, shaking hands.

"When he rides by, you hit him with it," my dad said, then went back to his tinkering in the garage.

Along came Chris, unaware that he was about to reenact a scene from *Tom and Jerry* with me. As the nose of my bike and the kid's smirking face appeared from behind the wall, I swung with all my might. *Clunk!* The bat made contact and clotheslined Chris right off the back. His head banged on the street, knocking the wind out of him. I'd never heard such wailing.

I picked up my bike, climbed on, and didn't stop to watch Chris run back to his house.

I'd learned one thing. The bat was my justice.

My dad's job was no ordinary nine-to-five. Most officers were assigned to a division, or precinct, under the four bureaus—West, South, Central, or Valley. Within those four bureaus, there were eighteen geographic divisions, and each officer was usually assigned to one. My dad was assigned to Metro Division, which worked the entire city and ran the K-9, Equestrian, and SWAT Units, the last of which he played a key role in revitalizing.

My dad's was a high-risk occupation, and there were days I worried about him. One of those days was May 17, 1974. At eleven years old, I watched the live televised events unfold as my dad's team converged on the residence at 1466 East 54th Street, where six members of the Symbionese Liberation Army were holed up and firing shots outside. With every angle change, I searched for my dad, but the TV cameras were in the front. He was in the backyard, where most of the bullets were flying. When he came home the next day, he didn't make a big deal about it at all.

The one day I thought I'd lost my dad came when he told me he'd be up in a helicopter, running training insertions and extractions with the rest of the SWAT team up in Saugus Canyon, about thirty miles north of Los Angeles. That afternoon, the news reported an LAPD helicopter crash in Saugus Canyon and the death of one SWAT member and horrible burn injuries for several more.

My mother, sister, and I anxiously waited in the living room for a phone call or some kind of word from my dad or his department. I was never as relieved at the sight of his unmarked police car as I was that day.

As fate would have it, a high-ranking commander had come up for the training and my dad had given him his seat in the helicopter. The commander was decapitated as the helicopter crashed just over a hill.

My dad raced toward the blaze of twisted metal and saw many of his colleagues on fire. He picked up SWAT member Rick Kelbaugh and placed him in the back of his car to drive him to the nearest hospital.

Rick was in shock. "You gotta cool me off," he mumbled from the backseat.

My dad stopped to search for a hose. When he trickled water over Rick's head, his skin started to roll off like crepe paper. Rick would spend many months in the Sherman Oaks Burn Center.

Sometimes my dad was called away for what seemed like days on end, which made the time we did have together more precious than anything.

There was a five-year span when we had season tickets for the Rams football games held at the Los Angeles Memorial Coliseum. Every home game, my dad and I could be found in our seats near tunnel twelve, aisle twelve, by the end zone. We've kept up our tradition. Today, we still meet and watch the Rose Bowl on New Year's Day every year.

When I was nine, the day before a deep-sea fishing trip with my dad, I broke my collarbone. Outside the school, my friend had been dragging me on my skateboard behind his dirt bike when I missed a turn and slammed into a wall. I didn't want anyone to find out about the accident because I'd need my arms to crank on the lines. I'd be damned if I let a little broken bone stop me.

So I sucked it up and hobbled home, trying not to let on to my mom that something wasn't right. But she noticed I was standing funny, and when she poked and prodded, I couldn't hold back my wincing and tears.

I was sent to the hospital and was put in a brace, but the next day I was with my dad on the Pacific Ocean, happily balancing my rod on the boat's rail and catching my fifteen-fish limit.

When my dad could, he'd bring me along on his job too. Yes, his occupation was taxing, but it also afforded me exciting opportunities.

When SWAT simulated hostage recovery scenarios in the

Universal Studios back lots, I ran the streets that appear in so many Hollywood movies. As I got older, my dad allowed me to try some of the exercises there after his team had left. I rappelled off rooftops and rode on the helicopter's skid at 120 miles per hour over the terrain's hills and dips. I also got to try spy-rigging, latching onto a rope with harnesses and clasps to hang from the bottom of the helicopter in formation with the group. When the helicopter gained enough speed, the rope went horizontal and I'd extend my arms like Superman.

My thrill-seeking tendencies came from my dad, no doubt about it. At forty-eight years old, I've tried almost everything like skydiving, bungee jumping, shark diving, quad riding, dirt biking, and sand railing. Any kind of crazy riding or driving is right up my alley.

Of course, not all of my childhood was extraordinary. Most days were of the normal variety, and I had the usual trials of kid life.

When I was five years old, my family moved up the 60 Freeway to Hacienda Heights, about twenty-five minutes west of Los Angeles. There, I attended Wedgeworth Elementary School, which was about 300 yards from my house, one of a dozen or so identical cookie-cutter models on the block.

My monumental event during this time was getting eyeglasses. I hated them. I enjoyed seeing but not being different.

I was one of the bigger kids in my class, but I wasn't nearly the towering figure people see me as today, which made me a choice candidate for every bully who thought he ruled the school.

Kids can be mean, but they're also not that creative. "Four Eyes" was the name they came up with for me, and there was a stretch of time—maybe from the age of five to eight—when Four Eyes had to defend his honor on the playground, after school, and even on the street outside his own house.

When it came to facing my antagonists, my dad gave me words I would learn to live by. "What you allow people to do, they'll do. If you don't like what's happening, make a stand." There was one stipulation, though. I was allowed to take said stands, which usually included punching people square in the mouth, only if they'd done something to me first. If someone called me a name, he was fair game.

Following this advice didn't always work out. There were older kids who'd clock me and send my glasses flying. Dr. Giordano finally switched me to thick, plastic, horn-rimmed frames. I know, the irony of it all. Luckily, my aim got better fast.

In junior high, I dumped my glasses to make way for sports. On the football field, I would usually tackle any moving blob in the opposite team's colors.[1]

Sports were another way for me to spend time with my dad. Starting at age six or seven, I shot hoops, ran the football, and played catch with him. He often took me to a field near Dodger Stadium, where he played flag football for his division in the LAPD league. He always wore this stupid brown hat, which he called his helmet, that made him look like he'd just stepped off *Gilligan's Island*. My dad was a gifted athlete and a lot of fun to watch from the stands. He'd never tell you that, but he was.

My mom, a PE teacher and cheerleading coach at John Glenn High School, was also a stud athlete. She was so good at sports, in fact, it was embarrassing. During one of the parents' games in my baseball league, she hit four out of the park. I'd hit two home runs the whole season.

---

1. A salute goes out to the LAPD, whose insurance program paid for corrective surgery as soon as I joined up. My Herman Munster–sized hands weren't made to handle contact lenses.

Growing up, I was allowed to play anything as long as it involved contact. If it didn't, my dad didn't consider it a real sport.

It wasn't until sixth grade with Mr. Culley that I learned about soccer. He was obsessed with it, and his enthusiasm was infectious. Eventually he got the whole class playing.

Not only did Mr. Culley introduce me to soccer, but he was the greatest teacher I ever had. Not satisfied to merely teach out of a book, he brought out our passion for competition in the classroom with head-to-head spelling bees, geography tests, and math races. Whichever teams earned the most points got two days at the end of the semester to do anything they wanted. They didn't have to do schoolwork. They could play at recess all day, bring in a TV, or have a party for all he cared. Mr. Culley's example taught me that if you made learning fun and interesting, people listened, a lesson I would take with me into my careers.

I was a decent student but only because Mr. Culley was a great teacher and my dad was keeping a watchful eye. In our house, if you didn't get good grades, bad things would happen to you. As and Bs were the only marks allowed. Anything lower and you were in trouble. Your life would be coming home from school and sitting in your room. Needless to say, I managed to keep As and Bs in grade school.

Anything that captured my imagination, I excelled at. I loved history and still read a lot of nonfiction books to this day. Math and English were boring. Science was super easy. And of course, I also had those lapses of stupidity we all go through. One day in grade school, I hid in the classroom closet until everyone left, then opened the locked door from inside for my friends. We rifled through all the papers the teacher had on us, sharing and scrutinizing the comments she'd made. Masters of espionage we were not, and a disheveled paper trail led to a phone call to my mom. My dad told me I was no better than any other burglar on the streets, then spanked the thievery right out of me.

I also had times when I lost my temper. Once I started a fight with another student for hitting the chessboard when I was close to winning a game. Now, by today's standards, this student would have been popping Ritalin for hyperactivity, but back then ADD was just something you did with numbers.

That day we had a substitute teacher. She couldn't control me and told the principal, "If he hadn't stopped fighting when he did, I would have fainted."

I wasn't a bully, but I had been raised to not take crap from anyone. To toughen me up, my dad often roughhoused with me, twisting my arm or grabbing my ear or pulling my lips or nose. I grew a thick skin fast. I was confident and sometimes a bit bolder than I knew was good for me.

I couldn't help myself, even from an early age. When I was five, my mother tried to spank me. I turned around and said, "That didn't hurt."

Before I knew it, my dad was in the doorway.

"Oh, it hurt, it hurt," I said in panic.

"No, but it will," he said.

Sometimes my mom would go to slap me, and I would grab her hand.

"Just settle down, Mom," I'd say, which would infuriate her.

Discipline went both ways in the McCarthy household, and I could be a mean little bastard. I got one golden opportunity for revenge when I was twelve years old. I know every boy grows up hating his sister, but in my case I had a really good reason. My sister, Sheri, who was two years older than me, beat the snot out of me every chance she could get, and there was little I could do because I'd been taught to never hit girls. That is, until one day when my dad caught Sheri slapping me.

"Has she ever done that before?"

I nodded.

"Sheri, who the hell do you think you're slapping like that? Have you ever done that before?" My dad was interrogating his suspect.

"Yes," she said.

"Okay." He calmly took her by the hand and led us both to the garage. "All right, here's the rules. John, you can hit her from the neck down. Do not hit her in the face. You hit her in the face, and I'll wallop you. Other than that, she's fair game."

"Sheri, you can hit him anywhere you want."

I don't think an act of God could have stopped the smile that flashed across my face. I'd been wrestling down at the YMCA a little bit, so I shot in on her body with everything I had, grabbed her legs out from underneath her, and started kicking like she was one of Mr. Culley's soccer balls. When Mom heard the commotion, she went running outside to find my dad.

"He's killing her," she yelled in utter terror.

"No, he's not," he said. "Just let it go. She deserves it."

After about thirty seconds of pure glee, my dad came back into the garage and told me to stop. Sheri was balled up in the corner of the garage, sobbing. She never touched me again.

I've never had a fear of fighting. In fact, as you can probably tell, I would say I was enamored with it. I loved to watch Bruce Lee as the sidekick Kato on *The Green Hornet* as he punched and kicked the bad guys, leveling them all with superhuman speed and accuracy.

My dad didn't buy into it. He thought TV fighting was BS, and he hated pro wrestling. If it was real, it was all right with him, but he had no time for anything he considered fake. "Lee's an actor, not a fighter," he'd say.

I knew better. I was ten years old when Lee's blockbuster film *Enter the Dragon* was released in United States theaters in July of 1973, just six days before his mysterious and untimely death. I got myself a pair of wooden nunchucks and set out to become my own martial arts master in the McCarthy garage. I wasn't smart enough to get a practice set, but after just a few hundred bumps and bruises, I felt I was pretty decent at it.

When a karate craze swept the nation shortly after, I begged my parents for lessons.

My dad said, "If you're going to do something, you're going to do something real," then signed me up for boxing lessons. He took me down to the Grand Olympic Auditorium in Los Angeles to watch the fights, and I ate up every minute of it. For a wide-eyed eleven-year-old boy, there was a grittiness and danger about boxing. The crowds would get raucous and throw their beers at the ring if their guys lost.

I loved the fights, and Joe Frazier was the man. He was the champ when I grew old enough to understand the sport. Frazier always came to fight. During their epic three fights between 1971 and 1975, my dad took great offense to Muhammad Ali's calling Frazier everything from ugly to a gorilla to an Uncle Tom just to sway the black fans against his opponent. My dad felt Ali was a racist and that this was one of the cruelest and most dishonorable things a man could do to Frazier and his family.

Years later I met Joe Frazier when a local California TV station interviewed us about the UFC. As we were getting our microphones in place, I told Frazier I'd watched and admired him from afar for years.

Ironically, the vaunted boxer knew little about mixed martial arts. "They kick people in the groin, right?" he asked.

From SWAT ride-alongs to garage battles to boxing events, I was raised differently than other kids, but I don't think I'd change any of it if I could. I'm sure there were people who looked at my dad like he was Attila the Hun, but I'm also sure most adults saw him as a good guy.

I've thought about how easy others may have had it because their parents weren't as strict as mine, but I wouldn't change it. As a father myself, I now believe it was a good way to be raised because life isn't easy. It's full of good and bad people, and you need to be able to deal with all of them, to treat the good people right and to let the bad people know bad things will happen to them if they screw with you.

I raised my kids softer than my dad raised me, no doubt about it. It's a different world. What's allowed and what's acceptable in today's society is nothing like it was in past generations. When I was a kid, there were no video games or Wiis or Internet or 300-plus channels to choose from on your flat-screen, high-definition TV. Everybody played outside, and not everybody made the Little League team. You learned to deal with disappointment.

My dad grew up in much harsher times, which is why I appreciate what he taught me in my childhood. The lessons I learned from him made me the man, the police officer, and the referee I would be in years to come.

Being a gentleman and helping Mom put on her water ski

What family vacations were like for the McCarthys: water skiing on Lake Havasu, Arizona

CHAPTER 2

WATER BALLET AND BLOODY NOSES

Serious sport is war minus the shooting.

—George Orwell

I was going to be the greatest lineman ever to play in the NFL. At least that's what I thought when I was nine years old. Pro football players like Los Angeles Rams quarterback Roman Gabriel and defensive tackle Merlin Olsen were my heroes.

My dad, who had every expectation that I'd play sports, must have been encouraged by my size. Though I was never the biggest kid, I was always above average, a definite plus for any aspiring pigskin practitioner. At age eight, I even tried out for the Junior All-American team a year early alongside about 200 kids ranging from nine to eleven years old. There were thirty-three spots, and I was the last kid to be cut during hell week after my dad had given me a crash course in tackling to help me hit with power.

When I made the team the next year, the coach wanted to put me at tight end because I could catch any ball thrown to me.

But there was one problem: I was as slow as a friggin' turtle. So he started putting me on the offensive and defensive lines instead. They couldn't let this big guy go to waste, could they?

For my first few years of football, I had to diet to make the eighty-five-pound cutoff. I ate a lot of steak and stewed tomatoes, then salivated as the other kids scarfed down potato chips and candy. It didn't make me the happiest camper.

Honestly, I never thought about my size. I wasn't the biggest or the tallest kid out there. I fell somewhere in between.

From the age of six and into high school, I also played baseball, though I wasn't what you would call an all-star. I was assigned to pitching and first base because I had a really strong arm, which was both good and bad. I could hum a ball, and it mostly went over the plate. The rest of the time, I had no control over it, which meant it sailed past the batter or beamed him. It happened just enough that kids would take to the plate with their feet slightly turned outward, poised to make a quick getaway. My mom and dad watched from the stands and laughed.

As I got older, my issues with my speed, or should I say lack of speed, became more prominent. I walked with a bounce, and my heels were always sore. I don't know if this was because of growth spurts or what, but the doctor said my Achilles tendons became too short and began to pull away from their attachments.

Between my freshman and sophomore years, I had surgery on both of my Achilles tendons. The surgery left me immobile for months, and the doctor told me I couldn't play football. The one activity he did recommend for my rehabilitation was swimming.

In California, almost all of the high schools have swimming pools, so I headed off to mine to find the coach, Scott Massey.

"Okay," he said, looking me up and down, "but instead of just swimming, why don't you play water polo?"

I couldn't even describe what water polo was, but summer was coming and it was something to do. I couldn't go back to football in the fall, and I definitely couldn't run cross-country, so I thought I might as well find something to keep me in shape. Water polo it would be.

If you're picturing me in tight briefs, a cap pasted around my melon, you're not far off, though I'd recommend keeping that image to yourself. One of the immediate benefits of water polo was that it helped tame my asthma. Something about the humidity allowed me to breathe easier, which meant I didn't get tired as fast. I was able to go and go and go.

The season came and went, and although my plan had always been to return to football come next season, Coach Massey approached me with another idea. "If you want to go back and play football, I understand that," he said. "But I'm telling you, if you stay with this, you'll get a college scholarship. Can you say that about football?"

I couldn't answer him, which tells you the decision I made.

In the beginning, my dad didn't like water polo because he didn't understand it. My entire first year, he didn't watch me play. He rationalized that I was doing it as a part-time gig that would pass once I could get back on the football field the next year.

When I did start running again, I wasn't slow anymore. I was catching people, even passing them. All signs pointed to me returning to football and, believe me, I thought about it. But there seemed to be more opportunity for me in the pool.

My dad wasn't thrilled with my decision to stick with water

polo until I got him to come to a tournament at the LA Watts Summer Games.

Water polo is hard for a new spectator to follow. There are whistles and flags and referees kicking players out when they foul. I'd equate it most with basketball, with its strategic passing and scoring setups, except water polo allows you an extra man and a goalie covering the net.

Water polo can be played on two plains: above and below the water. What you see above the surface can be quite athletic, orchestrated like a water ballet as players stretch their torsos and arch their arms to launch the ball the length of the pool to their teammates.

It's what you don't see that's the best part. Most of the real action is taking place underneath the water, where players can control position by grabbing, kicking, or colliding into their opponents' legs and bodies. It's all absolutely illegal, but players can make it look like they aren't doing anything wrong.

When my coach had first sized me up, he hadn't seen a swimmer. I couldn't swim with these guys—they were rockets compared to me. In a line of speedboats, I was a tugboat. What he'd seen was an enforcer, a player who wouldn't be afraid of dishing out or taking a few shots in order to score. My coach thought if I could just be kept under control, I could benefit the team. He was right.

I compensated for my average swimming abilities by playing dirty. I played the position of two-meter man, or the hole man, which is like the center in basketball. You take an ass-whipping because the ball is always coming to you and, like a football quarterback, you have to toss it to someone or take it to the net to score.

I didn't shy away if I got hit. In fact, I went after the person to get back at him. Obviously, I knew what cheap shots and clean shots were, so I could usually weave my way in and out of the system without getting caught. When someone would cheap-shot me, I would try and be smart with my retaliation, but subtlety sometimes went out the window and I'd grab them and just start punching.

The pool we played in had an underwater viewing tank for spectators, and in the crowd my dad could see the guys getting hit and kicked under the water with elbows and knees flying everywhere. Water polo wasn't only the hardest game I ever played; it was also the most violent, even more than my beloved football. Suddenly my dad didn't have a problem with water polo anymore.

In fact, he started coming to all of my games, and it was hysterical to watch him in the stands.

In the summer league tournament finals one year, I had a problem staying in the game. When I was hit, I would start fighting. I got smacked one time too many and snapped, grabbing the guy's cap and punching him in the face. I was swiftly ejected from the game.

On the sidelines, my coach ripped into me. "You won't become anything. You can't control your temper. You're useless to me."

All I could hear was my dad: "That's awesome. Way to go, John!"

Meanwhile, the other parents stared at him like he was an escapee who'd forgotten to take off his straitjacket.

My dad wasn't the typical parent, and I wasn't the typical water polo player. A lot of these kids had grown up swimming competitively, which must have been nice for little Stevie with all his 100-meter butterfly medals. There was never any contact for these kids, however, and when little Stevie got hit and his nose started bleeding, his parents thought he would die.

With that kind of player out there, you wouldn't be surprised to learn that I probably hold the distinction of being the first water polo player ever kicked out of the Junior Olympics. I wanted everyone to be afraid to come near me so I'd have more room to hustle my ass up and down the pool.

At Glen A. Wilson High School in Hacienda Heights, the football team during my junior year was the strongest squad my school had ever produced. Most of my friends were on the team and questioned my choice of surf over turf. They even started bashing the water polo team, so I made a challenge to them.

"I'll tell you what," I said. "I'll go on the football field and do any drill you want against anyone you want; then you can come into the pool and drill against any of us. We'll see how you do."

I knew I could handle any defensive or offensive football drill, but if they got in the pool, they would probably drown. Nobody took me up on the offer.

When I got behind a cause, I pushed it to the hilt. I had a T-shirt printed up with balls stuffed inside two nets dangling side by side. I think you get the visual. It read, "It takes balls to play water polo." I was suspended a day for wearing it to school, but my dad was proud of me for standing up for what I believed in.

In high school, I was proud, confident, and considered a jock. I didn't do clubs because they weren't the cool thing to do. I was one of the guys pranking teammates by rubbing Icy Hot in their straps. Sports and friends—that's what it was all about.

From the age of sixteen on, I always had a girlfriend and was never home. I was into dirt bikes, and when I was old enough, I graduated to street bikes. I saved enough money from my summer job as a pool lifeguard to buy my first bike, a black Yamaha XS850. The one thing I didn't do was drugs—no pot, acid, mushrooms, or any other illegal substances.

My dad was scared to death of his kids doing drugs and wouldn't have a user under his roof. He brought home pictures of overdose victims to show us more than a few times. In the pictures, we'd see people with stuff coming out of them that wasn't supposed to or corpses bent in unnatural positions and staring vacantly at us with flies on their eyes.

It worked. I've never taken any kind of recreational drugs to this day. I can't say it was entirely the pictures, though, because I think I was more scared of my dad and what he'd do if I touched them.

Alcohol was another story entirely. From the age of five, I'd been allowed to drink. If my dad was hanging out with friends and I wanted a drink, I could get a sip from my old man's beer can or even have one of my own.

I drank with my friends throughout high school. One time I got so inebriated that I crushed my friend's nose with a head-butt and didn't even remember doing it. I didn't like being out of control like that and not being able to remember anything, so at age twenty I cut back on drinking.

Genetics and economics took care of that for me eventually anyway. By the time I'd reached adult size, it would take twelve beers to give me a buzz and a case of beer to make me really feel it. Who wants to go through that, bathroom runs and all, to get a quick high? Not to sound cliché, but I don't need a drink that bad to have a good time. Even today, I have only the occasional drink or two but nothing more than that.

My dad's view on drugs was fairly predictable if you knew

him, but there were some things from my teenage years that I could never anticipate.

My parents' separation during the summer between my junior and senior years was totally unexpected. No one would have ever known it was coming. It wasn't like they fought or anything like that. In the open, my dad always seemed loving toward my mom.

I'd noticed that my dad seemed a lot more miserable the last couple of years, and it had caused some friction between us. I hadn't liked being around him. I thought he was a pain in the ass, always pissed off. Whatever I did, it wasn't good enough. If I scored four goals, there were still those two I missed. So I started drifting my own way and doing things completely the opposite of what he wanted.

When my dad asked me not to remove the roll bar off the truck he'd bought for me, I did it anyway. When he confronted me, I turned my back on him to walk away. He threw me over the rail onto the living room staircase for disrespecting him.

On the surface, the disagreement was about a rebellious adolescent trying to challenge his father. But there was more going on with my dad.

Of course, you find out those things later in life. People get married and believe someone is a certain way, and things turn out differently. Some people are compatible; some are not. Over time, some grow together, and some drift apart.

According to both my parents, my dad's exit wasn't particularly dramatic.

"You're not happy," Mom pointed out as they lay awake in bed one night.

"No, I'm not," he answered.

"Then just leave," she said.

My dad complied, stuffing some belongings into a garbage bag, then walked out the door while my sister and I slept.

When I found out the next day, I was angry he'd hurt my mother's feelings. I'm embarrassed to admit I punched a hole through the front door. When he came back to the house a few days later, I confronted him. Most importantly, I wanted to know why.

He explained it all to me. He'd been unhappy for quite a while and had been trying to figure out how to take care of it. I think he'd thought of leaving when I was much younger, but he didn't want me to grow up without him. He was just waiting for the right day, and to him this was it.

For the first time in my life, I didn't look up to my dad quite as much. He seemed much happier, though, and gradually we would spend more time together again.

In the meantime, I took my frustration out in the pool. Coach Massey had been right on the money with me. In my junior year, the water polo team finished in second place in our league, and we qualified for the California Interscholastic Federation finals. In my senior year, I earned Sierra League first-team honors, was named the league's player of the year, made all-CIF, and was an all-American honorable mention. Even without glowing SAT scores, I got a college scholarship.

I chose California State University Long Beach because the water polo coach, Ken Lindgren, was also the assistant coach of the Olympic team. Even though CSULB was thirty miles from my house, I *had* to live on campus. I'd become friends with a rival player from Los Altos, and we'd decided to room together.

At the age of seventeen, I set off for my first year of college in the fall of 1980. It was a rude awakening. At six feet three and 210 pounds, I was perfect for college water polo. But I was all wrong for college. I was young and free but didn't have the right mind-set or the discipline for it.

The professors didn't give a shit if we went to class, and who was I to argue with them? Still, it certainly made a difference come exam time.

I did excel in one way: I partied like a champion, and I was a shoo-in for any get-together because I never got carded. On every other dorm floor, an unlimited supply of girls pranced in and out while parties raged. I still have scars from getting drunk and falling off my bunk bed onto the furniture.

Things really hit the fan in the pool, though. My technique wasn't even close to the other swimmers', and there was a world of difference between the twenty-five-yard pool I'd plundered in high school and the fifty-meter pool in college.

On some level, I'd known this going in. I have to admit I was petrified the first day of practice. While the coach timed us, the team swam 16,000 yards—that's ten miles of hell—with our shoes on for part of it. With each waning stroke, the thought ran through my mind that they were going to kill me. By the time the ball hit the water, I didn't have the strength to pick it up.

I hadn't come to college to swim; I'd come to play water polo my way. That wasn't really an option here.

Since it turned out that I majored in failing and minored in partying, by the end of the first year I was on academic probation. This made it easier for my coach to approach me about redshirting the next year, meaning I would train but not compete.

I had a friend who'd redshirted the year before, and he told me it sucked. Being the levelheaded, rational guy I was, I said, "Shove your red shirt," and walked out the door.

I try not to have regrets, but being a dummy during my abbreviated college career would probably be one of them. When I dropped out, my dad blamed himself for not being around enough. I moved in with my mom, who was now living in Irvine, and enrolled at Orange Coast College, a two-year junior college. But like CSULB, that wouldn't last long.

One day, I got on my motorcycle and just started riding. To where, I couldn't really tell you. Both figuratively and literally, my life suddenly lacked any sense of direction. We are all creatures of habit, and sports had always been mine. Without sports, what was I supposed to do?

On my way back home, I stopped at a random gym on East Chapman Avenue in the city of Orange. Samson's Gym was a no-frills operation, where only serious lifters needed apply. In the corner, the gym had what they called the Power Pit, littered with racks of black weights, dumbbells, plates, and benches.

I worked out at Samson's Gym for the next few months and caught the eye of the owner, Jim Dena, a former Anaheim police officer who would often come onto the floor and lift with me. Jim turned me on to bodybuilding and eventually gave me a job at the gym.

A group of powerlifters also worked out at Samson's Gym, and one day they called me over to them. "You shouldn't do that pretty posing lifting," one of them told me. "It's always better to be stronger than you look than to look stronger than you are."

Turns out, I wasn't getting advice from your typical muscled meatheads. These were some of the greatest powerlifters of the time. Terry Shaw had been a world's record holder in the dead lift, and Terry McCormick was the world's record holder in the dead lift (848 pounds), while Marv Phillips, also a police officer, held twenty world records and was called the King of the Squat.

So I dropped my weights and migrated to their side of the Power Pit to do some powerlifting. You know those lifting competitions you see on TV, where a constipated-looking guy in a uni-tard and tube socks squats, grunts, and huffs and puffs to stand with a massive weight bar on his shoulders? That's powerlifting. It's pure strength lifting and differs from bodybuilding, where you build and tone specific muscles to get an aesthetically appealing appearance.

In powerlifting, there are three lifts: squats, dead lift, and bench press. There is no powerlifting in the Olympics, but there is Olympic lifting with maneuvers like the clean and jerk and the snatch, which require speed, agility, and of course strength. However, Olympic lifters' weights are light compared to the ones professional powerlifters use.

When I started lifting with the pros, it was a rush to feel myself getting stronger. I dedicated so much of my time to it that they decided I should try a competition. At my first show, down in Camp Pendleton, the Marine Corp Recruit Depot in San Diego, I took third place.

After I got a taste, I didn't want to stop. My lift numbers kept going up, and I started entering competitions every couple of months. But my body could go only so far on its own. It was time to take the next step, my teachers told me, and if I was serious about lifting and keeping up, there was something else I had to do.

This is when I started taking steroids, which at the time weren't illegal or frowned on. In these circles, it was just a part of the program. The pros gave me the name of a doctor who gave me a prescription. Always careful to follow his cycle instructions, I took them for about two years.

I won't lie. Back then, I didn't think there was anything wrong with it. And you could certainly feel and see a difference. In steady increments, my squat increased from 535 to 802 pounds, my bench press from 320 to 455, and my dead lift from 505 to 802. You couldn't argue with those types of gains.

I guess if steroids had been illegal back then, I would have thought twice about taking them, but they wouldn't become a political hot potato for another five years, when Canadian sprinter Ben Johnson ran against Carl Lewis at the 1988 Olympics and won, then tested positive for Stanozolol. I was off them long before then.

As an MMA referee years later, I could usually tell which fighters were on steroids. You'd be surprised to know how many fighters were taking steroids and other performance-enhancing drugs. It's illegal, and I don't think it's ever right to break the rules, but I understand why fighters do it. Yes, it's cheating, but sometimes it's cheating for a paycheck to feed their families. Sometimes it's to work through or prevent injuries. I'm not saying all this to condone steroid use. I don't. The bottom line is that it's illegal and shouldn't be done, but I'm smart enough to know guys still do it, cycle off, and never get caught.

I won't say steroids are addicting physically, but I think they can be psychologically. People start to see results and want more. Human beings are that way. We think if two will do, then four is better, eight is even better, and so on. People can start to abuse, and I think that's where problems arise.

The one issue I had with steroids was 'roid rage. I didn't get mad easier, but if I was going to get mad, I'd get *mad*. And once I did, I couldn't let things go. I wanted to hurt whoever had done me wrong.

PHOTO COURTESY OF THE MCCARTHY FAMILY

Dead-lifting 730 pounds at a competition in Pomona, California

If the image of an albino Incredible Hulk comes into your head, you're on the right track. I was 300 pounds strong. I was winning a lot of local tournaments and was getting ready to go to the Junior Nationals.

But there was one small problem. Powerlifting would never pay the bills no matter how much I lifted, and someone was about to enter my life who'd cause me to reassess my priorities.

My first picture ever with my squeeze, Elaine

ELAINE

To get the full value of joy you must have someone to divide it with.

—Mark Twain

Some men promise their women riches and a life of luxury. Others—mostly the poor ones—promise the sun, moon, and stars. I bribed my wife to marry me with a five-gallon tub of peppermint ice cream.

Romantic, I know, but it's a true story. I swear. In my defense, have you seen a five-gallon tub of ice cream?

But I'm getting a little ahead of myself. I should probably tell you first how I met Elaine, the woman I've been married to for twenty-seven years now, because she plays an intricate role in my story.

Die-hard UFC fans might have noticed the beautiful blonde sitting cageside at virtually every event I've ever refereed. Elaine has been with me from the start, before I became a police officer or a world-traveling referee or anything else of any substance. She is the one person who truly knows me. She's seen the good and bad in me and has stuck with me through all of life's ups and downs, even when we didn't have the money to buy food. She's stood with me through it all, and she will forever be the love of my life.

I met Elaine by chance. While I was working at Samson's Gym, a coworker named Mark helped me clean and organize at night to get the gym ready for the next day. One evening, he confided in me that he really liked this girl who worked across the street at Del Taco, but he was having trouble getting up the courage to speak to her.

"Dude, you can sit here and look stupid, or grow a pair and go talk to her," I told him. "She's no better than you."

Each night at the gym, I took my best stab at being Mark's relationship coach. At one time I'd been just like him, shy and afraid to talk to girls I liked. It had finally dawned on me that if I was waiting for the girls to come flocking to me for my looks, I'd be waiting a long time, so I'd quickly learned that holding a conversation and scoring some laughs went a long way with the girls.

After I'd done my best to get Mark feeling confident enough to go ask this girl out, he finally found his balls and made his way across the street to sweep his damsel's feet right off that fast-food joint's floor.

A few minutes later, he walked back.

"How'd it go?" I asked.

"It was good. We talked," Mark said, busying himself at the gym counter, "but she likes you."

"She likes me? She doesn't even know me."

"Yeah, she says she saw you run across the street and thinks you run good."

Run good? I tried to think of all the times I'd sprinted across the street to Del Taco. I'd gone over a few times to get their chicken taco salad, but of all the things to notice, my swagger wasn't one of them.

Mark watched me contemplate the situation. "Do you want me to go tell her anything?" he finally asked, resigning to his new role in the matter.

"Yeah, tell her I like the way she walks," I said. I was being a complete smart-ass, but I couldn't help myself.

I think Mark got the picture pretty quickly. He never talked about Elaine again.

If you ask Elaine, she'll tell you I started going over to see her, but she actually made her way to the gym more, even if she won't admit it.

It was attraction at first sight. Elaine reminded me of Princess Diana, except she was far cuter with her short, blonde bob to complement her tall, thin body. She lied and told me she was eighteen years old. I was nineteen at the time, and it didn't take me long to figure out she was really sixteen. For our first date, I took her to dinner and a walk in the sand in Newport Beach.

Elaine was nice and sweet, but I actually broke up with her after two months. One night, I was supposed to pick her up for a date and just didn't show. I stopped calling. I know it was wrong and cowardly, but it just seemed like the easiest way.

Generally speaking, at times I wasn't a good boyfriend for any girl. I'd treat them fine while we were going out, but there would come a time when I'd get bored and stop calling. I would basically disappear. Right after I turned twenty, I did it to Elaine.

Imagine my surprise when Elaine walked into Samson's Gym about four months later. She'd thought I'd left the gym because I'd traded in my car, a 1966 Ford Econoline surfer van with a 302 V-8 engine and jacked-up Cragar rims, for a black Pontiac Trans

Am. When she didn't see the van parked outside the gym, she assumed I'd moved away.

When she ran into one of my gym buddies, though, he told her I was still around, so she decided to pay me a visit. Shockingly, she wasn't all that mad. We talked a bit and ended up going on another date. Elaine was tenacious, I'll give her that.

When did I know Elaine was the one? It was when she played the theme to the film *Ice Castles*, "Through the Eyes of Love." I know it sounds crazy, but she played the piano so beautifully and looked so pretty in that moment that I told myself, *I'd better not screw this up again.*

Elaine proved to be my match in every way. In the past, I'd always gotten tired of being around girls, but after that I never got tired of Elaine. Okay, I'll admit I did get tired of talking to her on the phone—the girl could go on for hours—but our time together was fun.

Elaine became my best friend. She took a great interest in me and everything I was into, like my lifting, motorcycles, and suped-up cars. She never tried to change me but allowed me to be who I was, for better or worse.

I'll admit that couldn't have been an easy thing for her to do sometimes. Did I mention I have a temper and a stubborn streak? But Elaine was always brave enough to tell me when I was acting crazy or getting out of control. This is not a feat for the fainthearted.

Elaine's and my unique relationship dynamic was clear the day we played Zimm-Zamm, an inane game involving paddles and a tennis-sized ball attached to a pole with a cord. It's like tetherball, except one player is trying to get the cord wrapped around the top of the pole while the other is trying to hit it to the bottom.

After playing a couple games, Elaine sat down to take a break, while I kept hitting the ball.

Elaine got annoyed. "Stop hitting it so hard," she said. "You're going to hit me."

Now, I was standing there with a ball on a cord attached to a stake pounded into the ground. There was no chance of that ball going anywhere outside of the arc the cord allowed it to travel.

"Elaine, it's physically impossible for me to hit you with the ball," I said with complete certainty. "You're sitting ten feet away."

But she insisted I was hitting it too hard.

One of us was wrong, and it wasn't going to be me. I'd prove it. I tossed the ball up and swung the paddle like I was Pete Sampras at the US Open. Sure enough, I knocked the ball right off the cord and hit Elaine in the throat. A direct hit.

She staggered back, eyes big as saucers, and started gasping for air.

"I'm so sorry!" I told her. I couldn't say it enough.

When she could finally speak, all she said was, "You did that on purpose."

I'm not sure I've ever fully convinced her I didn't.

To this day, when my stubbornness clouds my judgment and I think it's no way but my way, my wife has to utter only two syllables: "Zimm-Zamm."

Elaine and I became inseparable. We went to parties and the movies together, I took her to her junior and senior proms, and I got to know her family.

Elaine's mother's side of the family had come from money.

Elaine's grandfather had run Farmers Insurance, a nationwide operation with millions of customers. I wouldn't say Elaine's family was rich, but she lived in a middle-class neighborhood and got most everything she wanted.

Elaine's mom, Lynn, was always working. She was a computer wiz at a time when one computer system would fill an entire room. Lynn was a little savant who could write super complex computer programs, but nobody knew how she did it.

Elaine's father, Ted, was a smart man and had graduated from California Polytechnic State University in San Luis Obispo. He'd even worked on the rockets that allowed the Lunar Excursion Module to land on the moon, but from the day I met him, Ted never had a job, and I never figured out why.

I usually have a hard time respecting someone who doesn't work, but I always seemed to get along with Ted. I also would not have normally associated with someone like him. Not only was he an intellectual, but he belonged to clubs that had table tennis and pellet pistol shooting and was always trying to figure out what activities he could beat me in. These clubs definitely weren't the types of places you'd find me in on my own, but it made him happy, so I went along.

I always thought Ted should have been a politician. The man loves to talk and meet people. If it's a homeless guy on the street, Ted will strike up a conversation like that guy's the most interesting person in the world.

Ted's gift for the gab got us all into some sticky situations, and sometimes I had to jump in and get us out of them. One time, Elaine and I went on vacation with Ted and Lynn to Cabo San Lucas. Ted struck up a conversation with a little Norwegian man sitting at a nearby table during breakfast, and before we knew it, we were all on a boat with this perfect stranger heading off for a day of diving.

The boat driver dropped us off on a shore about twenty-five feet long and ten feet deep. While the Norwegian and Ted prepped the diving equipment, Elaine and I swam. Then I noticed a boat hauling ass in our direction. Once it got close enough, I could see the Federales symbol on its side. I left Elaine in the water and started swimming for shore.

It was as if we were in a scene of a Chuck Norris movie. Two of the four uniformed men, one of them toting an AR15, jumped out of the boat, grabbed the Norwegian guy, and proceeded to kick the shit out of him. Ted started yelling at me to help the guy, but I glanced at the officer holding the AR15, then at Ted as if to say, "Are you fucking kidding me?" then back at the Federales, who dragged the Norwegian man onto their boat and split his chin on the rail.

It turns out our friendly tour guide had been warned numerous times not to poach business from the local dive shops.

Diplomat Ted tried to tell the Federales they didn't need to use so much force on our Norwegian guide, but I told him to can it and tried instead to negotiate our trip back to shore. The head Federale said another boat would be by shortly to pick us up, revved his engine, and sped away with his men just as quickly as he'd arrived.

There we were on a shore that was about to go bye-bye with the tide coming in.

Minutes, then hours passed with nary a boat in sight. Ted kept talking, trying to minimize his involvement in marooning us in the middle of Cabo San Lucas Bay.

Meanwhile, it was obvious to me that we'd soon be climbing the rocks. I said good-bye to Elaine, put on some fins, dove into the water, and started swimming in the direction of the harbor. About an hour of swimming later, I made it to the marina.

By the time I returned to Marooned Island on a rented boat, Elaine and her family were huddled on the rocks like a pack of pelicans. Ted tried to sputter out his reasons why he shouldn't be blamed for all this, but the last thing I remember was telling him to just shut up and sit down.

My fishing improved over the years: a dorado (mahi-mahi) I caught in Mexico

I know everybody has crazy stories about their in-laws, and I have a ton I could tell you about Ted that still make me chuckle. Unfortunately, Elaine never really got along with her dad, so I felt like I was always trapped between them trying to keep the peace. Based on my own experiences, especially my own relationship with my dad, I valued family greatly and always felt she should try to work things out with her own dad.

I figured he loved her and Elaine just didn't understand him. I always encouraged her to talk to him, but it would take me years to understand her point of view. I learned later that just because someone is family doesn't mean you have to love them, like them, or even put up with them. Some relationships work, and some don't.

Whoever came up with that "for better or for worse" phrase was a freaking genius. When Elaine met me, I was living on the edge. Some days I think back and wonder why she wasn't scared off altogether. I guess I was lucky she was into the rebellious type, because I had plenty of that to go around.

I was a big, immature twenty-year-old powerlifter who thought he could handle just about anyone. I know now there were plenty of people who could've handed me my ass, but back then I was a six-feet-four, 300-pound guy who thought he was invincible.

At the time, I was driving a Jeep CJ-7. I was so big the back of the seat had broken off at its hinge and I couldn't sit in it anymore. I started driving Elaine's car, a tiny Datsun truck, with the window rolled down so my arm and shoulder could hang out to give me more room.

One night, I was driving Elaine home so she could change for a party. When I slowed down at a stoplight, I saw a green MG compact sports car ahead of us with its top up and the rear window open. Then I caught the driver's eyes.

"What the hell is that guy winking at?" I asked.

"Certainly not at you," Elaine said.

That was it. I snapped. I pulled up behind Mr. Green MG, honking my horn and flashing my lights to get him to pull over.

Instead, he turned in to a McDonald's drive-thru, where I boxed him in from behind. Then I jumped out of the truck, went up to the driver's door, and told the guy to get out of his car.

He looked at me as if he'd just dropped his grandmother off at church. "What's the problem, buddy?" he asked innocently.

Wrong answer, buddy. I tried to rip his locked door off its hinge, and when I remembered the open back window, I fished inside, tearing out a big piece of his shirt and then a clump of his hair.

The guy was grabbing as much floorboard as he could, screaming for help while this big lunatic attacked him.

"Get out of the car, or I'll crush it around you," I said, and when he didn't obey, I hoisted the tail end repeatedly as if I could shake him out.

Meanwhile, I was vaguely aware of Elaine standing there calling me every name in the book, which only enraged me more.

I beat the soft top down flat and jumped on the hood and trunk, denting both ends beyond recognition. I picked up the back of the car again and bounced it off the ground, bottoming out the suspension and crushing the underside. I was out of control and breath when I finally realized I had an audience. As the sirens gained, I jumped into the truck with Elaine and drove off.

"You're a psycho," she yelled.

She was right.

I was lucky I didn't get caught.

Of all the times for me to go off the deep end, this wasn't the best. You see, I had planned to propose to Elaine that night.

So I did the one thing I could think of to right this sinking ship. I bribed her.

Leaving her huffing away in the parking lot of an ice cream parlor, I went inside. A few minutes later, I reappeared with a tub of peppermint ice cream. It was Swensen's, her favorite, and these 5 gallons would go a long way with a girl who weighed only about 115 pounds.

At least it was enough to get Elaine to agree to come to the party.

Outside of the house full of partygoers, I stopped her. "You have every reason in the world to turn me down, but if you would like to, I want to marry you."

It was the worst proposal in the history of mankind.[2] Still she said yes, and for that I am eternally grateful.

Looking back on that day, I realize I felt as if that stranger had spit in my face right in front of the girl I was going to marry. I couldn't let that happen. But my behavior spoke to a larger issue. I was heading down the wrong road.

I wouldn't say I looked for fights, but I certainly didn't back down when they fell in my lap. For some reason, they did a lot. It was probably because I was now bouncing in nightclubs and country bars.

My dad saw the writing on the wall. He knew I'd been doing steroids off and on the last two years, and it scared him because it fueled my aggressive tendencies when people pushed my buttons just right. "You're going to kill yourself one of two ways," he warned. "By getting into a fight or by driving your car or motorcycle so fast you crash and burn."

After getting into a big argument with Jim Dena, the owner

2. A few years later on a cruise ship, Elaine and I won an award for the worst proposal story ever.

of Samson's Gym, I left the powerlifting world. To make ends meet, I started picking up odd jobs: painting streets, working at a packaging company, taking on heavy lifting projects, and anything else I could find.

One day while I laid down cement blockades for parking spaces at Chapman University, the head of security drove by in his golf cart. "Do you want a job working security?" he said.

Drenched in sweat from head to toe and burning under the brutal sun, I gave him the no-brainer answer.

Being a security guard was quite boring. I didn't have a gun or any real authority outside of the college campus, so I'd just cruise around in my golf cart, stopping to talk to people.

The "scenery" at Chapman was fantastic, but Elaine couldn't stand me being around so many other girls. It didn't pay well enough for me to argue anyway, so I lasted nine months.

That's when I turned to what I knew: the police force. It was either go to jail for losing my cool in the wrong moment or put others there in my place. It wasn't a hard choice when you thought about it that way.

With my dad's overwhelming blessing, I applied for both the Los Angeles County Sheriff's Department and the Los Angeles Police Department and waited to see which one would take me first.

You'd probably be relieved to hear that sheriff and police departments require a lengthy interview process, including a written test, an oral interview, physicals, background checks, and the all-important psychological tests.

At first, the LASD system seemed to be moving me through faster, so I thought I'd be heading there. When I went to complete the background info stage, I had to fill out all this paperwork on my family and personal life.

"I see your dad worked for the police department," the deputy sheriff said as he looked over the paperwork. "Why aren't you interviewing there?"

"My sister's a deputy for the sheriff's department," I said, "and there seems to be more opportunity for me here."

This deputy sheriff had worked for the Special Enforcement Bureau, which is their version of SWAT. "I really don't know the LAPD, but we did some training with their SWAT Unit. There was this one crazy guy who would stick his badge pin in his arm."

If I could've shrunk into the chair and disappeared altogether, I would've. He was talking about my dad. As he talked to other officers, my dad liked to sterilize his pin with a lighter and sit expressionless while he stuck the three-inch steel spike into his arm. He wanted people to think he didn't feel any pain. His forearms had loads of tattooed dots, permanent marks from the burned carbon.

"Have you ever heard of him?" the deputy sheriff said.

I just looked at him. "I haven't."

It wasn't that I was embarrassed. I just didn't think they'd look at the relationship as a plus. *Yeah, let's hire the son of the wacko guy.*

In the hiring process, I also had to fill out a questionnaire that listed recreational drugs. As I've mentioned, I never tried anything other than steroids, which were legal at the time, and alcohol, so I marked that down, handed in my sheet, and waited to take the mandatory polygraph test.

Shortly after, a woman came into the room. "I don't think you understand the way this test works. If you lie, you will be disqualified. It's okay if you've experimented with marijuana."

"I haven't," I said again.

She looked at me like I was a kid elbow deep in the cookie jar.

"You're telling me you never experimented with marijuana? At all? Not even a little puff?"

"No, ma'am."

"Well, you realize you're going to fail the test if you lie." She shrugged, fed up with the game she thought I was playing.

But I wasn't playing. Not even close.

Screw this, I thought, but I collected myself. "Ma'am, I told you how many times, I've never used marijuana. I have never taken any drug. Either you believe me or you don't."

I passed the test, though I'm sure I got no extra points for congeniality. The woman and her polygraph test irked me so much I told myself I wouldn't go into the LASD if the LAPD made an offer.

Thankfully, I passed all my tests with the LAPD as well, so the choice was mine.

The thing about this whole interviewing and testing ordeal is that you don't get paid for it. It's like one long, maniacal interview from hell where you wade through medicals, background checks, physicals, and other evaluations just to wait to see if you get a job, which could take months or years depending on how many slots need to be filled at any given time. After all this, they give you a hire date and you're off to the academy for training.

At the time I applied, the LAPD was brimming with about 6,400 officers, which was a relatively robust number. Newspapers today say the LAPD underpays and is understaffed. When I was looking to get hired, the process was slow and arduous because the 1984 Olympic Games were taking place in Los Angeles and eating up the city's budget, so the department had instituted a hiring freeze.

A year and a half passed from the time I started testing till the day I was hired. In the meantime, I had to stay busy with other work and keep out of trouble. I accomplished one of the two.

A good distraction for me was my upcoming wedding. Since I was twenty-two years old and Elaine was eighteen, you can imagine our parents' reaction. None of them had a problem with our chosen mates, but they all thought we were way too young to get married. Elaine's parents pretty much paid for the entire thing, so we planned a Presbyterian church ceremony to make them happy. On the rainy day of November 24, 1984, in Orange, California, we made our vows.

On our way to the reception, the rain leaked into our limousine and Elaine had to navigate the raging river at her feet when she stepped out in her long, frilly dress.

The weather followed us to our honeymoon in Hawaii, which had its worst storm in ten years. No structure could seem to keep out the downpour. After mistakenly sticking us in a bungalow with two twin beds, the hotel manager upgraded us to their presidential suite. By the time the rain stopped, which was pretty much at the end of our trip, we had a couple inches of water on the floor.

When we finally did get outside, I wanted to visit Pearl Harbor. Since we were dirt poor on this trip, we decided to take a public bus. We found a seat behind a little old couple.

At one of the stops, five local teenage girls boarded, not one less than 250 pounds. They sat behind us and started talking loudly enough for the entire bus and probably the drivers outside to hear.

Now, I can handle a lot, but they started talking about their sexual exploits, and it got pretty graphic even for me. The old woman in front of us was even squirming in her seat. While I sat there swearing off public transportation forever, I told myself to mind my own business and keep my mouth shut. This is why I blame Elaine for what happened next.

"Say something on her behalf," Elaine said. She pointed at that poor old woman, who was all but sliding out of her seat and onto the floor.

I turned around to the group and said, "Listen, if you want to talk your dirty little talk, just please do us a favor. Not everyone on the bus wants to hear what you're saying. Can you please quiet down?"

"Fuck you, asshole," one said. "This is our fucking island."

When the bus made its next stop, Elaine and I stood to exit, but the group followed us and one girl went to hit me. I sort of deflected her right out the door, where she rolled onto the sidewalk on her back like a beached whale. Her friends followed to attack me, and I pushed them out the door in quick succession. They rolled out onto one another in a heap.

Unfortunately, the bus driver called the police on me, but the little old lady spoke up and saved me. We were free to go.

However, my run-ins with the police were far from over.

When I say I got into the LAPD by the skin of my teeth, I couldn't be more serious. While I waited for my hiring call, I managed a miniature Indy car track in Fountain Valley called the Malibu Grand Prix. Elaine would even come in and volunteer for small tasks because she wanted something to do. It was a great place to ride out the months.

Finally, I got a call from Lt. Mike Hillman. "They're picking your academy class tomorrow," he said, "so don't screw this up.

Don't make an officer even look at you funny. Don't do anything, and you'll be in."

One more night to close the Grand Prix and Elaine was there with me. What could go wrong?

You can probably guess who came prancing in the front door. Yes, my good old friend trouble. Of all nights, two guys in the arcade decided this was the one when they'd ignore closing time. I got a call from the girl working in the store. These two men had racked up another game of pool.

"I'll go talk to them," I said. Mistake number one. I should've stayed in the office counting the money.

At first I tried the diplomatic approach. "We're closed, but go ahead and finish your game. Have a good time, but please don't put any more money in the slot." Then I went back to the office but was soon interrupted by another call.

"They're racking up another game," the girl said.

I walked back into the arcade. Mistake number two.

The two guys eyed me, pool cues in their hands. I'd bounced enough to recognize that there were different species of idiot and that this particular species didn't understand verbal commands.

They hadn't been drinking, but I figured they'd been smoking something. I removed the cues from their hands, placed them behind the counter carefully, and stacked their quarters for the last game on the edge of the pool table. We'd been closed for twenty-five minutes, and I was giving them a refund. Apparently, that wasn't enough.

"What's your fucking problem?" one of them asked.

Now, I was about 265 pounds at the time. One of the guys was about my size. The other moron was about 190, not a small guy.

"I don't have a problem," I said, but there are only so many times I will tell somebody to move. I finally gave them the ultimatum: "Either you leave or I'm calling the cops." I went behind the counter and got on the phone with the police dispatcher, but these guys kept mouthing off.

Then one of them did the unthinkable. He spit on me.

There are certain things I can't accept, and being spit on is one of them. I stopped long enough to think, *I'm going to spend the rest of my life buckling bratty kids and their parents into miniature race cars*, and a split second later my hand was putting down the phone and my body was vaulting over the counter in one succinct motion.

I hit the big guy first, which left the smaller guy on his own. Divide and conquer at its best. The big guy went reeling across the room, slamming into a magazine rack, which sent periodicals flying everywhere. He landed on an arcade game, shattering the screen.

I grabbed the other guy next and leveled him before doing what I'd done for so many years. I started stomping and pounding the piss out of him. He was out, but I just didn't care.

By the time I was done, my customers were a heap of blood and bruises on the floor and the police were on their way. I grabbed both guys by their shirts and dragged them toward the door.

Elaine, who'd watched the whole thing play out, was in shock. "Why are they bleeding so badly when you didn't hit them hard?" she said. "Your punches didn't make that much noise."

Little did my young, naive wife know she would later watch fight after bloody fight when we'd both get involved with the UFC.

A few minutes later, justice's black-and-white sedan pulled into the parking lot. I told the officers what had transpired, trying to keep my cool as sweat dripped down my forehead.

When a man walked toward us and said he'd witnessed the entire thing, I almost lost it. He was an off-duty Orange County sheriff out with his kids. After explaining everything, he turned to me. "Son," he said, "that was the bitchinest thing I've ever seen." Then he walked away.

Without another word, the officers jotted something in their notepads, handcuffed the men, escorted them to the car, and drove off.

As soon as I was alone, I called Mike Hillman and forced the words out. "I'm in trouble."

Mike told me not to say a word to anybody. He would call the police department and make sure nothing came of it.

Elaine and I didn't sleep a wink that night as we waited for my lifelong career at the Malibu Grand Prix to be green-lit come morning. But the only call that came was from the LAPD. My delinquent butt was expected to report to the academy in a month.

HAWAII 1984

The only sunny day of our honeymoon in Hawaii until the last

CHAPTER 4

THE BADGE

Live as if you were to die tomorrow.
Learn as if you were to live forever.

—Mahatma Gandhi

Even at twenty-two years old, I knew I never wanted to spend my life behind a desk. I wasn't built that way physically or mentally, and I knew from watching my dad that police work would present a fresh challenge each new day. I never imagined some of my greatest challenges would come from inside me.

I thought there was nobility in the act of protecting people who couldn't protect themselves. In my mind, there were three kinds of people in the world—wolves, sheep, and a sheepdog that protected them—and the police officer was the last kind. I wasn't altogether right or wrong on the matter, but I learned later that there were some things I could change and other things I would never be able to. That was something I had to learn to live with over time.

Honestly, though, one of the immediate allures of crime fighting for me was a steady paycheck and health insurance for my family. When I reported to the training academy in July of 1985, I was hired for $2,204 a month. It was a big step up from what I'd made at the Malibu Grand Prix and allowed us certain luxuries, like being able to go grocery shopping. (Elaine and I had become quite the hot dog and nacho connoisseurs at the Grand Prix.) And the great thing about the academy was that I got paid the moment I stepped onto the training grounds.

I spent the next six months at the Los Angeles Police Academy in the twenty-one-acre Elysian Park complex, located outside the cluster of skyscrapers and government buildings of downtown Los Angeles. The academy is actually quite a beautiful place, with buildings atop a sprawling hill, surrounded by fountains, waterfalls, and streams. It wasn't what you'd expect from a police academy at all, and you might mistake it for a well-kept private college.

Elysian Park was the location of the 1932 Olympic Games pistol and rifle competitions and has been immortalized in countless films and TV shows, including *Dragnet*, which portrayed officers in a dignified light. In fact, creator and lead actor Jack Webb often visited the park in the 1950s and '60s to observe the training and boost the authenticity of his show. When he passed away in 1982, his character Sgt. Joe Friday's badge number 714 was permanently retired by the department.

Among the buildings at the police academy at Elysian Park, you could find the outdoor shooting ranges, classrooms, and even a cafeteria. This is where I and seventy-two other cadets reported for training Monday through Friday at 5:00 a.m. dressed in our navy-blue sweats, with our last names plastered in bold white lettering across our chests and backs so our instructors could tell us apart.

As a class, we all quickly figured out who excelled at what. I'd handled a gun before, so the firearms training wasn't a problem. My dad had allowed me to hold a gun, in his presence of course, from the age of ten on. He always told me if I wanted to pick one up, all I needed to do was ask him. Still, I'd sometimes sneak behind his back for the thrill of ogling one on my own. In fact, the bigger the gun, the more I liked it.

A part of our tactics training took place in the DEFT simulator, which stands for "development and evaluation of fire-arms training." In 1985, the DEFT simulator in Los Angeles was cutting-edge technology. Inside, you shot wax bullets at a large aluminum screen on the wall while a film projector ran different vignettes for you to react to. It was as lifelike as it could get, with real actors playing out the parts. The scenario itself lasted about a minute, but it took about twenty for the instructors to get the results, then reload the program for the next cadet. You were evaluated based on when you drew your firearm, where you landed your shots, your verbal commands, and taking cover.

In my six months at the academy, we were put through just two scenarios in the DEFT simulator. I got in a little trouble with one of them, which had me standing in line at a bank waiting for a teller when an armed robber suddenly pushed his way to the window and demanded money. There were civilians everywhere, so accuracy was key. I unloaded six rounds into the robber. Later models of the simulator would compensate for gunshot wounds and a target would fall when you hit him, but this guy just kept going, so I kept shooting and reloading, firing a total of eighteen rounds into his head. I got reamed by my instructors for that.

We also practiced at the standard outdoor firing range and Hogan's Alley, where we'd have to shoot on the move against targets popping up or coming at us. We were taught tactics, the universal guidelines for dealing with specific scenarios in police work, such as the proper technique for stopping cars or pedestrians and how to react in high-pressure situations. We also took classes on applicable law and learned the definitions of robberies, burglaries, and domestic violence. We studied traffic law and how to fill out reports, took a required eighty hours of Spanish, and watched lesson videos with instructors acting out family disputes or robberies. I got caught at my cubicle falling asleep to the recordings more times than I'd like to admit.

What I really excelled at were the self-defense classes, which included wrestling and other types of one-on-one combat. When a student was what we called HUA (because he had his head up his ass) and the instructors wanted to give him a hard time, I was the one they paired him up with.

I could also handle a squad car and was good at physical training, or PT, except for the running. Unfortunately, running was a big part of the program.

PT was broken down into two different regimens. Two or three days a week, we'd complete our fieldwork, which consisted of situps, push-ups, burpees, and other basic calisthenics, along with running around the track. On alternate days, we'd jog the hills, which is where I ran into trouble.

A cadet with asthma couldn't graduate from the academy, so I hid my inhaler in my jockstrap. Every time my lungs would clinch up, I'd take out the inhaler and sneak a deep breath. I was pretty good at that but got caught during one excruciatingly hot August day when temperatures soared to 118 degrees.

I made the run for the most part, but when we came back and stood at attention, my instructor noticed me leaning like the Tower of Pisa. After they pulled me out of the lineup and dumped me in the pool to cool me off, the inhaler bobbed to the surface and gave me away.

"What's this?" the instructor asked, snatching it from the water.

"It's an asthma reliever." I gasped, trying not to show my discomfort.

The officer in charge of PT reported me that day and asked to have me dismissed.

However, my drill instructor, Jerry Stokes, happened to be a fair man. A few days later, as I awaited my fate, he pulled me out of class. "Mr. McCarthy," he said in his slow drawl, stressing each consonant, "are we straight with everything?"

"Yes, sir," I said.

"Then don't worry about what's going on," he said. "Some people are saying you're not the best runner around here, and I think that's true. But I watched you wrestle yesterday and, son, you don't need to be a good runner."

Luckily, Sgt. Stokes took the time to evaluate my overall progress at the academy and reported it back to the higher-ups. I was cleared to continue.

I'd say my fondest memories of the academy were meeting and training with the other cadets, forging long-lasting relationships with some. On the second day at the academy, we were told to run from one fence of Dodger Stadium to the other, up the hill and back. A classmate named Joe Johnson threw up on a parked car at the finish line. We both laughed, and I knew right then I was going to like the guy. I ended up working with Joe for the bulk of my career.

One benefit of the endless running was that I got in better shape and lost more weight. I'd had to diet to start at the academy because I wasn't at the designated height and weight ratio. The doctor said I wasn't fat, but I still had to drop 20 pounds to make the requirements. Once I hit the academy hills, I went from 250 to 225.

As part of our training, we accompanied officers on calls. I saw my first real crime scene during my second ride-along, when two officers were called to the scene of a shooting at Tam's restaurant in a seedy downtown neighborhood in Southwest Division.

An employee's head was canoed down the middle with a shotgun blast, and blood splatter and brain pieces covered every possible surrounding surface. I looked at the scene and thought, *Whoa, the real world's not that pretty. Hollywood gets it pretty right.* The motive? A customer had ordered fries at the counter and hadn't gotten them the way he'd wanted.

Rather than scaring me away, the scene made me want to continue my training. At the end of six months, fifty-five of the original seventy-two cadets graduated. Of those, Southwest chose five, and I was one of them.

My police graduation ceremony (January 1986)

PHOTO COURTESY OF THE MCCARTHY FAMILY

Just as I graduated, Elaine was rushed to the hospital with what we thought was a case of appendicitis. It turned out she was pregnant.

I remember exactly what went through my head. *Holy shit, oh my God, I'm not ready for this.* We'd always wanted to wait five years, but you know how it is. One thing happens after another, and suddenly your life is taking off without you.

As a police officer, I was resigned to the fact that I'd never be rich. It was a decent living, though, and about six months later, Elaine and I were able to buy our first home for our growing family. Our single-story, two-bedroom house was in Covina, about twenty-five miles from the academy.

I felt prepared for what lay ahead. Looking back, I had no idea what was coming.

Under badge #10238, I entered my probation period at Southwest. In California, the standard training for police officers is called Peace Officer Standards and Training (POST). All probationary officers, or P1s, have to get a basic certificate to be considered full-fledged officers. I'd be on probation for the next year, paired with a training officer, or P3, and put to work on the streets. That training officer would become my partner until I was assigned to another when I switched watches, or shifts.

Every day I was out in the police car on patrol answering calls. In Southwest, we had five calls holding most of the time. As soon as we cleared one listing, another one would take its place. It was busy but fun.

Some of the calls would amount to nothing. We might get a burglary call and report to the building only to discover the alarm had been set off by the wind. Then there were very serious calls, for rape or child abuse, for example. Some calls I'd never forget, no matter how hard I tried. Some people are capable of the unthinkable at any given moment, hurting their friends, wives, husbands, even their own children. You never know when someone is going to snap.

Thankfully, not all of my calls were tragic. Some were quite comical, in fact. On one occasion, we were called to a domestic dispute. An old couple who had been together about forty years thought it was time to part ways.

My training officer listened to each side's complaints, then calmly slipped his badge off his chest and placed it in his open, outstretched hand. Remember, his job was to keep the peace—no more, no less. As serious as a minister on Sunday, he said, "You both really don't want to be together anymore. Do I have that right?"

"Yes, sir, I'm tired of her. She's just a nasty woman," the old man said.

"He's a son of a bitch," his wife said.

"Well, all right," my partner said. "Put your hands on my badge. By the powers vested in me by the state of California and the city of Los Angeles, you are hereby divorced from one another."

The couple looked at my partner.

"So I'm not married to her anymore?" the old man asked.

"Nope, not anymore," the officer said. "You feel better?"

"Goddamn right I do. I'm a free man."

As my partner and I left the house, I saw the old man beam.

"Did they really believe that?" I asked.

"Hell, yes, they believed it," my partner said, "and they're gonna be making love tomorrow anyway, so it really doesn't matter."

Some calls defied logic. Sometimes survival trumped everything else.

On Thanksgiving, we were sent to a family dispute and arrived to survey the father sitting at the dinner table with a fork stuck in his hand and his son shot dead in the chair across from him. It turned out the son had been mad at his father for taking the piece of turkey he wanted, and this was the end result.

Because of what we saw as officers every day, we all had to gain a sense of humor about things. Otherwise, the scenes would drive us crazy. I don't want to say we became desensitized. There were sobering images we'd never get over seeing again and again, but we made light of things to get through the days.

I learned how to be an officer when I started working patrol in the divisions. At first, I struggled to fit in with the realities of being on the force. The LAPD wasn't quite what I'd imagined, and I have to admit I was disappointed after my first month. I'd grown up around my dad and his fellow officers within the Metropolitan Division of SWAT, a unique breed. They were honorable brothers who worked together and backed each other up.

The first training officer I worked with outside the academy had been at a desk job in the communications department fourteen years before he'd been bumped back to patrol. Most officers didn't like the communications department because it was so boring, but this guy liked sitting at his desk and not having to do anything. He was scared to death to work in Southwest Division. On our first burglary call, I had to enter the building myself because he was too frightened. When he got to know me a little better, I became his protection.

As a child I'd watched my dad and his coworkers and listened intently to all their stories. I'd seen their gratification when they'd put away somebody who was a threat to the rest of society. In the beginning, that was missing for me. But in my third month of probation, I was moved to the morning watch, 11:30 p.m. to 7:45 a.m, and my view of police work completely changed. Leonard Mora, Nick Savala, Ron Barker, Tommy McMullen, and Carlos Velasquez hit the street and made a difference.

By now, I'd noticed there seemed to be three types of officers.

The first type were ticket writers or radio followers, who always picked up the little calls because they wouldn't require much from them. They did police work with people who would never be a problem. These officers would even write their mothers tickets. They chicken-shitted their way through their jobs.

The second type were middle-of-the-roaders, who pulled status quo and did just enough to handle their areas. However, they didn't go looking for what wasn't right in front of them.

The third type were big game hunters. These officers didn't hunt rabbits, which couldn't hurt them back; they hunted lions. They answered the hardest calls, went looking for bad guys, and put them away. That's what I wanted to do.

My training officer, Leonard Mora, and the others on the morning watch were the hunters. It wasn't a free-for-all, however. They taught me the balance between the letter of the law and the spirit of the law. That the law is an immense power, but it's there to protect people, not to crush them. That it's all about dispensing the law in a rational way, with care and compassion. Under Mora's lead, I found my place within the LAPD and my strengths were utilized.

As an officer, the more situations you get involved in, the more likely you'll encounter a suspect trying to get away or fight. The less you do, the less chance use of force will be needed. It's just basic math and odds. Every time you use what the department considers force, you have to file a report. If you file three in a month or six over a six-month period, the department can counsel you about use of force and even take you off the street if they feel there is a pattern.

In any profession, some people are more suited to certain tasks than others. I quickly gained a reputation for being willing to roll up my sleeves and get a little dirty. More often than not, I'd be called when others were having trouble controlling the situation. On a public street where a naked, sweaty guy on PCP was swinging a steel pipe, Tasering usually didn't work well, and we never wanted to use deadly force. A sergeant would just have to point and tell me to take the man into custody.

I wanted to put bad guys in jail and didn't mind dropping a few on their heads in the process if I had to. I was getting plenty of on-the-job training for my future profession as a mixed martial arts referee. Lateral drops and other wrestling takedowns worked well. I did as I was told, and it made me a viable part of the force.

If there was a job for a tunnel rat—a smaller guy who wasn't particularly physical—I wasn't the guy to send. But a few guys and I were the first ones sent to the front lines. We were also the first to reach the quota for use of force reports. I didn't mind, though, because I finally felt like I belonged and was accomplishing something positive.

I stayed on morning watch with Mora and the others for about six months. They requested to keep me there, which was a good fit for me. I admired Mora so much that when he left the department two years later, I traded in my badge number for his to keep his presence on the street in some small way.

About nine months into probation, on September 28, 1986, I made my next contribution to the world: my son Ron, named after my dad, of course. While I was carefully inspecting Ron's ten fingers and ten toes, his tiny hand grabbed my little finger. It's difficult to explain the love I felt in that moment. This little person had just come into my life, but I would have died for him. If a four-year-old had come up and tried to hurt him, I'd have punched the kid in the mouth. That's the kind of love you have for your child when he's born. He was the cutest, most perfect thing I'd ever seen.

I think all guys want their first child to be a boy, even if they won't admit it. They want to play catch and put them in Little League and take them to karate or wrestling class. They want that boy to protect his sister, who will be born next. I wanted the experience of teaching my two-year-old son to take a football stance and come at me so I could toughen him up, just as my dad had done with me.

I made it through my one-year probation unfazed and graduated to a full-fledged officer, or P2, then moved to night watch. Everything was going fine for the next few months, until I ran into an issue with a new captain who'd transferred into Southwest. We all called him Nick the Knife because of his awful reputation for stabbing everyone in the back. I thought he wasn't good at his job, and Southwest went downhill fast because of it.

My partner was accused of mishandling a suspect when we'd been called to a disturbance at a party. The suspect complained that she'd kicked him. Our supervisors both came to us separately, and we told them the truth: yes, we'd stopped the suspect outside the party and searched him, but other than that, nobody had laid a hand on him.

Nick the Knife called me into his office. "If you need to change your story now, you won't get in trouble," he said. He obviously didn't believe us.

I knew he didn't like my partner. She was a tough cop. Nick didn't like the fact that she didn't say nice things about him, so if I altered my story it would clear a path so he could punish her.

Nick tried a variety of ways to persuade me to squeal on my partner for something she hadn't actually done. He even brought up my dad. "Just because Ron was who he was doesn't mean you owe it to others to cover up for them."

He also tried to get something out of me by telling me about an experience he'd once had. "This drunk spat on me," he said, "and I went to hit him. My partner stopped me and said, 'We don't do that.' He handcuffed him, and you know what? My partner was right, and I was wrong."

I didn't know whether I was angrier with being pressured to lie or being forced to listen to his stupid story. "If someone spat on me," I said, "and I went to do something and my partner tried to stop me, the first thing I'd do is beat the piss out of the person who spat on me. Then I'd beat the piss out of my partner for trying to stop me." I ripped my badge off and threw it at him. "I don't want your fucking job. You guys are a bunch of candy asses."

As I walked out the door, I realized I'd screwed up in a major way. My temper had gotten the best of me. I had more people than just me to think about. I had a wife and son relying on me.

I was immediately suspended for forty days with no pay and

had to hand in my badge. My case was sent to a board of rights, a committee that would decide if I got to keep my job. Three captains listened to my testimony, and I ended up getting ten days of unpaid suspension for blowing my lid.

Next I was supposed to report to Hollywood Division to work the Prostitution Enforcement Detail (PED), a special assignment. However, when Bob Taylor, captain of Hollywood Division, found out I was coming off a ten-day slap on the wrist, he sent me back out on patrol. I will forever thank Bob for making this decision because it taught me some invaluable lessons.

On my first day on patrol in Hollywood, my new partner and I pulled over a car after observing it swerving in traffic. The driver, a fifty-year-old black man, danced through his sobriety test, and it was my inclination to let him go. But my partner wanted to take him in and have him screened by a drug recognition expert (DRE) at the station because he really thought the guy was on something illegal. Personally, I believed my partner was intoxicated on his own authority.

It's true that a police officer can stop anybody for virtually anything. I tried to do so for the reasons I'd been taught, such as for drivers running stoplights or exceeding the speed limit. But I wasn't the guy to write tickets if I believed I was staring into the eyes of a good person who'd made a mistake. He'd lose money or his car insurance would go up, and that didn't seem fair to me. I'd say, "Slow down" or "Watch the stop signs," and let the person off with the warning.

When you take someone into custody, it's even worse. You're having his car towed and impounded. I didn't do that to someone for just anything.

But demonstrating letter of the law versus spirit of the law at its best, my partner insisted we take this man in. At the station, though the man passed all drug tests and the expert couldn't determine if he was really on anything more than a prescription drug, my partner still pushed to book him.

"If you're going to book him," I said, "keep my name off the report."

It was another sobering day for me. I hadn't gotten into this line of work to screw with people. I wanted to go after the bad guys, and this guy wasn't one of them. I drove home that night disenchanted and disappointed, thinking it might be time to get another job.

My second day in Hollywood couldn't have gone more differently. I was assigned to work with a great officer named Jimmy Barlow, a six-feet-two, 140-pound black guy we all called J-Bone.

While we were driving about midnight, we noticed two guys cruising along with their lights off, a definite red flag. We were in the process of pulling them over when the car took off. We went into pursuit. After about a minute into the high-speed chase, the car suddenly screeched to the side of the road and one man jumped out with something in his hands.

On impulse, I jumped out and started chasing him as he hopped over a nearby fence, tossed something underneath another car, and scaled a second fence. I didn't know the neighborhood at all and it was pitch black, but I could track him because of the two blinking red lights on the backs of his sneakers. Note to would-be criminals: functionality always outweighs fashion.

Meanwhile, Jimmy was in pursuit of the driver, who'd peeled out.

Behind a run-down apartment building, I caught up to my

suspect, cuffed him, and dragged him back to where he'd tossed his package. By now, a few other police units had arrived on the scene.

When I opened the parcel, I found about eleven pounds of fifty-dollar rocks of cocaine worth hundreds of thousands of dollars. Miles away, I'd learn, the other suspect crashed his car into a tree, and Jimmy apprehended him. The car was full of guns.

I'd made my first serious bust in Hollywood Division, and it couldn't have gone any better if it'd been written for *Law & Order*.

This is what I'm talking about, I thought. It was quite a bit of loot for a young police officer to find during his first arrest in a new division, and I felt really good about it. I didn't even mind filling out all the paperwork, which included the traffic accident, a foot pursuit, and use of force.

My morning watch sergeant, Chuck Wampler, wanted to write me up for a commendation. It was the first time I interacted with this hardworking second-generation officer. He had a lazy eye and didn't look at anything directly, but he was one of the straightest shooters you could ever meet. I would work with Sgt. Wampler throughout my career, and I loved him.

Though Sgt. Wampler was impressed with my work, the lieutenant pointed out how I'd failed to follow procedure. I'd called dispatch to tell them I was in foot pursuit, but I hadn't told them where I was, so they couldn't send backup. The truth was that I didn't know the Hollywood streets well enough yet to report my position.

The bigger problem to them, though, was that I'd separated from my partner. I hadn't even realized Jimmy left me until I was running up the alleyway and heard on my belt radio about his vehicle pursuit.

The lieutenant had to settle for giving Jimmy and me a stern talking to, though, because the department couldn't ignore what we'd hauled in.

Jimmy joked with me after that first day together. "I can't take too many more days like this."

I laughed, feeling a little more secure about the people I'd taken up company with, and I drove home that night smiling.

This is what happens when your partner is a part-time photographer.

Three generations of McCarthy men

I asked for the double lucky number seventy-seven; Ron liked putting on my uniform.

VICES

Not everything that can be counted counts,
and not everything that counts can be counted.
—Albert Einstein

When people tell me they want to become police officers to help people, I recommend firefighting instead. People like firefighters because they come to their aid when they're sick and can't get out of bed or when they're stuck inside a burning building or a mangled car that's just hit a telephone pole.

But police officers usually come on the worst days of people's lives, when something bad has happened to them or someone they love. Sure, police officers are protecting and helping them, but that's usually hard for people to put into perspective when the most traumatic event of their lives is flashing before their eyes. Sometimes they want you to deliver instant justice, which is almost always impossible to do.

Being a police officer can be a thankless job. I once broke a guy's car window and pulled him out of his burning vehicle. He sued me for tearing his Ralph Lauren shirt. The city had to pay him $75 to make him happy.

Something I gradually learned as I moved through different units during my twenty-two years on the force was that you will do positive things in life that no one will ever see or recognize. And then you will perform seemingly small acts that mean the world to others. Accolades may be few and far between. You don't get to choose the value of what you do in others' eyes, so you have to take stock in knowing that doing the right thing is enough, no matter who notices.

After I worked for Southwest and Hollywood patrols for about the first year and a half, Captain Taylor transferred me in September of 1987 to the Prostitution Enforcement Detail (PED) in the Vice Unit of Hollywood Division. Captain Taylor thought it would be fun for me, and at first I thought so too. Instead of handling general radio calls, we'd be out observing illegal activities and making arrests, which was called "snooping and pooping." After sixteen months of being chained to the calls screen, that sounded refreshingly liberating to me.

A vice is defined as a practice or habit that is considered immoral, depraved, or degrading in normal society. That includes what we consider the public order crimes, such as prostitution, pornography, gambling, and a little drug trafficking sprinkled in for good measure, though Narcotics is really a separate unit unto itself. When I thought of Vice, I thought of Las Vegas. Later, I referred to it as the "crap crimes" because in my mind it never really amounted to much in the way of getting the true bad guys off the street.

My main job in Vice was to find ways to pull prostitutes off the streets for whatever amount of time I could. We had to catch them accepting money for their services, but they were usually smart enough to wait until they were out of sight to do that. Without the transaction, it was just consensual sex.

So we had to get creative. We busted them for breaking city ordinances like jaywalking or soliciting too long in front of a particular store or on a certain street corner—anything we could do to get them off the streets, even for just a few hours.

A prostitute's job is to manipulate, not only to get people to accept services but to get more money out of them. That's how they make a living. Sometimes they'd put up a fight when we'd try to arrest them, because having to get an angry pimp to bail them out or sitting in a jail cell until they got a court date equaled minutes ticking away without pay.

When I confronted prostitutes, my goal was to find a reason to either take them in or let them walk. Prostitutes' ears were always to the street. If they had some type of information that could help us in bigger cases, such as local murders or robberies, we'd let them go.

The offer of sex in exchange for freedom was always there, but no sane officers would do that. If they did, they'd become the john and could be arrested themselves.

My first partner in Hollywood Vice was Maria Gonzales, a five-feet-two bodybuilder who scared all the female prostitutes to death. They knew if they didn't listen to her, she'd make their lives miserable. Even though they weren't afraid of any of the male officers, they feared Maria.

I couldn't help feeling for some of the women. I thought they were simply trying to get on with their lives, make money, and survive. They weren't bad people. One girl I met was a crack addict who'd been in a few porn films. Her mom contacted me through the station, and I told her where her daughter was and tried to reunite them to get her off the street. In the end, it didn't work. Prostitutes were what they were, and the problem was that they were addicted to the lifestyle. It didn't matter what was right or best for them; they had to fuel that addiction.

My second Vice partner was Danny Molieri. Danny had already worked in Southwest with me. One of the sergeants had been impressed with him and plucked him out to come work in Holly-wood Division.

Danny had an unshakable confidence, and I swear he thought he was the best-looking guy in the world. He wasn't, but he did have the gift of gab, which came in handy when we were out working together. Danny and I gradually became friends. This bothered Elaine because she thought he was a player with the ladies, and she didn't want that rubbing off on me.

I couldn't blame Elaine for being worried. Many marriages fail when one or both spouses are in law enforcement. When I was coming home at 8:00 a.m. and had just enough time to kiss my wife on the cheek as she rushed out the door to her day job, it was taxing. And none of the other shifts were any better, especially when I was pulling double duty to make court appearances for my arrest cases when I wasn't on duty.

We also met a lot of women, and not all of them could resist a man in uniform. Unfortunately, a lot of police officers don't know how to say no in the face of temptation either. I wasn't one of those officers, though.

Danny and I worked Vice together, so we spent a lot of time around the Hollywood prostitutes. I have to tell you, I wasn't tempted in the least. Everybody thinks when you work Vice, you're in contact with a lot of women, and you are to a certain degree. But in Hollywood, there are about five male prostitutes to every female working the streets.

Sometimes I would work in plainclothes pretending to be a john looking to try something new. In my Mercedes rental car, I'd pull up wearing a suit and my wedding ring and tell a male prostitute I was from out of town and just wanted to experience a different side of me.

They'd climb into the car every time. The ones that groped first and asked questions later got crushed into the floorboard of the car. I have to admit, in those situations, I much preferred the females.

And then there were the transvestites. We called them Dragons, and I didn't like any of them. Dragons never hit on officers when they were in uniform, but they'd stand around taunting us with "Oh, jou are so good-looking" or "Oh, jou so fine." It made my skin crawl.

During one of my least favorite arrests, I was sent into a porn theater on Santa Monica Boulevard to look for lewd activity. I hated those places because of the sticky floors. You wanted to think you didn't know what you were walking in, but you always knew. That wasn't the worst of it. What I saw in places like that would turn my stomach. Once a priest was on his knees in front of another man, and, trust me, he wasn't praying.

On this occasion, I found my suspect in the far corner. I flashed my light and had to look twice because I couldn't believe what I was seeing. Under the cover of dark, wearing a little lace bra, a pink baby doll nightgown, red fishnet stockings, and brown Oxford walking shoes, a man was whacking his meat to the movie.

I didn't want to touch him but still managed to get him out-side, where my partner, Maria, and Sgt. Rick Webb were waiting. They started laughing and elected me to search the guy, who started sobbing uncontrollably, but I just couldn't make myself touch someone who'd been doing what he had just a few minutes before. On top of that, I later found out this guy was a teacher.

Transvestites weren't my cup of tea, but you'd be surprised which people were interested in them. I used to follow one of the biggest celebrities of all time through Hollywood as he picked up Dragons and drove them back to his Beverly Hills home—and there was nothing we could do about it. I did stop him and ques-tion him about his activities and acquaintances once, but since we didn't see any public sexual activity or money transactions, I never had the legal justification to arrest him or the Dragons he'd picked up.

For the next year, Danny and I usually had the highest recap, or number of suspects put in jail, during each twenty-eight-day deployment. We actually made a ton of narcotics arrests because, surprise, surprise, drugs and prostitution often seemed to go hand in hand. Our supervisors called us in frequently because, though narcotics wasn't really our detail, I couldn't help but sniff out a drug deal going down. I knew where to go, and I knew what to look for.

Aside from the drug busts, I hated every aspect of Vice and was ready to do some work that counted for something. My prayers were answered after one year, when the department busted me for working a second job, one of many off-duty jobs I'd have over the years because my family needed the extra cash. On this occasion, I'd been working as a bouncer at a nightclub called Fantasia. I was supposed to work the parking lot only but would often get pulled inside to man the floor. One night, I took an inebriated customer to the manager's office when he got a little out of control. He decided it would be a good idea to grab my sweater, and when he wouldn't let go, I blasted him with one punch. He went down and out, and I cut his face in the process.

The guy ended up suing me, and the department got wind of it. They didn't really care that I'd punched the guy, but they were upset that I hadn't gotten the necessary permit to take on the second job. The truth was that working as a bouncer was considered a no-no for an officer, and I hadn't applied for a permit because I'd known I wouldn't get it. I was suspended for five days and removed from Vice, which suited me just fine.

I returned to Hollywood patrol but for less than a month. Word of my knack for narcotics busts must have preceded me, and I was quickly offered a position on the buy-bust team with West Bureau, which covered the Hollywood, Wilshire, Pacific, and West Los Angeles Divisions.

West Bureau Narcotics was one big search and destroy mission, and we were always doing one of those two things. We were the undercover buyers or chase team members waiting to pounce on the sellers. Either way, we were arresting the bad guys, and I thrived on that.

You could say I was pretty zealous when it came to my busts. Drug dealers tend to run when they know they're about to get arrested, and this was one situation when I didn't mind pounding the pavement. If you were running from me and I was after you, I wouldn't just grab you. I'd tackle you into the concrete.

Rather than being known only as Ron McCarthy's son, I started to make a name for myself on the force, though my dad's presence was still everywhere. When I mentioned that my dad revolutionized a lot of programs inside the LAPD, I wasn't just referring to procedural or tactical advances. To win a bet, my old man had started the LAPD football program, which is still running to this day.

The bet had stemmed from what used to be called the Death Valley Relay, another scheme my dad had concocted in 1978 when he'd taken his SWAT team running across the famed southwestern desert to set a world's record. That race later became the Challenge Cup/Baker to Vegas Relay, beginning in Baker, California, and stretching across the highways through the desert for about 120 miles into Sin City. In 2009, 247 teams made up of about 8,000 runners from all over the world passed the finish line. The race has become so well-known that NBC's *CSI* shot an episode around the race.

Back in 1979, the Arizona Department of Public Safety had been one of the first teams to enter the Death Valley Relay. The Arizona DPS and LAPD started arguing over which state had better high school football players. In the end, Arizona DPS challenged the LAPD football team to a game. My dad gladly accepted on the spot, but there was one small problem: at the time, the LAPD didn't have a football team.

A little detail like that wasn't going to stop my dad, though. He recruited his first team from Metropolitan Division's flag football team, and on May 5, 1979, the first LAPD Centurions football team stormed the Jackrabbit Stadium in Mesa, Arizona. The Arizona DPS team didn't know what hit them, as the Centurions took home the 21–0 victory.

The idea to form more teams spread like wildfire through police departments across the country, and today the National Public Safety Football League hosts twenty-two teams nationwide.

In 1986, I joined the Centurions and had a blast playing for the next eight years. While some of my teammates had been college and pro ball players, I hadn't played since my freshman year of high school, so it wasn't easy. However, by my third year, I made team captain.

We traveled to New York, Phoenix, and Austin to scrap against other teams, and we did it all on our own time and dime to raise money for the Blind Children's Center of Los Angeles. In 1989, we even had over 40,000 people watching us win our first national championship against the Metro-Miami Magnum Force at the Orange Bowl Stadium in Miami.

Being a part of the Centurions was one of the things that saved me as a police officer. Those were the guys I wanted to be next to.

Leading the Centurions out for another game

PHOTO COURTESY OF THE MCCARTHY FAMILY

It wasn't about individuals; it was about what we could do together. That sense of camaraderie helped fortify me on the tougher days.

Though I didn't mind West Bureau Narcotics, I'd had my eye on another unit since I'd become an officer. I submitted my application and five months later got the call to transfer to the Community Resources Against Street Hoodlums program, the stupidest unit name I've ever heard. It was cool when you heard the acronym CRASH, but when you realized what it stood for, it sounded a bit ridiculous. I didn't join this antigang unit for the name, though.

CRASH wasn't a promotion, but it was what the department called a coveted position. It was made up of twenty patrol officers and fifteen detectives who handled gang-related radio calls, and we got to work more than one area at a time. I was still within West Bureau, so I continued to bounce between the Hollywood, Wilshire, West Los Angeles, and Pacific Divisions.

I'd wanted to work in CRASH because I felt it made a difference. We got to deal with the scumbags who intimidated others and set a lot of crimes in motion, so in a way we were getting to the heart of the matter.

I stayed in CRASH for the next four and a half years. It was like navigating through a separate society with its own set of rules, relationships, and vocabulary. My main job was to makes arrests and collect data by talking to the members of the gangs I was assigned to. I had my regulars, but new guys were always popping up into the mix as well. We took down information on everyone, including gang tattoos and secret hand signs, and recorded them onto field identification (FI) cards, which we sorted into each gang's pile at the end of the day. When a gang-related crime was

Top left: Those glasses, and the body attached to them, took one hell of a beating.

Top right: My short-lived stint as a tight end in Junior All-American football: I was quickly moved to left tackle.

Above: My second powerlifting competition at 525 pounds: I was eventually able to lift 802 pounds in the squat.

PHOTO COURTESY OF THE MCCARTHY FAMILY

Above:
Elaine and I at her senior prom:
look at that hair! (May 1984)

Right:
Me with my Princess Di

PHOTO COURTESY OF THE MCCARTHY FAMILY

Left:
Graduating from the Los Angeles Police Academy, and this time my hair is much better than Elaine's. (January 4, 1986)

Below:
Between two LAPD greats: my father, Ron McCarthy (L), and Chief of Police Daryl Gates

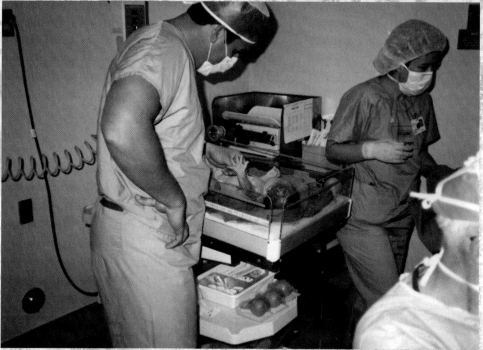

Above: One of the best moments of my life: the birth of my first child

Below: Coming out of the LAPD Centurion locker room with my personal water boy, Ron

Above: My favorite Christmas card ever (1993)

Below: With Rorion and Royce Gracie at an early UFC: What was I thinking with that vest?

Above: Checking in on Patrick Smith after his loss to Royce Gracie in the finals at UFC 2 "No Way Out" (March 11, 1994)

Right: Instructing last-minute alternate Fred Ettish prior to his bout with Johnny Rhodes at UFC 2

PHOTO BY SUSUMU NAGAO

PHOTO BY SUSUMU NAGAO

Above: The media often interviewed me about the UFC.

Bottom right: I took my shirt from UFC 5 and added two numerals to update this one. What a cheap bastard!

Left: Let's . . . get it . . . on!

PHOTO COURTESY OF TOM PALMER

Above: Paul Varelans vs. Marco Ruas at the UFC 7 final in Buffalo: Who says there's no MMA in New York?

Below: Getting a closer look during the Oleg Taktarov-Dan Severn final at Ultimate Ultimate (December 1995)

committed, we could use the cards to find the members who probably were involved or knew something about it.

For a long time, I was assigned to the 18th Street gang, one of the biggest Hispanic gangs throughout Los Angeles and eventually the world. I was also assigned to the Mara Salvatrucha, a ruthless Salvadoran gang. The School Yard Crips was another one I had. There was a turf war on the Venice boardwalk between the Venice Shoreline Crips and the Playboy Gangster Crips out of West Los Angeles in the Cadillac-Guthrie area.

We were in uniform, driving through the gang-infested territories in unmarked vehicles. We could make legal detentions, stopping suspects to talk with them and investigate if we had reason to believe they had done something.

Sometimes I'd stop gang members during what's called a consensual encounter. I'd pull up in the squad car and ask a gang member to come talk to me. Many of them didn't know they could just say no and keep walking. I wouldn't be able to follow them, but I wasn't about to tell them that. They'd always agree.

Some were no older than ten or eleven and were usually victims of school yard or neighborhood abuses. They'd been harassed enough and thought it was better to join a gang than get the piss beaten out of them until they did.

I understood that these kids were just trying to survive, and sometimes it was hard not to feel bad for them. However, they all had a choice, and they made it. And there were enough kids who said no to it. I knew this was a hard thing to do, but gang life was no joke. One thing TV doesn't sensationalize about gangs is their finality. There are only two ways of getting out: you die or you move to another county, state, or nation for good.

I arrested one kid when he was twelve years old for being part of a drive-by shooting. He was a member of 18th Street and had been a passenger in the car, so he ended up going to court and being placed in juvenile hall. He was back on the street in about four months.

When he was thirteen, I arrested him again when he was involved in another drive-by shooting. This time he was the shooter. He was sent to the California Youth Authority (CYA), where he stayed until he was sixteen.

He was out for two days before he executed four TMC gang members at a 76 gas station up on Hollywood Boulevard. Not only did he put them down with his first round of shots; he popped an additional bullet in each of their heads with a Calico 9mm, loaded with a 100-round magazine, not your standard choice of weapon for a gang hit.

I'd arrested that kid three times in four years, but he kept committing crimes. I saw this often and couldn't help but feel frustrated with the system for spitting him back out every time I put him in jail.

Because they chose this life, I never had a problem with gang members shooting other gang members. To me, that was part of natural selection, like animals in the wild. It was survival of the fittest.

The worst part of CRASH was pulling up to see an innocent old man shot on his porch or a little kid dead on a sidewalk after a drive-by shooting. That would get to you and drive you mad. It was all so senseless.

In CRASH, I was considered one of the go-getters and usually brought in high stats. I think I did well because I saw the big picture and knew when to pounce or to hang back and wait. Sometimes keeping a lowlife out of jail would lead to them owing me info on the street, and that could pave the way for the bigger arrests.

I didn't have a problem giving members and their gangs respect as long as they showed me the same in return. I never downplayed a gang, which sometimes wasn't easy, especially when they had names like The Magician's Club or Rebels. If they believed you were decent to them, occasionally they'd give you info because they thought it would screw over a rival gang.

I also liked CRASH because it was the place where I worked with some of the best officers, many who'd go on to really big details, including Bomb Squad and SWAT. It was satisfying to be a part of a team that got results from working hard.

We also played hard, and practical jokes were pretty common. If you were young and new and pulled a practical joke on another officer, they'd call you Morton for being salty, not doing what was expected of a newbie, or they'd call you a boot. Boots had to be careful.

Luckily, I wasn't a boot any longer and could appreciate a good practical joke. I knew they weren't meant to ridicule anybody but just to be fun. We dealt with a lot of serious stuff, and laughter helped relieve the stress of it all.

Some of the pranks were quite elaborate. Sometimes we'd put shoe polish on the handle of the squad car's door or behind the steering wheel, glob Vaseline onto the windshield wipers, run invisible fishing line from the car lights and siren to the door handle, or plug up the air vents with talcum powder. You learned not to be surprised when a beanbag came flying through your patrol car window as you passed another patrol vehicle. Whoever had the beanbag at the end of the day would have to buy everybody else drinks after work. Even sergeants dished out the pranks, and we dished them right back. In CRASH, we were all one.

During my fifty-two months at CRASH, my personality started to emerge on the force, and I also hit a few milestones in my private life.

On November 24, 1989, just eight months after I'd joined the unit, my daughter, Britney, was born. Elaine went into labor on our fifth wedding anniversary, which killed the plans I'd made for a nice dinner in Palmdale, where we'd moved from Covina.

Prior to Britney's big debut, we were told she was breach but would turn around in time. She didn't, however, and the doctor decided to perform a Cesarean. Then, just before the procedure, it was discovered that she had suddenly turned into the proper position.

It was a typical Britney move, we'd learn. Like her father, she liked to do things her own way. We'd gone into the hospital at 10:00 a.m., and by the time Britney was born it was 12:13 a.m. She had to have her own day.

Another life change came after a dinner out with friends. A few months after Britney was born, Elaine and I spent an evening with John McKnight and his wife. Both worked for the LAPD. Donna was a public safety radio operator manning the calls coming in from the other officers in a compound four stories under the ground. Elaine mentioned how she wanted to try something new, and Donna suggested she become a radio operator as well.

I knew Elaine was looking for some excitement and this wasn't the gig for that, but I didn't say a word till we got home. "Some days," I said, "you'll get these high-pressure calls from officers in pursuit, shots will be fired, and you'll have to stay really calm while you take down the information and call for backup. Other days, you'll be bored out of your mind, sitting around waiting for calls to come in.

"The difference between that and my job is that at least as a police officer, if I don't like doing traffic, I don't have to. I can go do Narcotics or CRASH or SWAT. There are all kinds of jobs within the job. But with the radio operator position, if you don't like it, there's nothing else you can go to."

As the words left my lips, I realized I'd just opened a can of big, fat, ugly worms.

"Okay," Elaine said. "Then I'll become a police officer." She started talking about all the fun positions she could try. She wanted to be a detective and maybe work in child crimes.

I knew there was nothing fun about either of those things, but there was nothing else I could say. Elaine liked being a part of what I did, and I guess my role as a police officer wasn't going to be any different.

For the next few months, I watched Elaine go through all the testing I'd taken to secure a place at the police academy. She asked me to help her study and prepare. Of course I did, but I kept thinking she'd give up on the idea.

She passed her written tests and then her orals. During the physicals, she had to scale a six-foot wall, and I thought for sure she'd hit her limit here. But she scaled that wall and all the other obstacles placed in front of her. What had taken me a year and a half to accomplish, she got done in three months. She got her letter of assignment to the academy's class starting in November of 1990.

At the academy, I thought Elaine might buckle with all of the running or self-defense classes. She wasn't an athlete, and she'd be the first to tell you she wasn't that coordinated.

I also thought she'd miss our children, Ron and Britney, who were now being taken care of by a nanny at home.

Another thing I thought would change her mind was being yelled at. The training officers got in your face and broke you down, then built you back up the way they wanted. Once again, Elaine proved me wrong and handled it all.

In June of 1991, she graduated and reported to Hollywood for her year's probation. Although I'd never wanted my wife to become a police officer, I was extremely proud of her accomplishment. It was one of the best things she ever did for herself. It helped her understand a lot about what I did, and it changed her views on the world and people just as it had changed mine.

However, I didn't want Elaine going out on duty thinking the techniques she'd learned for subduing suspects would work against just anybody, because chances were they wouldn't. What I knew she had going for her was that she was incredibly bright and would listen. I needed her to understand that her greatest asset as an officer wouldn't be a choke hold; it would be her mind.

At first she thought I was belittling her. "I could use a choke if I had to," she said.

"Well, come over here and choke me then," I said.

She couldn't.

I hadn't asked her do it to prove her wrong, but I needed her to know that just because an academy instructor had taught her something and a classmate had tapped when she'd put a choke on him didn't mean she could do it effectively to anyone.

"Don't believe the crap they told you about physically controlling people. What you really need is the ability to realize you can't handle every situation on your own. There's nothing wrong with asking for help." Then I taught her to watch the body language of a suspect and told her to get on the radio and call for backup if she saw any warning signs.

As she went out on patrol in Hollywood and began to see the sad and sickening situations I'd been exposed to a few years earlier, she began to understand the gravity of it all. It wasn't an easy time for me either. I was afraid for her.

Every time I was in Hollywood, I'd have one ear to my CRASH radio and the other to Hollywood's frequency. She'd get a call, and I'd go spy on her. That was the only way I could make sure she was safe on the job.

Elaine was a police officer for the next three years and patrolled the streets for about a year and half of them. Those were years I really had to stay on my toes, and what monumental years they'd be for me.

Posing for a picture in Hollywood, California

Visiting my dad when he worked for the International Association of Chiefs of Police in Gaithersburg, Maryland

THE RIOTS

A man travels the world over in search of what he needs and returns home to find it.

—George Moore

I suspect you can recall where you were on September 11, 2001, when two commercial airliners crashed into the World Trade Center in New York City. Your life and how you looked at it may have changed after that day. Maybe you reevaluated your priorities. Drastic events can lead to dramatic change.

For me, one of those life-altering events happened on April 29, 1992, when four LAPD officers were acquitted of the charges brought against them for the beating of Rodney King. Nearly fourteen months before, in the early hours of March 3, 1991, they had pursued and then pulled over King during a high-speed chase.

The morning after King's arrest, my dad called me from Gaithersburg, Maryland, where he was living and working for the International Association of Chiefs of Police. "What the fuck are you guys doing out there?" he asked.

I had just woken up, so I didn't have the faintest idea what he was talking about.

"Turn on the TV," he said. "Any station."

I did, and that's when I first saw the dark, grainy images that would become the centerpiece of most newscasts the world over for months. An amateur cameraman had been woken by the sounds of sirens and had captured the video of a black man on all fours surrounded by four white policemen beating him repeatedly with their batons. King attempted to rise as the officers continued to take swings at him. One officer then began to stomp King's body, while another group of officers not involved in the actual apprehension watched a few feet away.

I didn't recognize the suspect, but I was pretty sure I could pick out two of the officers right away. One had worked in CRASH with me until he'd taken an opportunity to become a temporary P3, or training officer, at Foothill Division. I'd had my opinions about this officer. He wasn't a bad guy, but I thought he was a putz who couldn't fight his way out of a wet sack. With the badge on, sometimes he'd act much tougher than he really was. I'd told my supervisors, "You need to set him straight. He's going to get himself in trouble." But then he'd left the unit before anything had been done about it.

You can imagine the irony of it all when I watched the video and wondered if he was the one beating King. I thought, *Well, if that were me getting hit all those times, I'd want it to be him holding the baton. He can't hit that hard.*

There was more to this story, a longer version of the video that the masses didn't see. The beginning of the encounter between King and the police had been cut out of the version that looped over and over on the nightly news. Additional footage showed King going after the officer before it got rough. Of course, the edited version made for a much juicier story, so that's what the networks aired.

In the unedited video, King was pulled over in his Hyundai with two other male, black passengers. These men did what they were told and were taken into custody without incident. However, King, in whatever drug- or alcohol-induced state he was possibly in, decided he didn't want to follow the program.

When he came after the officer, he was met with a baton and then a Taser, which slowed but didn't stop him.

The officers wanted to get King into a certain position: proned out, or lying on his stomach, arms out, palms up, legs spread. King wouldn't comply, so they used the batons to make him, but it went too far. There's no doubt it went beyond the type of force that should have been used in the situation.

When the four officers were arrested and charged with using excessive force, their fates became a national obsession, just as the trial of O. J. Simpson would a few years later.

Another officer I thought I'd recognized in the King video was a supervisor on the scene. He was a good guy. He wasn't afraid to put his hands on suspects, but he wasn't a racist in any way. I'd watched him give mouth-to-mouth to a Dragon in the holding cell. This black man had vomit coming out of his mouth and hadn't showered in weeks, but this officer hadn't hesitated in trying to save his life. Here was a sergeant who hadn't shown prejudice in the past. Watching this officer in the video, I figured he'd been paired up with guys who didn't really know how to handle an aggressive, high-pressure situation.

I remembered this when my dad called again and said, "The district attorney asked me to testify as an expert witness against the four officers." The DA wanted him to speak about the incorrect procedure they'd used. My dad was pissed off about what had happened and that the whole episode had hurt his friend Daryl Gates, the chief of police at the time, so he'd agreed to do it.

Not only did I know this move was going to ruin my dad's reputation at the LAPD, but I also knew he didn't really have a handle on what was going on. "Don't sit here and judge somebody you don't know based on your experience as a police officer," I said. "You got to work with the best, so the results you got were the best. When you work with crap, you get crap, and you can't always blame the supervisor for what's happening."

Thankfully, my dad listened to me and withdrew from the trial. But the real fireworks were yet to come.

On April 29, 1992, in a court in Simi Valley, about thirty miles outside of Los Angeles, with a jury absent of any black members, one of the four police officers was acquitted when the jury couldn't come to a decision on one of his charges, and the other three were exonerated of the charges altogether.

Much of the Los Angeles South Central community, made up of many black and minority residents, took to the streets immediately in sporadic groups. At first, they yelled obscenities at passing cars. Then they threw rocks and other objects at them. The more brazen groups of disgruntled teenagers and adults then swarmed on the vehicles, smashing out the windows with pipes, as other terrified drivers looked on in horror.

Officers were dispatched to the disturbances, but quickly there were too many instances with too many aggressive civilians involved for the police force to handle. Officer reserves quickly ran dry. Unable to control the tide, a supervising lieutenant from 77th St. Division ordered every LAPD officer off the streets altogether. That proved to be an unwise decision because the groupings combined and grew, then migrated to the streets of South Normandie and West Florence Avenue, in the heart of South Central.

On that corner, a white man driving an eighteen-wheeler was stopped, dragged out of his cab, and thrown onto the street. Six black men, all between the ages of nineteen and twenty-seven, beat Reginald Denny with their hands, feet, and random objects they found on the ground. The final blow came from Damian "Football" Williams, a nineteen-year-old gang member who knocked the battered and bloody Denny unconscious with a slab of concrete, then did a jig over his body. Not a single officer came to Denny's aid. He eventually came to, blood streaming down his face as he writhed in pain next to his red truck.

A news helicopter caught the attack overhead and aired it live for the entire country to see. This was the flash point of the Los Angeles Riots.

The court's verdicts had come in just as my unit had been finishing roll call at our station next to the West Los Angeles Courthouse. When I heard that the officers had been acquitted, I knew there would be hard feelings in the community. I didn't realize how bad it would get.

My partner and I were scheduled to go out into Pacific Division that afternoon, and we started to drive down toward the Oakwood area to check on the Venice Shoreline Crips. I had no idea what was beginning to bubble over at the corner of West Florence and South

Normandie, but all hell was about to break loose.

My sergeant called for a Code Alpha at the nearby Wilshire Division's parking lot, which meant my entire unit was ordered to meet up at that location and wait for further instructions. We congregated with our two sergeants, Chuck Wampler and J. P. Williams, and waited. From every direction we could hear shots ringing out.

Soon a call came over the radio. "Officer needs help, shots fired." The location was a block away at the Shell Station at Venice and South La Brea.

We all jumped into our cars, but another order came over the radio from the area captain, J. I. Davis, which stopped us in our tracks: "Stay at the station. Do not respond to the call for help."

The order went against everything we'd ever been taught. When another officer's call for help came, you dropped everything and went. This order just proved what I'd always thought: the command staff of the LAPD were cowards who would run and hide when the shit hit the fan.

It took me and a few of the other officers about two seconds to make up our minds that we were going to disobey the command. It took Sgt. Williams about three seconds to officially order us to disobey and leave the parking lot. Within fifteen seconds, we were in vehicle pursuit of the suspects who'd been shooting at the officers at Venice and La Brea.

The suspects shot back at us as they tried to escape into the School Yard area that the Crip gang had claimed as its turf. A shooting occurred shortly after as the suspects attempted to run from their vehicle. It was the first shooting I witnessed over the next six days, and it wouldn't be the last.

From that point on, I was out on the streets attempting to

stop the bad people from hurting the good people. For me, it was as simple as that.

It's hard to explain what I saw in those next two days, but imagine a war breaking out in your neighborhood, where no home, store, building, or car is spared from senseless destruction at the hands of an endless, angry mob.

It seemed everywhere I turned, buildings and cars were vandalized and on fire. The stench of burning buildings was heavy in the air. I could hear glass breaking as looters hurled garbage cans into storefront windows to gain entry and take merchandise they couldn't possibly have any use for. Some of the overconfident looters pulled U-Haul trucks up to the exposed storefronts. In Koreatown, I watched store owners shoot at the ones who entered to rob them in plain sight.

People randomly shot at us as we moved from situation to situation trying to regain some semblance of order. Shots were even being fired at firemen as we offered them extra body armor so they could save some of the buildings from burning down to their frames.

Victims stood on the corners pleading for help, but there was just too much to respond to at once.

I watched looters get run over by cars as they left a store across the street. *Good,* I thought. *You deserve what you just got.*

The natural order of things was out of whack, and the police, of whom there weren't nearly enough, had to adapt. We set up an abbreviated justice system in which normal procedure and paperwork went out the window. We stripped it down to the basics. Some of us took to the streets and apprehended lawbreakers, jammed them into police cars, vans, and buses, and sent them off to the stations where other officers would do the paperwork, book, and jail them.

When one station radioed back that it was full and couldn't possibly take another body, we took them on to the next station.

At a Vons grocery store where the sprinklers had been triggered at full blast, we watched as shoplifters waded through several inches of water, sweeping items off shelves into big garbage bags. There were so many of them ignoring our commands that we finally stood at the entrance and clocked anyone trying to leave with anything more than the clothes on their backs.

For two days it was absolute chaos, but they were the greatest two days I'd ever worked for the LAPD. I didn't have to worry about use of force reports or paperwork or procedure. It was a free-for-all, and the world suddenly became clear to me. There were good people trying to save their businesses, homes, and families; they weren't doing anything wrong. The rest of them, regardless of color or race, were animals.

I was scared to death for Elaine, who'd just finished the day watch and was on her way home when the riots broke out. I'd called her and told her to not answer her phone when the department rang to ask her to come back in for duty. It was wrong of me, but I was afraid she'd get hurt. She did the right thing and went to work the next day when she was called. Her station assigned her to security on the rooftop with a shotgun. She completed her shifts there for the next two weeks.

For two days, the LAPD used every resource it had to regain control of its hostile city. President George H. W. Bush even authorized and mobilized members of the National Guard before it started to calm down. By the sixth day, a citywide curfew was lifted, signaling the end of the riots. For the next two weeks, I and other officers stayed on the streets to make sure nothing flared up again.

The riots left undeniable damage in their wake. It seemed as if every corner I turned on had buildings and cars gutted by fires. Graffiti and vandalism were also rampant. In the aftermath, 53 people had died, another 2,000 had been injured, 1,100 buildings had been destroyed by about 3,600 fires, and material damage to the city was estimated at somewhere between $800 million and $1 billion.

What impacted me most was the feeling that the LAPD couldn't handle a crisis of this proportion and our leadership was downright pathetic.

Honestly, though, I don't believe the riots themselves had anything to do with Rodney King, the police, or the perceived racism between them. Yes, there were people who were frustrated that the police were acquitted. But if you look at the case, including the missing moments of video when King attacked the officer, you can see why the jury came to their conclusion. It was hard to find the officers guilty based on the letter of the law.

However, a lot of the black community honed in on four white officers beating on a black man and getting away with it. "That's our lot in life," they said. "This is the way we get treated, and we just got screwed again." They were upset and felt cheated. I understood that. They were cheated in some ways, but it didn't give anyone the right to harm others.

And during the payback moments of taking or wiping out what others had, looters and vandals destroyed their own neighborhoods and belongings without even thinking about it. I looked at people differently after the riots, just as people had looked at officers differently after the King arrest.

An officer couldn't walk into a restaurant to pick up his dinner without hearing people whisper, "I wonder if he was one of them." In their eyes, anyone who wore a uniform was guilty. Every time we'd go to do something, people would yell, "Rodney King! Rodney King!"

I was never embarrassed to be a police officer, but I was embarrassed by the way people perceived what had happened when they didn't really know anything about it. I also knew some people were looking for reasons, contrived or not, to blow the whistle on police officers. Videotaping became a big trend, so officers had to be smarter about how they went about their work on the streets. I changed the kind of police officer I was; I didn't go about being as free-willed as I'd been when I went after suspects. As a result, I didn't put as many bad guys in jail.

The LAPD had been forced on the defensive.

About four months after the Rodney King beating, the Christopher Commission report was released. Chaired by attorney Warren Christopher, who later became the secretary of state under President Bill Clinton, the commission had been formed in 1988 to identify officers who were considered heavy-handed.

The commission came up with a list of forty-four repeat offenders, officers who had received six or more allegations of excessive force between 1986 and 1990. However, the screening process was flawed because they looked only at police reports, and officers' definitions of use of force varied. While one might write up a report for grabbing a suspect's wrist, another wouldn't consider that worth reporting at all. Some who made the list were clearly not offenders.

I wasn't on it, but one of my partners from Southwest made number one. He was strict about the way he did his police work, but I never saw him use force when he shouldn't have. He was a great cop who just got caught up in the political game and didn't survive it.

I didn't need the Christopher Commission report to tell me what had gone wrong during the Rodney King incident, the first falling domino that had set a string of destructive events in motion. The problem was that too many limitations were being placed on officers in the heat of the moment and they didn't know how to react. For instance, we had been told we couldn't use chokes on suspects. In fact, the officers' unofficial slogan in 1984 had been "Smoke 'em, don't choke 'em." The academy's take on chokes was much the same as uninformed people's perceptions of chokes in MMA today. They didn't understand them, and the general consensus was that if you choked someone, they would die.

Previously, there'd also been some choke-related deaths when officers had tried to apprehend suspects who were on PCP. The drug was especially popular in South Central Los Angeles at the time, and users were typically easy to spot, often found talking to someone they alone could hear and naked because they felt like they were burning up. They weren't able to engage in rational conversation, and any stimulus could set them off. They didn't feel pain and seemed to have superhuman strength, which made it difficult for officers to control them. They wouldn't quit fighting or attempting to flee.

During struggles with officers, some suspects' tracheas were crushed, although I believe it had more to do with the execution of the technique than its appropriateness. Still, many on the force questioned why an officer would attempt to use a choke hold on a suspect who was trying to cause him serious bodily harm when it would probably be much more effective to shoot the aggressor instead.

I thought this way of thinking was ridiculous and went looking for my own answers. What I discovered was that Sgt. Greg
Dossey, who had once run the PT Self-Defense Unit, had studied
and categorized the instances of use of force within the LAPD
in 1988 and again in 1992. Both years, he determined that two-
thirds of the altercations had ended on the ground with the officer applying a joint lock and handcuffing the suspect. I thought
Dossey's research could point us all in the right direction. If so
many altercations ended on the ground, why weren't we focusing
on training officers there?

At the time, my knowledge of ground tactics was minimal. I'd
wrestled and boxed, but my best friend, Joe Hamilton, also an officer, had studied karate and judo. Joe, a few other officers, and I
exercised together regularly. During one workout, Joe mentioned
some South American brothers who had their own ground art he
thought I'd love. Joe couldn't remember the family's name, but I'd
later come to know them as the Gracies.

I didn't seek out the Gracies, but we all found each other eventually.
In the wake of the Rodney King incident and the riots, the LAPD
organized a Civilian Martial Arts Advisory Panel led by Sgt.
Dossey, to come up with new tactics an officer could use in appre-
hending a violent suspect. Because I had a great interest in combat sports, I was asked to join to represent the police force. Aside
from me, the panel included a who's who of martial arts figures in
Southern California, from kickboxer Benny "The Jet" Urquidez
to judo expert Gene LeBell to the determined-looking Brazilian
jiu-jitsu black belt Rorion Gracie.

The panel, which started meeting about once a week, was a

mess from the get-go. There was no way these practitioners, all experts in their chosen arts, would agree on doing something one way. Each one thought his art was superior to the other's.

For the first few meetings, I sat quietly and watched them demonstrate their disciplines on dummies or assistants they'd brought. They'd throw the dummies around or subdue the assistants, and I have to admit they all looked great doing it.

However, it wasn't realistic to think what they were demonstrating could be used by an officer on the street. After a few meetings, I decided to speak up. "I mean no disrespect, but your techniques work on your subjects because they're letting you do it. On the streets, a suspect will put up a fight. They're not just going to let you do it."

The expert du jour said, "Do you want to come try being my subject?"

"Okay, I'll do it," I said, "but I'm not going to just stand there."

The martial artist, who'd incidentally been on the cover of *Black Belt* magazine a few times, went to grab me, and I took him down, sat on his chest, and trapped his arm around his neck. I'm not sure what overcame me, but I started to slap him lightly across the face with my free hand. "What are you going to do now?" I asked.

I looked up at the rest of the congregated experts and realized I should get up. I hadn't meant to make the man look bad, but my frustrations with the panel had overtaken me. I'd made a mistake, and Sgt. Dossey wasn't happy. But Rorion Gracie, who usually yawned out loud at the demonstrations, seemed rather pleased.

Afterward, Rorion invited me to his academy to experience his art, Brazilian jiu-jitsu, firsthand.

At the Gracie Jiu-Jitsu Academy in Torrance, California, Rorion introduced me to his skinny younger brother, Royce, who would demonstrate. Rorion's family preferred to call the art Gracie Jiu-Jitsu because they'd perfected their own variation that utilized positioning and leverage to overcome strength once a fight hit the ground. I was impressed immediately with Rorion's confidence. If you wanted to fight, the Gracies were ready to fight, and that said everything to me.

Usually, when I'd tried out other martial arts, I was told I couldn't do this or that because I could get hurt. Rorion placed only one restriction on me during Royce's demonstration: no biting. Otherwise, I could do anything I wanted: punch, kick, or tackle. At any point, we could stop if I tapped out by slapping any part of Royce's body or the mat. We decided this time we'd grapple without punches or kicks.

I grabbed Royce's legs and lifted him off the mat fairly easily—he must have been 100 pounds lighter than me—then took him down onto the mat. I didn't realize I'd landed in his half guard, with one of my legs laced between both of his and my other leg on the outside of his. While I tried to crush him on the mat with my body weight, he started breathing in short, focused spurts. I actually thought I was doing well.

Royce began to talk to me. "You watch this movie *Rocky*?" he said in his Portuguese accent. He kept wiggling while I tried to squash him.

I didn't know how to answer.

"You watch *Rocky*," he continued. "Everybody think he lose too."

I thought that was funny.

With that, Royce draped his legs over my shoulders and

straightened out my arm by pushing his hips up underneath it. My elbow joint extended at an uncomfortable angle, and I tapped out immediately.

"How did you do that?" I asked.

Royce flashed his all-knowing smile.

I'd have to return to find out.

Rorion, Royce, and I started training together almost immediately after that. I became a student in the subtleties of Gracie Jiu-Jitsu at Rorion's academy, and he tried out his suggestions for the police panel on me.

I had no idea what it was like to be a jiu-jitsu expert, and Rorion didn't know what it was like to be a police officer. Whenever he said, "This is the way I'd do it," I'd give him the gun belt and let him try the technique on me.

In any situation as a police officer, a gun is involved. If you're rolling on the ground with a suspect, you have to be conscious of your weapon because the suspect could always reach for it.

The difference between Rorion and all the other panel experts was that he was willing to learn. Over time, Rorion would meet me at the police academy, where I taught him how to use a gun better, how to shoot on the move, take angles on suspects, and perform other police-related exercises. This was the beginning of our friendship.

And like so many others, I fell in love with Brazilian jiu-jitsu. It was a simple but highly effective art, and it was real. I appreciated the fact that there was no mystic element to it. You trained hard with your partner, and the longer you practiced, the better you got.

The Gracies didn't just dole out ranking belts, a problem I saw with other martial arts academies. You had to earn them, and the only way to get to the next level was to work hard and dedicate yourself.

That wasn't a problem for me. I became a disciple. These guys had the knowledge of life. To me, this was it. They fought. They competed. They were honest. I was convinced, hook, line, and sinker.

I even tried the Gracie diet, which involved eating a lot of watermelon and cream cheese. I got sick of watermelon really fast.

I started going to the Torrance academy twice a week and even started taking my kids to the academy to train. I'd drive home to Corona from the academy in Los Angeles, pick up my seven-year-old, Ron, and four-year-old, Britney, and take them down to Torrance. I was putting in some serious miles.

Twice a week was already pushing it, but I had to train more. Three times a week was the ultimate commitment, so I made it and then also paid for private lessons with Royce on the side.

As my knowledge of Gracie Jiu-Jitsu grew, my faith in the martial arts panel dwindled. Amidst all the bickering and posturing, the panel was never going to produce anything of use to police officers. Yes, they came up with great ideas and techniques, but the real problem was the police department itself.

The LAPD kept asking the panel for ways to use force that wouldn't injure the suspect but would keep the officer safe. But when we suggested techniques like an arm-triangle choke, which has nothing to do with the trachea, the LAPD would reject them. They said officers couldn't use chokes.

It became a frustrating and hopeless situation. Though the police force eventually adapted the panel's recommended techniques and a few of them came from Brazilian jiu-jitsu, I felt most of them were watered down and would never work against a suspect.

Knowing some officers could get hurt while using these new techniques, I walked away from the panel after merely eight months.

Still, I was thankful for the panel because it had introduced me to the Gracies and Brazilian jiu-jitsu, which changed my life forever.

Easter with Ron, Charlie Brown (Johnny), and Britney

Another life changer following the riots came when Elaine and I learned we were expecting our third child. With both of us on the force, it had gotten to the point that nannies were basically raising our two kids, and our "riot baby" would make three. Elaine and I agreed we didn't want our kids being raised by strangers.

I told Elaine that if she loved police work, I'd quit my job once she returned from maternity leave. I felt she had much more of a chance of upward mobility than I did.

Instead, Elaine decided to leave the force altogether.

Johnny, our second son, was born on January 31, 1993, which was Super Bowl Sunday. I got to watch the Dallas Cowboys kill the Buffalo Bills through a tiny TV in Elaine's hospital room, which I didn't mind given the circumstances.

Eventually the world turned its attention away from Los Angeles, which began to rebuild and move on. Still, what I'd seen for six crazy days in April of 1992 didn't leave me. It's funny how resonating moments in your life can give you pause. The riots made me think about what I was doing with myself and my family. My schedule was impossible. I was reporting to roll call at 2:30 p.m. and was out on the streets for CRASH by 3:30 p.m. until about 2:30 a.m. Then I'd go home for a few hours of sleep and get up at 6:00 to make it to Los Angeles in time to appear in court as a witness for my cases by 8:30. I never had enough time to drive the seventy miles home and make it to roll call again by 2:30.

One morning I woke up, looked in the mirror, and saw my dad. It's not that this was a bad thing. I love my dad and all he stood for and accomplished. The LAPD and SWAT had been so important to him, and he was always there for it. But I realized I wasn't him and didn't want to be.

I knew that in the end, the LAPD wouldn't give a damn about me. It was how I raised my children that would define me. My kids were already getting older, and I felt like I was missing out on so much. I didn't want to struggle to make it to occasions like Ron's preschool graduation. It got to the point that I simply wouldn't do it anymore.

It just so happened that at that time in early 1993 a teaching position in the police academy opened up. The hours would be far better. I'd start at 5:30 a.m. and be done with my day at 2:30, right as the kids were getting out of school. I could go play in the backyard with Britney, take Ron to Little League games, and be home at night with Elaine and the kids.

I and a group of hopefuls applied for the position of tactics instructor and went through a battery of oral and written tests. During the orals, I had to do a presentation of my teaching skills. As a kid, I'd hated public speaking. It made my stomach turn, but now I had something to fight for. For the test, I taught a standard vehicle stop lesson, showing how I would disseminate the necessary information to a class of cadets and explaining why I would teach it that way.

Tommy McDonald and I were the two finalists for the position. Tommy had worked for SWAT and was Sgt. Frank Mika's choice. Mika was the officer in charge (OIC) of the Tactics Unit. Glen Hees, the assistant OIC, thought I was the man for the job. Both Frank and Glen had worked for my dad.

I'm told that in the end, Frank said to Glen, "You can have McCarthy, but you'd better be right."

There was a big difference between Tommy and me. I was surprised they gave me the spot. Tommy was a golden boy, and I was a bad boy.

The one thing I knew after getting the job was that I had to prove they'd made the right decision. I can't justify it, but I have always felt that whatever position I was in or whatever team I played for, others were always trying to replace me. I know it sounds crazy, but even if I was the captain of the team, I still felt that the coach was looking to put in someone else so I had to continually prove myself. It's my own personal paranoia that's stayed with me to this day. In this case, it did ensure one thing: the cadets would get the best I had to give, guaranteed.

The change of scenery and pace, both at work and at home, came at just the right time. I'd told Elaine one of the perks of working for the LAPD was that if you ever got tired of what you were doing, you could try something else.

I felt I'd accomplished a lot of good in the four and a half years I'd spent in CRASH, but there comes a point working with gang members when you just want to kill them all. There's something about them that makes you think you can change them, and I guess it takes about four and a half years to realize you can't.

Returning to Elysian Park seven and a half years after I began my career there, I was undoubtedly a different person. The academy had changed as well and mostly for the better. When I'd been a recruit, I'd gotten about 908 hours of training. When you think about it, that's pretty scary. I read somewhere that you needed 1,500 hours of training to become a cosmetologist, to carry around scissors and cut someone's hair. You need only 900 hours to be a cop, to carry a gun and potentially take someone's life. It doesn't quite add up, does it?

The academy hadn't offered nearly as much tactical training when I'd attended as it did by the time I was an instructor. For instance, my 1985 class hadn't been taught how to do a building search, but by 1993 the academy had a mock town with houses and buildings to maneuver through. I got to play every day alongside the cadets as I put them through paintball and grappling exercises, and I taught them the proper way to find and apprehend me in the mock town.

I felt being a police officer was all about tactics, learning how to handle oneself properly both physically and mentally in the field. After what I'd seen out there, I had a few pearls of wisdom to share.

In the classroom, I was assigned to teach the course on use of deadly force. Thankfully, it had been given considerably more hours than when I'd been a cadet, which was helpful as I instructed seventy students on department policy, including the proper use of firearms and chokes. All the time I was spending studying jiu-jitsu with Rorion Gracie gave me a better handle on how to train others in certain aspects of force.

Rorion was studying too, though I didn't realize it at the time. His weekly meetings with the rest of the martial arts panel weren't necessarily about improving officers' field techniques. In Rorion's mind, he was holding an audition, and the traveling show was about to come to town.

The family that started it all, the Gracies (from left to right: Rilion, Relson, Rorion, Helio, Royce, and Carlson)

THE BEGINNING

*When you do the common things in life in an
uncommon way, you will command the attention
of the world.*

—George Washington Carver

They say some of the greatest successes have come when someone wasn't afraid to look at what others had rejected and said,
"Let's try it another way." Rorion Gracie's mind had certainly
been churning during those weekly meetings with the other martial arts leaders on the advisory panel. When I'd been there, I'd
seen a roomful of well-meaning but stubborn zealots. Rorion had
seen an opportunity.

Each master was as dedicated to his own art as Rorion was to
Gracie Jiu-Jitsu, but Rorion wondered if they'd all be willing to prove
it. Would their students lay it all on the line? Pride can be a powerful
motivator, and Rorion knew firsthand that there was none greater than
a martial artist's. Not only was there no way they'd step down
from a challenge, but Rorion bet people would probably be willing
to pay to see who was the best.

Who was the best? The question buzzed around Rorion's gym in Torrance as he began to speak about his plans for War of the Worlds, a martial arts tournament he'd host in the coming months to decide once and for all which martial art reigned supreme.

Rorion's grand scheme wasn't all his own creation. There had already been a man who'd fearlessly tested his art against all who'd challenged him. That man was Rorion's father, Helio Gracie.

The Gracie family opened their first jiu-jitsu academy in 1925 in Brazil, nearly a dozen years after a Japanese foreigner named Esai Maeda, also called Conde Koma or Count Combat, had befriended Helio's father, Gastão, a respected politician.

Gastão and his family lived in the northern state of Pará in Brazil. Gastão helped Maeda, who was part of a Japanese colony there, establish himself in Para. In gratitude, Maeda, a champion martial artist, offered to teach Japanese jiu-jitsu to the oldest son of Gastão's family.

For the next few years, Carlos Gracie learned the self-defense art, then passed it on to his four brothers. One of those siblings was Helio, the youngest and frailest. Helio was said to get winded scaling a flight of stairs, but from the sidelines he intently watched his brothers master the moves on the mats.

One day when his brother Carlos was late for a private lesson he would be instructing, sixteen-year-old Helio offered to begin the session with the student. When Carlos finally did walk into the academy, the student asked if his brother could continue the lesson. Carlos agreed, and Helio became another instructor.

Helio was an innovator and could see beyond what others did. He realized quickly that many of the Japanese jiu-jitsu moves relied on strength, something he didn't possess. For the next few years, Helio modified every move he'd learned to manipulate leverage and timing in his favor. The eventual result was Gracie Jiu-Jitsu, also referred to as Brazilian jiu-jitsu today.

Word of Helio's new effective techniques spread throughout Brazil. Fighters came from far and wide to challenge him. Helio, whose small frame never surpassed more than 140 pounds, wasn't afraid to demonstrate his system.

In 1932, Helio submitted boxer Antonio Portugal in thirty seconds with an armlock. Helio would go on to fight seventeen more times, submitting wrestlers, judokas, and sumo wrestlers alike. Sometimes Helio would issue his own challenges to the well-known practitioners of the day.

Because of Brazil's fascination with combat sports, many of these battles were fought in stadiums filled with thousands of people. Helio didn't win every time, and on numerous occasions the bouts were declared draws, but no opponent ever spoke ill of Gracie Jiu-Jitsu when leaving the proving ground.

Helio's most famous match was against the much heavier judo expert Masahiko Kimura at a Rio de Janeiro stadium, where the president of Brazil and thousands of other spectators watched.

Because of their size difference, Kimura told Gracie, "If you last more than two minutes with me, you should be viewed as the winner."

The match lasted thirteen minutes. Kimura controlled most of it and finally caught Helio in a reverse ude-garami, a type of shoulder lock that eventually broke Helio's arm.[3] When the thirty-eight-year-old Helio wouldn't tap out to Kimura, Helio's older brother Carlos threw in a towel to stop the match. The results graced the covers of the local newspapers the next day.

3. The move would later be adopted by Gracie and renamed Kimura after its originator.

Helio also fought what could be considered the longest uninterrupted MMA bout in history when he grappled with his former
student Waldemar Santana for three hours and forty-two minutes
at a private event. Gracie lost due to a kick to the head as well as exhaustion. In 1967, fifty-four-year-old Helio fought his last public match.

Gracie Jiu-Jitsu and other forms of combat sports continued to
grow in Brazil. In the 1960s, the early forms of MMA, called vale
tudo, or "anything goes," found its way to TV on a show in Brazil
called *Heróis do Ringue*. Some of the Gracie family participated as
coaches. The bouts attracted all styles, including another popular
discipline called luta livre, or "free fighting."

Soon the popularity of the sport would cross national borders.
Rorion, the oldest of Helio's seven sons, was the first to come to
America to spread the gospel of Gracie Jiu-Jitsu. Out of his garage
in Southern California, Rorion taught private lessons and accepted
the frequent challenges of nonbelievers who would seek him out.
Some of those bouts, along with a detailed version of the Gracie
family history as told by them, were captured on the *Gracie in
Action* videotapes.

When Rorion decided to create the War of the Worlds tournament, it came from the greatest inspiration of all and one that I
could personally identify with: his father. At Rorion's gym, we'd
all watched the tapes of vale tudo fights from Brazil.

Rorion said, "I am going to bring these fights to America. It
will be like those fights you see on TV." The ambitious Rorion
wanted Gracie Jiu-Jitsu to become a household name in America
and knew the TV medium could do just that.

Since Rorion had arrived in California in the late 1970s, he'd taught relentlessly and collected a diverse clientele. One Gracie student, Art Davie, then an advertising executive, began to develop War of the Worlds with his jiu-jitsu teacher. John Milius, another client and the writer and director of *Conan the Barbarian* and *Red Dawn*, also joined Rorion and Davie. The three men brainstormed and developed the concept of a sixteen-man single-elimination tournament where each participant would represent a recognized combat art.[4]

Milius, who became the show's initial creative director, first conceptualized an eight-sided fighting structure, which Jason Cusson helped develop into an eight-sided cage with canvas-covered floor padding enclosed by fencing so competitors could neither flee nor fall off the sides or through a set of ropes. The cage was named the Octagon. Initially there was an elaborate plan to either surround it with a moat full of alligators or electrify the chain-link fencing. Cooler heads prevailed, and it was decided the cage alone would suffice.

Among Rorion's students, friends, and family, he and Art gathered enough investors to fund the event and formed a company called WOW Promotions to produce it. Davie then pitched the concept as a one-off event to a handful of pay-per-view producers, including HBO and Showtime.

Semaphore Entertainment Group, a New York–based company that had been successful in the growing pay-per-view market, agreed to broadcast the event. Michael Abramson, an SEG executive, suggested that the name of the event be changed to the Ultimate Fighting Championship, to which everyone agreed.

Now it was time to pick the fighters.

---

4. This was later pared down to an eight-man tournament for UFC 1.

To find the fiercest, deadliest combat sports practitioners in the world, Rorion placed an ad in *Black Belt* magazine that simply said, "Are you tough enough?"

Rorion got a few replies, but he wanted to include certain types of fighters he'd have to go after himself. "I have to include a boxer," he told me. At that time, boxers were seen as the baddest fighters on the planet.

Rorion and Davie approached both James "Bonecrusher" Smith and Leon Spinks to compete in the first tournament, but they turned it down because they didn't know what the UFC was and Rorion had no footage to show them. However, Sam Solomon, a trainer of Spinks, was hired as a cutman for the event.

Though a bit skeptical, Art Jimmerson, a thirty-year-old journeyman boxer who was in line for a shot at an aging Tommy Hearns, agreed to enter the tournament. Jimmerson's camp later expressed reservations and tried to withdraw him from the event. Acutely aware that much of their audience would recognize and relate to a boxer, Rorion convinced Jimmerson to stay on board by offering him $20,000 to simply show up, though most of the remaining seven fighters would be paid only $1,000 each to enter. The winner of the tournament, who'd have to survive three fights in a night, was promised a $50,000 prize.

Rorion and Art tried to recruit martial arts' heaviest hitters, such as Don "The Dragon" Wilson, Dennis Alexio, Ernesto Hoost, and Peter Aerts, but they all turned down the offer. Not convinced the whole thing wasn't illegal, Chuck Norris wouldn't even accept a cageside seat from Art.

Zane Frazier, a karate expert from Southern California, got into the UFC because of a fight against Frank Dux, the legendary and controversial martial artist whose story was loosely adapted into the Jean-Claude Van Damme film *Bloodsport*. Rorion and Art had been at a karate tournament called the Long Beach Internationals when a real street fight had erupted. Rorion and Art had watched Frazier punch the shit out of Dux over a few disrespectful words.

Afterward, Rorion had told Frazier, "You're a tough guy. You want to fight?"

Of course, one of the eight slots would go to a Gracie. The best jiu-jitsu black belt of all of Rorion's six brothers was Rickson. He would have been the logical choice, but since he'd opened his own school in West Los Angeles away from Rorion's Torrance academy, he wouldn't get that slot. Rorion was pretty savvy when it came to the business side of things, which led to squabbles with some of his relatives. With UFC 1, Rorion wasn't going to lose all those potential new students who would come looking for training after watching the show. He'd give the spot to his twenty-six-year-old brother, Royce, who taught at the Torrance academy.

I hadn't had the money to put in the show when Rorion had been looking for investors, so my own contribution to the first UFC was relatively modest. I was enlisted as Royce's sparring partner. Royce was six feet and about 176 pounds, which meant he would more than likely be the smallest fighter in the tournament, not that Rorion was worried about that. At nearly 290 pounds, I could help him prepare for the bigger opponents he'd be facing.

Rickson was still coming around to the academy to train Royce, but I could tell he was seriously pissed off with Rorion. Everybody thought Rickson was the better fighter by far, but he had to step aside and let Royce get the shot at glory.[5]

---

5. Rumors that Rickson was later offered the opportunity to replace Royce at UFC 3 are false. SEG approached Rickson to fight alongside his brother after Royce said Rickson was ten times better than him. Rickson priced himself out.

I was really excited about the first UFC and was sure people were going to love it. In my mind, there was no question it was legitimate, and I was protective of it.

A week before the event, I was listening to a local radio show and heard the hosts talking about "this ultimate fight challenge." I decided to call in and give them some information. No matter what I said, though, the hosts just blasted the event. I had to defend the UFC before it even happened. It certainly wouldn't be the last time.

I was so sure of the UFC that I even got Elaine a job as a travel assistant for the event coordinator, Kathy Kidd. Over the months and weeks leading up to the show, Elaine spoke to many of the fighters and their wives while booking flights and hotel rooms. Tina Shamrock was particularly confident about her husband, Ken, who had some experience fighting for a promotion in Japan called Pancrase. Tina basically told Elaine the UFC would be easy for Ken, he'd destroy everybody, and the $50,000 prize would be great for them.

When Elaine told me how assured Tina was during their phone calls, I took note, but I was far from convinced that Ken Shamrock would be the one to take it.

The week of the event, Elaine and I flew out to stay at the Executive Tower Inn in downtown Denver, Colorado, which was about six miles from the arena. Elaine spent most of the week prepping with the other staff members in one of the meeting rooms. Meanwhile, I joined Royce's group, which included his brothers Royler, Relson, Rickson, and Rolker, as well as Fabio Santos, who worked at the Torrance academy, training at a local gym reserved for the fighters.

When I wasn't with Royce, I was helping Rorion. There wasn't really a promotional model to follow for this type of show, so we were all just winging it, which meant there were tons of last-minute snafus to fix. When Rorion needed a certain fighter somewhere, I'd go retrieve the guy. People had to be picked up at the airport, and some would want to be taxied from the hotel to the local gym and back.

Behind the scenes, Rorion was dealing with much more than mounting his first UFC event. On more than one occasion, Rorion called me to his hotel room to discuss his issues with his family. The UFC was a reunion of sorts for many members of the Gracie family, some of whom had flown in from Brazil. A few of Rorion's relatives weren't pleased with the way he'd trademarked the Gracie Jiu-Jitsu name in the United States and felt he was trying to monopolize jiu-jitsu here. Rorion had even legally stipulated that his brother Rickson add his first name to his own academy so it wouldn't be confused with Rorion's.

Rorion told me he'd been physically threatened by one older family member, and he asked if I thought he should hire security or if I could get him a gun. I'd thought Rorion had all the answers, but in the end he wanted what I had. There's nothing better for self-defense than a gun. I didn't fulfill his request, of course.

The night of the show, a few of Rorion's friends stood within earshot of him, just in case a confrontation erupted outside the cage. It was the first time I saw these little cracks that are present in all families, whether they're a martial arts dynasty or not.

When I wasn't with Rorion, I had the opportunity to meet the other competitors, some of whom had larger-than-life personalities. Kevin Rosier, a lively New Yorker and former ISKA kickboxing champion, showed up at the hotel an unfit-looking 300 pounds or so, but he was funny as hell.

Kevin talked more about how much he could eat than anything else. "How many large pizzas have you eaten at one time?" He surveyed the people at the table at the hotel restaurant. "I've eaten four at once by myself in one sitting."

You could tell he was proud of it.

Naturally, we'd also talked about what was to come. Jimmerson, the boxer from St. Louis, Missouri, told me he doubted Royce would be able to get by his vaunted left jab. "How's he going to deal with that?" Jimmerson flicked out his fist a few times.

I asked him a simple question. "How many times per round have you ended up clinching with an opponent?"

Jimmerson looked confused and said, "I really don't know."

"Well, if clinching happens in boxing all the time and it's not a legal part of the sport, how are you going to keep it from happening when it is legal?" I asked him to indulge me and took him to a back part of the ballroom, where I proceeded to grab his two legs and take him down in just a couple seconds.

Jimmerson looked up at me and said, "Oh my God, he's going to break my arms and legs, isn't he?"

"If you get in trouble, all you have to do is tap out. That's always an option."

Jimmerson knew he'd be facing Royce in the tournament's first round because Rorion and Art had predetermined that match-up. They knew a win for Royce would be especially symbolic to a United States crowd who understood boxing.

This was the only time Rorion handpicked an opponent for his brother. Beyond the first round, the matches would be determined by the brackets they were placed in. For the next shows, the UFC would write all of the fighters' names on a board and assign each one a number. Then they'd pull numbered balls out of a bingo machine in front of all the fighters and assign the matchups in order.

There wasn't a weigh-in at UFC 1, as there was no weight limit. There was also little paperwork to be submitted and no medical testing required beforehand to verify a fighter's health other than a blood test and an on-site physical from a doctor who determined whether the fighter was fit enough to enter the cage.

In fact, Colorado had been selected as the site of the event because the state didn't have a boxing commission at the time, so medical tests and paperwork wouldn't be required. However, Art didn't consider that the event was over a mile above sea level and a bitch for any athlete who didn't have at least a couple weeks to acclimate. This would become an issue in some of the bouts at UFC 1.

At the press conference, there wasn't much press to speak of at all. The whole event was seen as more of an oddity and was covered as such. Reporters asked the fighters what they expected, but nobody had a definitive answer. Art Davie spoke most of the time, boasting that the promotion had gathered eight of the deadliest martial artists in the world.

Afterward, the fighters gave a quick demonstration on a Thai mitt bag that had been tied to a pillar with a monitor hooked up to it. To prove who had the hardest strike, each fighter took a turn hitting it with his punches or kicks. Ken Shamrock got up there and hit it pretty hard. Another competitor, Gerard Gordeau, kicked it.

I can't remember who had the highest score. I thought the whole thing was stupid.

Royce must have been thinking the same thing. "That doesn't say whether you can fight or not," he said coolly and walked right by it.

The day before the show, the rules meeting was a bit intense and kind of funny because there weren't many rules to speak of other than no biting, eye gouging, or groin strikes, all of which Rorion viewed as dirty tactics. Still, the fear of the unknown gave the fighters plenty to debate about.

The competitors and their entourages congregated in one of the hotel's conference rooms and tried to hypothesize what would happen, though no one really knew.

Amongst all of the discussion, a real controversy exploded over hand wraps. Zane Frazier, the karate fighter Art and Rorion had scouted themselves, wanted to wrap his hands. Rorion said he could but with the stipulation that the tape had to be one inch from the knuckles. Rorion didn't want the fighters to be able to construct a wrap that would give them extra padding to shield their hands and add to their power. Rorion was undoubtedly looking out for his little brother Royce.

But the strikers in the room wanted their wraps their way.

Frazier was particularly adamant. "Hey, my hands are how I make my living, and you want me to break them?" He even suggested that Rorion was changing the rules to benefit his brother and make the rest of them look like fools come fight night.

I think Rorion had prepared for this type of reasoning. "Are you telling me that before you get into a street fight, you're going to go wrap your hands? In the fight I saw that got you here, your hands weren't wrapped, were they?"

That answer seemed to shut down the argument.

The next commotion was over the forms WOW Promotions and Semaphore Entertainment Group had asked every fighter to sign releasing them of any responsibility if someone got injured or even died. Some of the guys said they wouldn't sign it.

Teila Tuli, a 410-pound sumo wrestler who'd flown in from Hawaii, was the first one up at the table. The room fell silent for a moment as the Samoan turned to address them. "I'm tired of all this," he said quite calmly. "If you want to fight, I'll see you tomorrow." Then he dropped his signed form in front of Rorion before walking out the door.

The Gracie brothers gave Tuli a standing ovation.

All of the remaining fighters followed the soft-spoken Hawaiian's lead and scribbled their names on their papers before handing them in as well. Nobody wanted to be labeled a coward.

On November 12, 1993, the Ultimate Fighting Championship got off to an auspicious start inside the McNichols Sports Arena in Denver, Colorado, when announcer Bill "Superfoot" Wallace goofed and welcomed everyone to the "Ultimate Fighting Challenge" preceded by one of the largest burps ever captured on live TV. Wallace, a well-known kickboxing legend who'd retired undefeated, was flanked in the commentary booth by five-time kickboxing champion Kathy Long and NFL rushing legend Jim Brown.

Jim Brown was an especially familiar face for another reason entirely. I'd been called to his Hollywood Hills residence a few times to quiet down loud parties.

By UFC 6, Brown asked, "Did we know each other before this?"

When I told him how we first met, he couldn't believe it.

Wallace had taken over play-by-play duties at the last minute when Brown had decided he wanted to fill the color commenting role instead. Unprepared, Wallace mercilessly butchered the names of secondary announcing team members Brian Kilmeade and Rod Machado throughout the night. Wallace also repeatedly made a mistake typical of newcomers to the sport, mispronouncing Royce's name. The "R" is pronounced as an "H" in Portuguese.

Not only were the names unfamiliar to them, but Wallace, Brown, and Long had little knowledge of the action they were calling and describing to the fans shelling out $14.95 to watch at home. They understood Gracie Jiu-Jitsu least of all.

Kathy Long made one of the sharper comments in the pre-fight banter with Wallace. When asked what her strategy would be, she answered, "I think the best thing to do is to go for something as quick as you can."

The McNichols Sports Arena was a nicely equipped 17,000-seat venue that housed the Denver Nuggets. This night, the UFC was handing out tickets, and about 5,000 spectators attended.

I didn't get to escort Royce or be in his corner—Gracies alone would be allowed—but as his training partner, I was given two front-row seats and laminated backstage passes for Elaine and myself. Rorion also gave me the important task of babysitting the gold medal to be awarded to the evening's winner at the tournament's conclusion. Helio, sharply dressed in a three-piece suit, sat a few seats down from me to survey the fruits of his early labors.

As the lights finally dimmed and the UFC's rambling guitar riff theme music was unveiled, everyone in the crowd stood. After his display the night before at the rules meeting, it was fitting that Teila Tuli was the first fighter to come walking out the entrance tunnel.

With the traditional Samoan sarong draping his shoulders and waist, former sumo wrestler Tuli climbed the stage's steps and entered the Octagon. Tuli, at six feet two and 410 pounds, was the largest and most physically striking of the eight participants, which was one reason why Rorion and Art had scheduled him for the first match.

Next to enter was six-feet-five, 216-pound Dutch savate champion Gerard Gordeau. The art of savate relies heavily on foot strikes and is also referred to as French kickboxing or French footfighting. Gordeau did most of his training as a kickboxer in Holland.

Referee João Alberto Barreto, Rorion's choice because of his experience overseeing vale tudo fights in Brazil, gave a few brief instructions through a translator—yes, the referee had a translator.

The Octagon door swung closed, the bell rang, and Gordeau and Tuli circled each other for only a few seconds. The heavier man charged at his opponent. Gordeau backpedaled quickly, throwing punches at Tuli's outstretched arms until the Dutchman's back brushed the fence and Tuli reached down for his legs. Gordeau simply circled out and Tuli fell forward.

Tuli's face, now level with Gordeau's prime weapons, was an easy target. The crowd exploded as Gordeau's foot cleanly hit it and one of Tuli's teeth went flying through the chain link. It landed just a few rows away.

"That's it," Elaine said, standing. She found her way to the nearest aisle, and I watched her climb the stairs to the upper level and walk right out of the arena.

Me? I thought it was awesome. Everyone had thought Tuli would win, but I'd known the heavy guy wouldn't be able to take this thing. I was enthralled by what I'd just witnessed, and I sure as hell wasn't going anywhere. I wanted to see what happened next and who the best was.

Inside the cage, referee Barreto had already made his first mistake of the evening. Under no uncertain terms, Rorion had explained that the fight could be stopped one of two ways: either the fighter tapped out or his corner could throw in the towel. Instead, Baretto himself had stepped in.

Rorion wasn't pleased. He hung over the cage's top while Baretto sputtered out his questions in Portugeuse and pointed to Tuli's bloody face and jack-o'-lantern smile. Rorion instructed Baretto to bring the fighter over to his cornermen, who were standing a few feet away.

Barreto asked, "Is he ready to go?"

One of Tuli's cornermen opened the door, and the rest poured into the Octagon. A doctor who was called to the cage inspected Tuli and deemed him unfit to continue. Then Tuli's brother threw in the towel.

In merely twenty-six seconds, by technical knockout, Gordeau had become the winner of the first UFC fight in history. He'd also taken a few souvenirs to remember Tuli by: a broken hand courtesy of Tuli's concrete head and one of the Hawaiian's dislodged teeth embedded in the instep of his right foot.

After the first fight, I went to see what Gordeau and Tuli looked like. Backstage, the whole mood had changed. Music wasn't blaring, and fighters weren't yelling or hitting their pads or chatting with their cornermen. It was a tomb, and everyone seemed to be thinking, *Oh my God, this is real. That guy's teeth just got kicked out of his mouth.*

It had been the perfect first fight. It hadn't turned out the way people had thought it would, but it'd sure woken everybody up.

I ran back out to my seat to catch the next fight, which matched Kevin Rosier against Zane "Hand Wrap" Frazier. The usually animated Rosier strode to the cage with his hood pulled over his head, his sweatshirt displaying the fitting words "Train as if your life depends on it. Someday it might."

Frazier entered the arena, chin raised, eyes focused on the Octagon, with a slightly peppier step. Frazier and his hand wraps were decidedly ready to go.

Rosier, his sweatshirt now gone to reveal his pudgy physique, paced the cage. If this was a battle of the bodies, Rosier had already lost. Luckily for him, it wasn't.

In Rosier's prefight video, he'd said his greatest weapon was his overhand right, and that's what he used to muscle Frazier down to the mat in the first few seconds. But as a kickboxer, Rosier didn't know how to keep Frazier there, and the two were quickly on their feet again.

Frazier went to work on Rosier and started to beat the piss out of him, landing a nice uppercut and straight right while they clinched and punched. But the altitude wasn't kind to Frazier, who was also asthmatic, and he started huffing and staggering.

Rosier went in for the kill with frantic haymakers, and Frazier wilted against the fence. When Rosier began stomping Frazier, his cornerman Frank Trejo threw in the towel. Rosier would advance.

Now it was Royce's turn to be introduced to the world. Of all the fighters' entrances, his was probably the most organized, and it certainly became the most beloved in those early days. With his brothers standing in front of and behind him in matching blue and white tracksuits, linked with their arms resting on each other's shoulders, Royce walked the weaving trail to the cage in what would later be dubbed the Gracie Train.

Dressed in the traditional gi, the white jacket and pants uniform many martial artists wear, Royce scaled the steps and walked into the cage while a strong contingent of his family members chanted, "Royce, Royce, Royce . . ."

By the look on his face, I could tell Royce was ready but nervous, which was understandable, but I wasn't nervous at all. I truly believed in his ability.

Jimmerson, the boxer, entered next, seeming anxious and not at all comfortable with his new surroundings. I immediately realized the quick demo I'd given him a couple days earlier had made a greater impression than I'd thought. On his left hand, Jimmerson wore a red boxing glove. I guess he counted on pounding on Royce while his free hand held him down. In reality, the single glove would be a hindrance.

As soon as Royce took Jimmerson down by grabbing his legs exactly the way I'd done in the ballroom, Royce passed over the boxer's legs and sat on his chest, which is called taking mount position. The audience didn't know it, but Royce had achieved in a few seconds what's considered one of the most dominant positions in MMA today.

Jimmerson's gloved hand wasn't able to grab a solid hold of Royce's body, which was now horizontal to his own, and I think he panicked as Royce began to successfully pry him off. Without a single hold or choke applied to him, Jimmerson tapped out and yelled, "Get off me." The fight was over in two minutes, eighteen seconds.

Rorion said in an interview directly afterward that he wished the boxer had put up more of a fight. "Royce didn't get a chance to do much," he said. He was probably lamenting over the $20,000 he'd just watched fly out the window. Then he threw me a look as if to say, "What the hell was that?"

I shrugged but knew my ballroom tutorial with Jimmerson had probably bungled the whole thing up.

As we moved to the last quarterfinal bout, I have to admit my interest was piqued. I knew Ken Shamrock had grappling experience because of his fights in the Pancrase organization. In fact, Ken had won his third fight and left Japan for Denver just four days earlier, bringing with him Pancrase regular Takaku Fuke to work his corner. Hands down, Ken had the most confident look and swagger of any fighter I've ever seen enter the cage. He gave off this aura that he meant business.

Ken's opponent, Patrick Smith, was a local tae kwon do fighter and kickboxer whom Art had scouted at a Sabaki Challenge when he'd visited Denver to select the venue. Smith had a large entourage, and when I'd passed them backstage in the tunnel, I'd heard them screaming, "We're gonna kill you," to Ken to psych Smith up.

Ken had been standing a few feet in front of them, getting hot. He turned around to Smith and said something like, "I'll see you in a minute."

Smith's record was listed as 250–0, which I'm sure raised a few eyebrows besides mine. I didn't want to miss this fight.

Ken's discipline was listed as shootfighting, which incorporates a multitude of martial arts to allow a fighter to kick, punch, wrestle, and grapple. Of all the participants at UFC 1, Ken was probably the closest example of a true mixed martial artist.

I wasn't surprised when Ken quickly engaged Smith in a clinch and took him down, then settled into Smith's guard, moving his body between his opponent's legs. From there, Ken tried to create some space to either punch or find a submission. After a few seconds, Ken grabbed Smith's leg and lay back with the append-age, torquing the heel with his arms. The move, called a heelhook, places a great amount of pressure on the opponent's knee and can also affect the ankle.

Smith didn't know what was happening to him or how to de-fend the hold. He kicked at Ken and landed a pretty good blow to his eye with his free leg. He even tried a few downward elbows to Ken's shin, but the pain washed over him too quickly and Smith tapped out.

After he was able to recover to his feet, Smith suggested, "Let's fight like real men."

Both sides' cornermen had to tangle themselves between the two hotheaded fighters.

The crowd, not understanding what they were watching, started chanting, "Bullshit, bullshit, bullshit . . ."

Though he was urging Ken to continue, Smith had already tapped out and the fight was over.

The semifinals were now set. Having observed the entire field of competition, I was more confident than ever in Royce's chances. Not a single fighter had the knowledge and experience to beat Royce's Gracie Jiu-Jitsu. It was as simple as that.

Watching Gordeau and Rosier make their way back to the Octa-gon, I knew one of them would face Royce, but they were practi-cally interchangeable. Without question, either of them faced the same fate: tapping out to a submission on the ground with Royce.

Gordeau's broken right hand was swollen like a balloon, and Tuli's tooth was still planted in his foot, which he'd covered with tape. Rosier's left eye was taped from a cut, and you could tell he was nervous, but he still came out aggressive at the bell. That wasn't enough to overwhelm Gordeau, though, who attacked with his legs and trapped Rosier against the fence. Again on instinct, referee Barreto stepped in as Rosier lay defenseless at Gordeau's feet. This time Barreto would be saved Rorion's diatribe because Rosier's corner quickly threw their white towel over the fence.

The other semifinal match was probably the most anticipated of the night. What Ken Shamrock lacked in actual skill, he more than made up for with his composure. He was captivating and immediately foiled Royce's stoicism.

At the bell, Royce shot for a double-leg takedown and Ken thrust his legs out behind in what's called a sprawl so Royce couldn't get ahold of them. Ken scrambled off the sprawl well, giving Royce a little challenge pulling Ken between his legs, or into his guard.

Many probably thought Ken, now on top, had the upper hand, but Royce was not in a disadvantageous position. From his back, he had a variety of submission holds and chokes he could set up on Ken.

From here, Ken resorted to his signature move, leaning back and trying to grab a leg for a submission as he'd done with Patrick Smith in his first fight. The difference was that Royce knew exactly what was coming and how to avoid it, and he used the momentum to roll himself to top position.

Ken squirmed and flipped over to his knees to escape, Royce secured the rear-naked choke, and Ken tapped the canvas violently five times. However, the referee, on the other side of the men, didn't see it. When Ken tapped, Royce let go of the hold altogether.

Now the referee wanted to continue, but to Ken's credit he manned up and conceded the win to Royce.

Interviewer Brian Kilmeade grabbed Ken as he exited the Octagon and asked him if he thought he was the second best fighter in the tournament. It was easy for all of us to see that was the case.

"I'm the third best person here today," Ken answered.

Right then, I knew Ken would go far in this.

I think Ken's sportsmanship helped the UFC in those early events. Spectators could relate to him and wanted to keep tuning in to see him.

As Gordeau and Royce rested backstage for the finals, the UFC held an alternates match between Jason DeLucia and Trent Jenkins. In theory, this bout was supposed to create a replacement should a fighter not be able to continue, but because it was held so late in the evening, it could apply only to the final bout. I doubted Gordeau, who'd already refused to stop despite a badly broken hand and punctured foot, or Royce, who was virtually unscathed, would bow out at this point.

Still, the alternates match turned out to be one of the most technical and competitive on the entire card. DeLucia and Jenkins were two of the fitter guys to enter the cage at the same time, and at twenty-four years old, DeLucia was the youngest in the tournament that night.

DeLucia studied a technique called five animal kung fu, which would lead one to believe he had no knowledge of ground techniques. But I'd seen DeLucia once before at the Torrance academy in a challenge fight against Royce. At the time, he hadn't had ground skills, but he was a good athlete with a ton of heart. After he'd lost to Royce in the challenge match, he said he'd start learning jiu-jitsu, so I knew to expect more from him.

The alternates match began, and DeLucia threw some fancy kicks that entertained the crowd. With surprisingly fast reflexes, Jenkins, an American kempo stylist, got out of the way. Then he fired back a few kicks of his own. DeLucia wrapped himself around Jenkins' leg and dragged him to the ground.

The crowd started booing, but DeLucia was doing everything right.

Then DeLucia grabbed Jenkins from behind and dropped backward, securing a hold called the rear-naked choke, wrapping his arm around Jenkins' neck and grabbing his bicep to squeeze while lacing his other arm behind Jenkins' head to lock the choke in.

Jenkins tapped out at fifty-two seconds, and the one sign of a fight was a small cut near DeLucia's eye. Jenkins' toenail had cut him during a kick.

Respectful and self-disciplined, DeLucia showed a lot of promise, and I think he got what we were trying to do right away. "Gracie Jiu-Jitsu had a big influence in the way I'll fight from this day on," he told the interviewer as he left the cage.

I knew we hadn't seen the last of this kid. Shortly after UFC 1, DeLucia would begin to train with Ken Shamrock.

With a few more minutes remaining until the finals, Rorion and his brothers, including Royce with his white gi peeking out of his blue Gracie Team jacket, entered the Octagon to make a special presentation to their father, Helio. One thing about Rorion was that he absolutely loved and respected his dad. Money, fame, and notoriety were all motivations that had brought about this night, but I believe one of the main reasons Rorion created the UFC was to honor his father. He was everything to him.

"What is the oldest question in the history of combat? Who is the ultimate fighter?" Rorion asked the audience. "We are here to pay our respects and to acknowledge the accomplishments of a pioneer warrior, who sixty-five years ago paved the way for this competition. He was a fighter who took on any challengers regardless of fighting style in the most bone-breaking, bare-knuckle fights that the civilized world has ever seen. We honor his fighting spirit, his teachings, his vision."

The crowd was unimpressed with the lull in action, but I understood that more than six decades of trial and error by that old fragile-looking man standing in the center of the cage had brought us to this moment. When people say today that Bruce Lee is the grandfather of MMA, it pisses me off. No disrespect to Lee, who was one of my childhood idols, but Helio was the guy. He's the one who started all of this, and he deserves the credit.

A stoic Helio stood there as his son handed him a plaque.

"This event that my children present here in Denver today is the prize that I receive for my sixty-five years of sweat and blood," Helio said.

If the majority of the audience didn't quite get the magnitude of this moment beyond the $50,000 purse on the line, there were still a handful of us aware. After the ceremony, Royce and Gordeau made their final trip that evening to the cage.

There were no surprises in this one. Royce immediately shot

for the Dutchman's legs, and Gordeau wisely tried to struggle free from the takedown but couldn't fend off Royce for long. Again, Royce moved to mount, and like Ken Shamrock, Gordeau instinctually flipped to his stomach to protect his face. Royce applied the rear-naked choke but this time held it until the referee stopped it even after Gordeau tapped the mat and Royce's shoulder to signal his submission.

Many people ask why Royce held the choke so long on Gordeau, but it's because Gordeau had bitten Royce's ear to try and shake his mount. Royce was dishing out a little payback.

I stood on the platform outside the cage and watched Royce receive his gold medal and one of those poster-sized checks written for $50,000 as Helio looked on from the floor. Royce was flanked by his brothers and his future wife, Marianne, all of them wearing grins and a hint of relief on their faces. Rorion's was the biggest smile of all.

I drove Royce and Marianne back to the hotel afterward, then dropped them off for dinner alone at a restaurant. On the way, Royce didn't say much to me other than that he felt he'd done well. He was a man of few words.

We all stayed in the hotel an extra night because Rorion had planned a big after party, a fancy Carnivale-themed masquerade ball. I wore a tux, and some wore tuxedos and masks, but most of the fighters showed up wearing T-shirts and jeans.

I spoke a bit with Ken Shamrock, who had a shiner from Patrick Smith's kick. "I'll be fighting only a couple more years," he said during our conversation.

At the UFC's first ever after party with Art Davie, Kathy Kidd, Rorion, Elaine, and the maître d'

It was a pleasant affair. There were no bad feelings among the fighters. They'd done their best and left it in the cage.

I didn't know then if there would be another UFC, though I was certainly hoping for it. I did know one thing: I was getting in that cage.

From UFC 2 on, I handled all of the fighters' rules meetings. (UFC 25, April 2000)

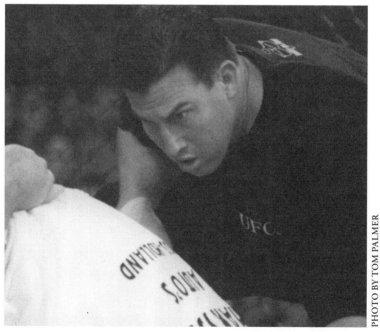

Remco Pardoel vs. Ryan Parker at UFC 7: trying to look like I know what I'm doing (September 1995)

BEST SEAT IN THE HOUSE

The secret of success is to be ready
when your opportunity comes.

—Benjamin Disraeli

Two weeks following the first UFC, Rorion called me at home. "Will you be coming to the academy anytime soon?" he asked. "I have something important to speak with you about."

I assumed he wanted to talk about the application I'd filled out and dropped off on Kathy Kidd's desk. If the UFC was going to continue, I wanted to fight in the next tournament.

When I came in for my next jiu-jitsu class, Rorion said, "What are you doing? You're with us, and Royce is doing this. You can't fight Royce. You can enter when Royce leaves."

I hadn't realized Royce would fight in the next UFC, and I certainly wasn't entering to challenge Royce. At the time, I hadn't thought so much of the UFC as a vehicle for the Gracies. But to Rorion, that's exactly what it was: an infomercial for Gracie Jiu-Jitsu.

And what an audience he already had. UFC 1 had already surpassed all expectations with its initial pay-per-view numbers—

it ended up with 86,000 buys—and SEG had given Rorion the green light to begin planning a second event.

Rorion had other designs for me. "John, how would you like to be the referee at the next show? You know what the fighters are supposed to be doing, and you can react in a split second to stop the fight if anyone taps out."

Rorion explained how the Brazilian referees at UFC 1 hadn't followed his directions. When Tuli took Gordeau's foot in the face and his tooth went airborne, the referee had stepped in to protect Tuli, but he didn't have the power to do so. Rorion wanted the fights uninterrupted, the way they had been for his father in Brazil.

To make sure it went right at the next UFC, Rorion had a few changes in mind, and he wanted me to help institute them. "John, we'll have you sit in a lifeguard chair outside the cage, and when the fight is over, you'll throw a red towel in so the fighters will know when to stop."

I had zero experience refereeing anything, but I'd seen enough street fights to know the idea was preposterous. Two guys going at each other wouldn't see the towel, let alone obey it. It was a disaster waiting to happen.

However, I wanted to be involved in the UFC whatever way I could. I felt it in my bones, so I made a deal with Rorion. If I could stay in the cage with the fighters to monitor the fights closely, I'd give refereeing a try.

Rorion finally relented.

At first, I didn't put much thought into refereeing. At the police academy, my good friend Joe Hamilton and I talked about it as casually as we would the weekend's upcoming football game.

"John, you ever referee a boxing match or a jiu-jitsu tournament?"

"Nope."

"Then what are you going to do?"

"I've got no clue." I laughed. "I'm just going to stand back and try to look like I know what I'm doing. It's No Holds Barred. Man, there's no rules, and they don't want me to stop it."

I really didn't think I'd have much to do come fight night. None of the matches at UFC 1 had gone five minutes.

My plan was to move around and act like I was doing something while really just watching two guys go at it from the best seat in the house. All I had to do was stop the fight when a guy tapped out or his corner threw in the towel. Other than that, I'd make sure nobody bit or eye-gouged, which wasn't hard to pick out. Pretty easy, I thought.

Everything else was legal. Groin strikes, which had been banned in the first event, would be admitted at UFC 2. A few of the applicants claimed they were a vital part of their disciplines and if they were allowed to execute them, they would perform better. Most of the fighters were wearing steel cups anyway, so Rorion said, "Why not?"

Rorion had an easier time scouting for the second event, I think because he now had something to show prospective fighters. Word spread through the martial arts community, and they came to Rorion like moths to a flame. Martial artists couldn't resist the opportunity to prove their discipline was the be all and end all.

With more fighters to choose from, Rorion decided to expand UFC 2 to a sixteen-man tournament, a dream he hadn't been able to realize with the first event. In keeping with the Brazilian marathon fighting tradition, Rorion also decided to get rid of those pesky rounds.

One of the common misconceptions of the early UFCs was that time limits and rounds weren't instituted until later. UFC 1 was actually scheduled for unlimited five-minute rounds separated by one-minute rest periods until a winner was determined. But because no fight had gone past the five-minute mark at UFC 1, Rorion and SEG didn't see the point of having rounds at all. It was decided that time limits wouldn't be necessary for UFC 2. The fights would go on for one endless round until one man tapped out or his corner threw in the towel, no exceptions.

Again there would be no weight limits, but all the sumo wrestlers must have been fond of their teeth because UFC 2 had no one to follow in Tuli's footsteps. The largest fighter weighed 275 pounds, and the lightest was 20 pounds below Royce's 176.

With the lineup set, Rorion moved on to the next details.

Though UFC 1's pay-per-view numbers were promising, the live event itself had failed to muster up enough of a paying audience to justify using Denver's McNichols Sports Arena again. On top of that, in the first of many political interventions to come, the mayor had said he didn't want UFC 2 there. So we packed up the circus and moved about seven miles down the road to the 2,000-seat Mammoth Events Center.

As a Los Angeles police officer, I was required to apply for a work permit to referee the event because I was going to get paid. On the form I wrote that I would be officiating a martial arts event. When my superiors asked me what kind, I told them, "It's mixed martial arts. It involves jiu-jitsu, karate, tae kwon do, wrestling, boxing . . ." I doubt they understood it was a combination of all those arts in one fight, and I wasn't about to overcomplicate things.

Satisfied with my answer, they finally signed off on it.

About a week before the show, I flew out to Denver with Elaine, who'd been asked back to help Kathy Kidd set up. In my new role as referee, I didn't seem to have much to do, so I hung around the production office with Elaine and worked out at one of the local gyms commandeered for the fighters. I had a few officer friends with me, too, who Rorion had flown in as extra security to work the event night.

A day before the show, we had our second rules meeting. The fighters sat anxiously at long tables set up classroom style as the matchups were selected randomly with the numbered balls pulled out of the bingo machine. Art Davie introduced me to the room as "Big" John McCarthy and asked me to come to the podium to go over the rules, or really the lack of them.

This was the first time I'd been called "Big" John in front of the fighters. My mother had called me "Big" John all the time when I was younger, but it was Art who reintroduced it a few weeks earlier at the WOW offices in Los Angeles.

The WOW offices were out the back door of the Gracie Academy, across the parking lot on the other side of the street, so I found myself there a couple times a week. On that day, Art and I had gotten into a little back-and-forth discussion. I don't remember what we were talking about, except that I told Art to shut up and when he wouldn't, I lifted him off the ground and over my head.

"Big John, Big John, let me down, let me down," he yelled, until I obliged him.

In this playful interaction between two smart-asses, I was marked for life.

"'Big' John. That's what you are from now on," Art said. And sure enough, each time he introduced me, a few other people would start calling me it, until the name finally etched its way into the sport's vernacular.

Standing at the podium in front of all of the competitors in UFC 2, "Big" John didn't know what the fuck to say. I was nervous, but from my years on the police force, I knew I had to at least give off the vibe that I was in control.

Certain things just stuck out in my mind that I had to get across. I remembered Jason DeLucia getting cut by Trent Jenkins' toenails at the first event, so I drilled home that the fighters had to cut their toenails and fingernails.

Then I said, "Look, if you want out, tap the mat." I hit the podium for emphasis. "You can tap the mat, your opponent, or even yourself if that's all you can reach. If your hands are tied up, you can tap out with your feet."

I also addressed the cornermen. Nobody had asked me to do this, but since the corners had the ability to stop the fight and I didn't, I figured communication between us all was probably a good thing. "If I think your fighter's in trouble or starting to have a problem, I'm going to point to you and say, 'Watch your fighter.' If they're really in trouble, I'm going to say, 'Throw your towel.'"

Soon the fighters were dismissed for their last-minute preparations. As they poured out of the room, Rickson Gracie walked up to me and said, "Hey, John, you're scaring everyone."

Apparently my nerves, stern delivery, and podium slamming had made an impression.

UFC 2 introduced another new player to the mix: Bob Meyrowitz, the owner of SEG. He'd watched UFC 1 on his couch back in New York City, and the smell of greenbacks must have wafted right out of his TV. He flew all the way out to Denver to see the second show firsthand.

I was sitting in the hotel restaurant's bar when Bob approached me for the first time. "John McCarthy, how are you?" he asked, extending his hand. Bob was a decent-sized man, maybe six feet and 200 pounds, with a distinguished salt-and-pepper beard, but his nasally voice didn't match up.

Truthfully, I had no idea who he was at the time. All I knew was that he owned the TV production company SEG. I had no idea that SEG might have ownership stake in the UFC.

Bob started describing to me what he wanted to see happen during the fights, as if I was the puppet master controlling the strings. "I want you to make sure the fighters are fighting good."

I wondered how the hell I was supposed to do that. Little did I know that TV producers and promoters would be saying the same stupid thing to me eighteen years later: "Make sure it's an exciting fight. Don't let them lay on the ground too long."

Here was this fortysomething TV guy doing what TV people do—trying to make the show better any way he thought he could—but I didn't understand any of that at the time. I just thought a lot of what he was saying was pretty ridiculous.

Rorion had never really spoken of Bob, so I just wanted him to go away. When it came to the show, I didn't take orders from anyone except Rorion. He was my boss.

There was one request that I did fulfill for Art Davie, though, and it was something that would become fairly synonymous with, well, me. A couple days before the show, Art asked me to come up with a catchy way to begin the fights. He thought a slogan and some sort of hand gesture would fit well.

"Christ, Art, I've got two guys standing in a cage waiting to knock the shit out of each other. I'm just going to ask this guy if he's ready and then ask the other guy if he's ready and then tell them, 'Let's get it on.'"

Davie loved the idea.

UFC 2 "No Way Out" was held on March 11, 1994, at the misleadingly named Mammoth Events Center, which had been incarnated as everything from a sports venue to a textile warehouse to an open food market. Compared to the McNichols Sports Arena, the place was like someone's armpit. It was old, outdated, and in a seedy part of town.

The arena didn't even have dressing rooms for the fighters to wait in before their bouts, so WOW and SEG rented a few rooms next door in a broken-down hotel full of prostitutes and drug addicts. The fighters pushed the beds against the walls to make space to warm up, and as the night wore on, they were ferried back and forth through the rat-infested alleyway between the two buildings.

Royce found that being Rorion's brother had its advantages. He was the only fighter given accommodations at the venue in an area behind some curtains.

This night there were sixteen participants and two alternates. There would be a whopping fifteen fights—nearly double the eight quick bouts that had transpired at UFC 1—and Rorion decided I would referee all of them. Only the last eight fights would be televised, and Royce's first-round bout would kick off the pay-per-view.

I don't know if there was a momentous realization when I

first stepped into the cage, which was officially dubbed the Octagon at the beginning of the UFC 2 telecast. I wore baggy, black Otomix weightlifting pants and a UFC T-shirt with the ironic words "There are no rules" across the chest. Standing there in the cage, I was nervous, I admit. I had no idea what I was doing. I just thought, *Holy Christ, don't let me screw this up.*

The first fight matched eighteen-year-old karate expert Sean Daugherty against Scott Morris, an American ninjutsu black belt at least ten years Daugherty's senior. Morris, a student of Robert Bussey's Warrior International program, was escorted to the Octagon by an army of teammates in matching button-down shirts, ties, and red-and-black letterman jackets. One of these dapper guys was Matt Andersen, half brother to future fighting great Jeremy Horn. Andersen himself would fight at UFC 9.

Once the fighters and their corners had settled at opposite ends of the cage, I walked to the center and motioned to each fighter one last time to make sure they were on board. "Are you ready? Are you ready?" I pointed to each fighter. My first "Let's get it on" was a far cry from its later glory. It was more like I was casually telling the guys I was going down to the store to pick up some milk. At least I accentuated it by raising my arm and throwing the imaginary gauntlet down in front of me.

As soon as the fighters engaged, I got out of the way fast.

Daugherty came out and threw a really fancy front hook kick, but Morris grabbed ahold of Daugherty's neck in their clinch and flipped him over his head in a backward roll before climbing on top into mount.

That's good, I thought.

Morris then cranked on Daugherty's neck, and I'm sure the karate kid had felt nothing like this in the dojos. He tapped the mat fast and hard, and I rushed in to separate them. Twenty seconds had elapsed.

That's it? I thought. *This is going to be easy.*

Before Morris could walk away, I grabbed his arm and raised it to signal that he was the winner and would advance. The two fighters left the cage, and the next pinball was in the chute ready to be launched on the first fight's heels.

Patrick Smith, a Sabaki Challenge champion kickboxer, was a returning fighter from UFC 1. I'd also seen his opponent, Ray Wizard, at a karate tournament in Los Angeles. Wizard was fast. I quickly realized fighter recognition would be important for me because it gave me at least a faint idea of what the dynamic of the bout might be.

I checked both fighters' fingernails and toenails to make sure they'd been cut down and then walked to center cage and repeated the starting words.

Smith flailed his arms above his head in some mock traditional stance, but what he really wanted was to lock up with Wizard and find a quick submission. Smith had learned his lesson from UFC 1. He clinched with Wizard and pulled him in tight as the two migrated to the fence. Finding a guillotine choke around Wizard's neck, Smith pushed his hips up to sink the choke in even deeper.

I was standing next to them. Rorion, dressed this time in a more practical tracksuit, squatted on the other side of the chain link. We both knew either the tapout or Wizard's unconsciousness was imminent.

As soon as Wizard went limp, I stepped in and he fell back to the canvas.

Two fights in under two minutes. No sweat.

The next fight paired Johnny Rhodes, another karate champion, against David Levicki, a kung fu practitioner and supposed Navy SEAL.

I took one look at all 275 pounds of Levicki and thought, *I don't think so*. I'd met a few Navy SEALs, and there was no way a man Levicki's size would be able to fulfill all those physical demands. Besides, the way Levicki talked about it set off my bullshit meter big-time.

Still, Levicki had Rhodes on the run right away. But when they clinched and fell to the mat, Rhodes landed inside Levicki's guard, then quickly hopped one of his own legs over Levicki's right leg into half guard. From there, the fighters pretty much stalemated in terms of punching, though Levicki regained his guard by pulling Rhodes' body back between his legs. I watched Rhodes try to push his fingers into Levicki's jugular, which was perfectly legal.

Levicki wasn't doing much from the bottom except trying to keep Rhodes close. As he hugged him, Levicki's legs naturally tugged at Rhodes' gi pants until suddenly we had a full moon rising inside the Octagon.

Son of a bitch, I thought. I didn't know what to do at first because I wasn't supposed to interfere with the fight. But the man's ass was staring me in the face, so I decided to move in and pull them up. I tried to offset this by blurting out, "Get to work," but Rhodes' pants just kept sneaking back down his legs. I must have yanked them up at least fifteen times.

Eventually, Rhodes' hugging, slapping, and sporadic punches opened a cut over Levicki's eye. The blood began to flow, creating a puddle on the canvas next to him, but there wasn't much I could do but grab those pants and try to keep UFC 2 from earning an X rating. The blood started to cloud Levicki's vision, so I asked him if he wanted to continue. Levicki finally tapped out by telling me no, he'd had enough.

At about thirteen minutes, it was the longest UFC fight so far, and I was thinking, *Shit, here I've been touching a man's ass on TV. This sucks.*

Little did I know a little nudity would be the least of my worries. It was all about to go downhill.

The first round's fourth fight matched the two greatest names I would ever hear in the UFC: Freek Hamaker and Thaddeus Luster. Hamaker was a student of Gerard Gordeau, the savate champion who'd made it to the UFC 1 finals against Royce. Gordeau had been announced as retired for this event, but I guess he wanted to keep his lineage alive by sending in one of his students.

Hamaker said his main discipline was sambo, which is Russia's version of wrestling with some effective leg locks and submissions. Luster was introduced as a seventh degree black belt in kung fu san soo, which he calmly explained on the telecast was the most potent fighting system on the planet.

As soon as this match hit the ground, the ponytailed Hamaker moved on top of Luster to half guard. Luster soon figured out that Hamaker's ponytail made a nice handle for keeping his opponent at an arm's distance. Hair pulling wasn't illegal, so I simply paced, waiting like the rest of the audience.

Hamaker kept trying to line up a shoulder lock called the key-lock or Americana. I was a Brazilian jiu-jitsu blue belt under Rorion at this point, so I could follow his technique. I was tempted to tell him he was doing it wrong.

Hamaker finally freed his now unruly hair and managed to create enough distance for a few punches. Then he mounted Luster.

Smothered underneath the Dutchman, Luster called out a muffled surrender. He'd had enough, and I stepped in fast.

It was the second verbal submission of the night, which reminded me that I had to listen just as much as I had to watch.

I was still thinking I was doing all right. I hadn't prematurely stopped a fight and was doing what Rorion wanted, and that's what I thought I'd been hired to do. The next fight would make me reevaluate my thinking.

Kickboxer Robert Lucarelli bobbed into the arena. At 245 pounds, he was bigger than opponent Orlando Weit, a slighter but well-conditioned muay Thai fighter, who bowed to each corner of the cage in the tradition of his art.

Lucarelli was soft and out of shape, so I was thinking he should go after Weit as fast as he could before he tired out. As if he were reading my thoughts, Lucarelli muscled Weit down and grabbed his neck in a basic bulldog choke within the first few seconds.

Weit was the better athlete, though. His instincts, agility, and a lot of hair pulling got him out of the hold and back on his feet in no time. When Lucarelli went to rise, Weit grabbed his head and launched a knee into his face. Lucarelli folded to the mat again, and Weit kicked his head like a soccer ball, then began to walk away.

I still couldn't do anything because Lucarelli wasn't tapping out, so Weit came back to finish the job. Honestly, I think Lucarelli was too dazed to signal that he was done, which left the only other option: his corner throwing in the towel.

Remember: I'd told the corners beforehand that if I pointed to them, I was signaling for them to think about throwing in the towel.

I pointed to Lucarelli's corner, but they didn't respond.

"Watch your fighter," I warned, but I didn't get a reaction. My eyes darted nervously between Lucarelli's corner and the beat down, and I knew I had to do something. I started yelling for the cornermen to throw in the towel, but they just stared at me.

With an elbow to the back of the head, Weit smacked Lucarelli's mouthpiece out. Lucarelli crawled away like his life depended on it—no exaggeration—and his corner finally tossed in the towel as Weit landed another devastating elbow to the back of their injured fighter's head.

It was a scary sequence that lasted no more than ten seconds, and it ripped the bloodthirsty crowd out of the seats. They were the most uncomfortable ten seconds I've ever squirmed through in the Octagon.

I walked a shell-shocked Lucarelli to his corner. "How much did you have to see?" I said. "How long was I telling you to throw the towel?"

"He told us if we threw in the towel, he was going to kill us," one of them sheepishly answered.

Holy shit, I thought, *this is a problem.*

I didn't want something like this to happen again, but there was nothing I could do. The next fight was under way before I could give it a second thought.

Remco Pardoel was a Dutch grappler specializing in jiu-jitsu, so I thought he must at least have a good understanding of base and where to position his body on the mat. I didn't know anything about Alberto Cerro Leon's style, called pencak silat, not even how to pronounce it. It was categorized as an exotics art along with the other obscure disciplines introduced during UFC 2.

They'd said Leon had broken bones, so I thought he would either strike hard or do submissions. At least Leon, who resembled a young Steven Seagal, looked the part in his black gi with matching grave demeanor.

Whatever his style, I can't imagine things went the way Leon had planned. After an opening exchange and a scramble to the mat, Leon found himself on his back with a rather large Dutchman pinning him down from side control.

Leon's discipline, which I would later learn was a culmination of Indonesian striking arts, didn't seem to cover this position in their manuals. So Leon did the only thing he could: he tried to stick his fingers in or over Pardoel's mouth whenever he could to slow him down.

Pardoel was in complete control, though. He mounted Leon and then shifted back to side control and isolated Leon's arm. He didn't have a standard armlock, but from his judo side control, Pardoel managed to get that arm into a straight lock, bending it backward between his legs at an uncomfortable-looking angle. After about ten minutes of getting smothered by Pardoel from multiple angles, Leon and his art of pencak silat tapped out.

Of the eight opening-round bouts, the seventh was a pretty good fight, mostly because both men had a little knowledge of jiu-jitsu. Jason DeLucia, the determined, athletic youngster who'd submitted Trent Jenkins during the UFC 1 alternates match, returned to face

Scott Baker, a Wing Chun master who'd been training in Brazilian jiu-jitsu with black belt Pedro Sauer in Salt Lake City, Utah. De-Lucia had been choked out by Royce at UFC 1, and I knew he'd sought out some jiu-jitsu instruction afterward, so I was a lot more familiar with his capabilities.

DeLucia sprang out of the gate and landed a traditional side-kick to Baker's body before he clinched with him. Though DeLucia was trying to initiate the takedown, he didn't resist Baker's instinct to push him to the ground. DeLucia now had guard from his back, but Baker was able to pass and get to full mount, where he was basically sitting on DeLucia's chest. DeLucia did a good job of using his hips to buck Baker off balance and take top position. It was solid Jiu-Jitsu 101 technique.

DeLucia then fell back and nestled Baker's foot into his armpit for a heelhook attempt. Amazingly, Baker countered the hold and escaped to his feet. Ladies and gentleman, we had a fight.

Another takedown and a reversal from each man later, DeLucia lined up a triangle choke, locking up Baker's head and arm by creating a triangle with his legs around them. Again Baker fought his way out of the finishing move. DeLucia found the triangle choke again from his back, but this time he flipped to top position with it. DeLucia was in perfect position to start punching Baker, who'd faded under all the pressure.

I was a little startled when DeLucia started speaking to him. "Dude, I don't want to hit you anymore. Just give it up."

After eating a few more fists, Baker did.

The final opening-round match, which would lead off the live pay-per-view, matched Royce against five-feet-seven, 160-pound karate expert Minoki Ichihara. Again, Royce's first opponent of the night had symbolic value. Karate had had a healthy run in the United States, thanks to films like *The Karate Kid*, and the Japanese Ichihara was viewed as mysterious and potentially dangerous. Of course, I didn't think Ichihara had a chance. We were talking about a man who'd dedicated his life to a discipline that doesn't allow strikes to the head.

If the other fighters had known I'd already studied jiu-jitsu under Royce for nearly a year, maybe they would have said something about me refereeing his fight. But I never thought I would have a problem with it, and I never did anything special for Royce.

In my mind, it was the same as being a police officer. When a child molester moved next to a school and the neighbors harassed him, I had to be impartial, protecting his rights just as I would any other citizen. I learned early on in refereeing that there would always be fighters whose personalities I liked more than others, but that didn't mean I could treat one fighter better than his opponent once the bell rang. I couldn't gamble with people's lives like that. So when Royce entered the cage, it was simply my eighth bout of the night; that was all.

The bout played out predictably with Royce taking Ichihara down with his trusty double-leg and mounting him. Ichihara had zero knowledge of ground technique, so he held on to Royce's body while Royce peppered him with the occasional punch. Royce finally pulled the lapel of Ichihara's uniform across the Japanese fighter's neck in a gi choke to coax out the tap.

The sixteen had been whittled down to eight.

In the first quarterfinal, my resolve was tested again. Patrick Smith was matched against ninjutsu expert Scott Morris. The two quickly clinched, but Morris lost his footing on his takedown attempt, allowing Smith to fall into full mount. Smith then proceeded to beat on Morris with fists and elbows.

Again I was pointing and screaming to Morris' corner to throw in the towel for their fighter, who had essentially been punched unconscious. The cornerman looked at me, turned his back, and threw the towel into the audience.

Smith stopped only because he thought my yelling was directed at him. He jumped off Morris, ranted, and paced around the Octagon. I quickly moved Smith away from Morris just in case he got any ideas to resume his destruction.

The fight lasted thirty seconds from start to finish, and in that half a minute I realized this system wouldn't work. Given the power, corners weren't coming through when their fighters really needed them most.

Already UFC 2 was unfolding much differently than its predecessor, and I didn't like what I was seeing. My view from the cage kept getting worse.

The next quarterfinal bout would become one of the most infamous of all the early fights because it included the show's second alternate, Fred Ettish. A kenpo karate expert from Minnesota, Ettish had flown to Denver for the tournament with no guarantee that he'd get to fight. When Ken Shamrock had withdrawn with a broken hand, the first alternate had been moved into the tournament. When Freek Hamaker couldn't continue with a hand injury, Ettish was called up.

Fred was like me. He believed in what the UFC stood for

and wanted to support it any way he could. With twice as many fights to deal with that night, SEG and WOW were short-staffed and disorganized backstage, so they'd asked if Ettish would lend some manpower.

Fred was ferrying the fighters from the hotel to the staging area when Rorion found him to say he'd be going on. Ettish had less than ten minutes to find his cornermen in the audience and wrangle them backstage, change into his gi, and warm up.

Ettish patty-caked early kicks with Johnny Rhodes, who'd battered his first opponent for nearly twelve minutes earlier that night. The 210-pound Rhodes swiftly stumbled Ettish with a counter right hand, then pushed him to his back with a few follow-up shots.

I knew right away that Ettish wouldn't be able to win.

Ettish tried to fend off Rhodes from his back by flailing his legs, but the next punch opened Ettish's forehead and sent him onto his stomach. He covered up, but Rhodes pummeled him with fists and knees. Propped on his left elbow, Ettish stretched his right arm to keep tabs on his standing stalker, shaking his head to get some of the blood out of his eyes.

All I wanted to do was get Ettish out of there.

Rhodes didn't have a lick of ground fighting knowledge, but he finally climbed on top of Ettish to find a way to finish the bout. Rhodes grabbed Ettish's neck with his right arm for an improvised choke and squeezed it with his bicep.

I followed Ettish's body as it flopped around the mat like a helpless fish pulled from the water. Then I saw the tap and jumped in.

A dazed and bloodied Ettish managed to blurt out, "I didn't tap."

Crouched beside Ettish, with his white gi and black belt

stained with blood, I said, "Okay." What else could I say? I knew I'd seen him tap. I guess he didn't remember it because he was going out from the choke.

His battle had just begun. Over the years, no other UFC fighter has been as ridiculed as Ettish. Fans denigrated him, called his style fetal fighting, and launched websites to crucify a man for those immortal three minutes and seven seconds. All because he had enough courage to go in there, do the best he could with what he knew at the time, and show an immense amount of heart. Since that day, I've had nothing but respect for Fred Ettish.

In the other pair of quarterfinal bouts, grappler Remco Pardoel knocked out Orlando Weit with elbows on the ground, and Royce armbarred Jason DeLucia. Both were over in under two minutes, but I performed poorly in the latter one.

During Royce and DeLucia's fight, I stood on the wrong side and missed the whole setup to Royce's armbar submission and the inevitable tapout. I think I'd overestimated what DeLucia would be able to do because he'd been training in Brazilian jiu-jitsu for a few months. DeLucia tapped Royce's leg nine times and tapped the mat seven times more when Royce fell to his side with the hold still in place.

Afterward, I told DeLucia, "I'm sorry I didn't get to you fast enough."

"Well, I was tapping," he answered, slightly perturbed. DeLucia received no lasting damage to his arm, but there's a famous picture of the armbar, Royce's tense body stacked and extended into the air with teeth clinched, that captures my mistake plain as day.

Needless to say, I learned that my own positioning was as important as the fighters' and I wouldn't be able to see everything from any one vantage point. I'd have to keep moving.

In the semifinals, Patrick Smith submitted Johnny Rhodes with a standing guillotine choke. I'm glad Rhodes had been paying attention at the rules meeting when I'd told the fighters they could tap out with their feet if they had to. Rhodes did just that at the forty-five-second mark.

As expected, Royce submitted Pardoel in the second semifinal match, which advanced him again to the finals to meet Smith. The much larger Pardoel put up a struggle when Royce tried to take him down, but the Dutch fighter was open season once Royce got him to the canvas. Mounting Pardoel's back and getting his hooks in, or wrapping his heels around the Dutchman's legs so he wouldn't slip off, Royce used Pardoel's own gi under his chin to submit him with a lapel choke.

After the bout when I presented the winner, Pardoel tried to raise his hand, but I pushed it down. I guess he was used to winning.

The fifteenth and final bout of the night was upon us with Royce meeting the strong, aggressive kickboxer Patrick Smith. We called this the classic striker versus grappler match. Again, I had no worries for Royce, and apparently he didn't either.

"If you put the devil on the other side, I'm going to walk into the fight," Royce told the cameras before the bout.

Smith, the local Denver favorite, was far from the devil. He didn't even connect with a kick before Royce had him in his arms to initiate the takedown. Once he got it, Royce mounted Smith's chest in seconds and threw six short, bare-knuckled punches straight at Smith's face. Smith looked like he was on the verge of tapping out, but his corner threw in the towel as I intervened. Seventy-seven seconds had passed.

I was surprised Smith had tapped so fast because he'd built up some steam during the show. Smith's UFC 1 introduction video kept running through my head. Pedaling on a stationary bike with his short dreadlocks swaying back and forth, Smith said, "Hi, my name is Patrick Smith. I'm impervious to pain. I don't feel pain."

In an ironic display of respect, Royce and Smith embraced and exchanged words.

"You're a tough man," Royce said.

"You're the best," Smith replied.

Again, Royce was hoisted onto the shoulders of his ecstatic family, Rorion and Helio included, as he held an oversized show check of $60,000 over his head for the world to see. The memo line said, "For: Being the Best!"

Nobody was there to tell me, but I was aware I couldn't congratulate Royce or celebrate with the rest of the team right then. I had to remain impartial.

Afterward, I met up with Elaine, and we went to the after party in a small ballroom inside the hotel.

"Mr. McCarthy, you're fantastic," Bob Meyrowitz said, handing me an envelope.

"There's something extra in there for you."

I'd been told I'd be paid $500, but they'd added an extra $250. They must have been happy with what I'd done.

I wasn't sure I was, though. I believed in the UFC's goal—to find the best fighting style—but I wasn't thrilled about the methods used or the role I'd played to get us there.

Keith Hackney, Kimo Leopoldo, Harold Howard, Roland Payne, and Royce meet the press at UFC 3 (September 1994)

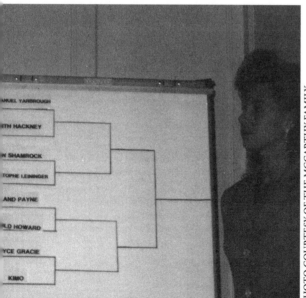

Royce's future wife, Marianne, placing names on the board after the fighters are paired by number with the bingo machine for UFC 3 (September 1994)

I was mic'd at every UFC event and hated it.

CHAPTER 9

THIS THING'S GOING

If a man does his best, what else is there?

—General George S. Patton

When I was sworn in as a Los Angeles police officer, I took an oath to protect and serve my community. For me that boiled down to one thing: I protected good people. Fighters were good people too. However, the rules laid out by the UFC didn't allow me to protect them. And if I couldn't do that, what was the point of being a referee?

When I saw Rorion at the gym again shortly afterward, I'd already made up my mind. "I'm never going to referee another UFC event again," I said.

"Why?" Rorion asked.

The answer was simple: "You're going to get somebody killed."

I could see the surprise on Rorion's face, but I didn't think I was overreacting at all. I'd already seen a lot in my life. I knew what real fights were and how far they could go. I'd gotten jumped by a group of people while trying to defend a friend, and I understood what it was like to reach a point when your mind says, *You*

can't win this; you're done. The human body can take a lot of punishment, but the brain eventually shuts off.

As an officer, I'd seen people get stomped to death, and if
you've ever seen this yourself, you don't forget it. The head crushes
and deforms, and the scary thing is that it doesn't take a ton of
pressure for it to happen. I didn't want to stand there in the cage
dreading that if I let it go just one more blow, that might happen.
I couldn't stand by as a fighter reached his breaking point and his
corner refused to throw the towel. I wouldn't stand there and let
that happen.

"Look, you care about your brother, and I understand that,
but these other guys don't understand what they're getting into.
They believe they're these awesome martial artists, their corners
think they're going to kill people, and they get punched in the face
one time and fold like a cheap tent. They won't tap out because
their brains are too scrambled. And their corners won't throw in
the towel because they're just too fucking stupid. I know someone's going to get seriously hurt."

Rorion wasn't convinced. He was so concerned about making
sure early stoppages never happened that he was overlooking the
obvious dangers.

"I'm not saying stop the fight because of a cut or the first sign
of damage, but I am saying there will be situations when we need
to step in." I said, "A fighter should be able to intelligently defend
himself, and when he can't the fight should be over."

Rorion said he would mull it over.

I left Rorion's office knowing I could be replaced easily. Rorion
could make a quick phone call and get someone else who'd follow
his guidelines to a tee. But as much as I wanted to stay involved

with the UFC, going along with what had happened at UFC 2 went against what I believed. Walking away was a decision I could live with.

One thing I had on my side was the public's immediate reaction to the UFC. While UFC 1 had 86,000 pay-per-view buys, UFC 2 jumped past that with 124,000 purchases. With virtually no marketing, this was just short of a broadcasting miracle. Apparently Rorion was so anxious to put on another show in September that finding another referee wasn't his highest priority.

When we talked about it again a week later, Rorion proposed that I could stop a fight only if someone either was too hurt to tap out or was already knocked out. In one of the biggest sport-influencing negotiations to ever happen outside the cage, Rorion and I debated terms that we would be comfortable with.

First, he said, "You can stop the fight at certain times."

However, it was all or nothing for me. "Either I can stop the fight as soon as a fighter can't intelligently defend himself, or I'm out of here."

Rorion thought for a moment, then said, "We'll give it a try." And "intelligently defending oneself" entered the MMA vernacular.

Another seed was planted about this time that would sprout deep roots and cause issues for the UFC later. The morning of UFC 2, WOW and SEG had managed to score an appearance on ABC's *Good Morning America*. They sent the promotion's most familiar face, commentator and former NFL superstar Jim Brown, accompanied by SEG executive Campbell McLaren.

During the show, McLaren uttered one of the stupidest but most famous lines: "You can win by tapout, knockout, or even death." That sure perked up a lot of ears. Little did anyone know that this controversial sound bite would launch the UFC down a path riddled with political land mines in the near future.

But first there was profit to be made.

With a moneymaker on its hands, WOW and SEG began preparations for UFC 3, and Royce was sent back into training. It didn't go smoothly for him.

Jiu-jitsu may not be as well-known as basketball or baseball, but it's just as exerting as any other sport out there. Anyone who's tried it knows the strains it places on the body while you stretch and bend into different positions.

A few months before the show, Royce hurt his neck badly and stopped training for a good chunk of time. He rested and got back on the mat as fast as he could, but with a few weeks to go, we all wondered if enough time had passed for his body to completely heal.

The show went on, and two nights before UFC 3, in Charlotte, North Carolina—another state with no athletic commission to speak of—I found myself with Royce, Rorion, and their older cousin Carlson Gracie Sr., an accomplished jiu-jitsu black belt and former vale tudo fighter in his own right. The beds in the hotel room had been pushed against the walls, and Royce and I were rolling all over the carpet as Rorion and Carlson gave Royce some last-minute fine-tuning.

Carlson wasn't pleased with the way Rorion had hoarded the Gracie name in the States, so Rorion would show Royce his way of doing a move, and Carlson, who ran an academy in Chicago, would demonstrate his own version. The two cousins went toe-to-toe here to gain the upper hand while instructing Royce.

While Rorion and Carlson tried to tell Royce what to do, I was stuck in the middle of it as Royce's grappling dummy. It was a mess.

Things were about to get messier for me.

The next night, Elaine and I had dinner with Guy Mezger and Oleg Taktarov, two fighters being considered for future events. I ordered swordfish, not knowing I was allergic.

That night, I woke up and felt like I was having an asthma attack. I sat up, sucked in some Primatene Mist, and then sat in a chair, but I couldn't get the feeling to go away.

After two hours, I finally had to wake Elaine.

When she saw the veins popping out of my face, neck, and chest as I strained to get air, she said, "I'm calling an ambulance."

"No, don't do that," I said, gasping.

Elaine knew Royce's fiancée, Marianne, was some kind of a doctor, so she wanted to go find her. I didn't have the breath or energy to tell her Marianne was a foot doctor.

When Marianne arrived and didn't know what was wrong with me, she called the paramedics. I was rushed to the local hospital as my body started shutting down. It was now the morning of the event, and I was stuck in an emergency room.

About four hours later, hopped up on some allergy medication and ephedrine, I was released. I was buzzing, and it was awesome. I'd never taken drugs like this, and whatever they'd given me kept me up like a wired rock star. I wouldn't sleep for two days, which wasn't an issue—there were fights to get to.

The Grady Cole Center, site of UFC 3 "The American Dream" was supposed to seat 3,500 people, but that didn't stop WOW and SEG from stuffing 1,500 extra fans into the stands and anywhere else they could fit them.

With North Carolina in its last days of summer, it had to be nearly 100 degrees inside the venue, and it was the humid kind of heat that makes everything stick to you. Under the scorching lights, it felt like 150 degrees. If there was a hell, this was it.

I don't know how some of the fighters made it through the night. I know I was sweating profusely, and I wasn't even exerting myself like they had to. "It was like trying to breathe in soup," Royce would say afterward. I'd say it was more like chili.

Prior to the first fight, I went backstage to meet with all the fighters. I'd been too stupid to think of doing it at UFC 2, but after observing firsthand what had happened with the fighters and their corners, I wanted to make sure everyone was on the same page.

I also wanted everyone to be comfortable with what would happen. This was why I started the ritual of talking to the fighters I'd be officiating beforehand, something I still do to this day. Giving them the chance to ask questions before they pressed into the unknown seemed to ease some of the anxiety.

This wasn't something Rorion or SEG asked me to do. Maybe part of it was that I was trying to keep myself busy, but mostly it just made sense to me.

UFC 3 showcased a handful of debut fighters along with returnees Royce Gracie and Ken Shamrock. The sixteen-man tournament had been a gruesome marathon with too many characters for WOW to handle and for the crowd to follow, so it was back to the eight-man scheme.

I performed my first referee stoppage when Harold Howard bludgeoned Roland Payne with his fist in one of the quarterfinal matches. Payne started to roll for cover before he went out, so I stepped in to make sure he didn't receive further damage.

"Intelligent defense" was a good term because it put the decision-making responsibility on me, and I had some leeway in my judgment. It was also a hell of a lot better than leaving it up to the corners.

In another quarterfinal, Keith Hackney whaled on Emanuel Yarbrough, a onetime world amateur sumo champion who out-weighed Hackney by more than 400 pounds. This was one of the saddest fights I've ever had to referee because Yarbrough was a nice man but could hardly move his 618-pound body. Once listed in *Guinness World Records* as the heaviest athlete, Yarbrough is to this day the stoutest man ever to enter the Octagon.

PHOTO COURTESY OF THE MCCARTHY FAMILY

Elaine posing with the promotion's largest fighter, Emanuel Yarbrough, at UFC 3

Hackney, a last-minute addition who'd trained in kenpo kara-te, had come to fight. After circling Yarbrough for a few seconds, Hackney knocked him down with an open-handed slap to the head. Yarbrough toppled, and Hackney rushed in. Yarbrough rose to his knees and pulled his tiny opponent into his refrigerator-sized chest and started assaulting the back of Hackney's head.

Hackney whipped himself around fast, but Yarbrough wouldn't let him go that easily. He grabbed and ripped Hack-ney's black tank top right off his body. Yarbrough then used his gaining momentum to push Hackney back against the Octagon's gate, which had the same flip-latch you would see on any backyard fencing. The latch unhinged under the pressure, and Yarbrough pushed Hackney right out of the cage.

We had to stop the bout momentarily, bend the latch's metal back into place, and restart the pair center cage.

The unexpected restart, the first one I'd ever performed in the Octagon, proved to be a tide turner. Hackney realized quick-ly he'd fare much better staying out of his opponent's reach, so Yarbrough plodded around the cage chasing him, chewing on his mouthpiece.

Hackney threw a kick, and Yarbrough caught it, again trying to suck his opponent back into his hippo hug. Hackney threw an-other haymaker, and Yarbrough went down again, rolling onto his stomach to find refuge from Hackney's punches. Hackney ended up beating down on the stationary Yarbrough like a kid who'd gotten a drum for Christmas. It was hard to watch a guy who couldn't get himself back up to a starting position because he was carrying too much weight.

"Tell me if you want out, and I'll stop it," I told Yarbrough over and over, but he didn't say a word.

Finally, he said, "That's enough," and I put an end to the punishment.

In Royce's quarterfinal bout, he met the dynamic fighter Kimo Leopoldo. The soft-spoken Hawaiian, whose discipline was listed as freestyle, had a foreboding look and a flair for the dramatic. Wide-shouldered, muscled, and heavily tattooed, with a trimmed goatee and hair slicked back into a thin braid that thinned to the bottom like a rat's tail, Leopoldo trudged through the crowd to the cage dragging a six-foot wooden cross on his back.[6]

Leopoldo's use of a prop in his entrance wasn't the only unique thing he introduced to the UFC. Like a professional wrestler, he also had his manager in his corner. Joe Son, a portly Asian man with a drooping mustache, would later tell reporters that by stepping into the Octagon, Kimo, who was also identified as a minister, had "answered the Lord's call."

Not long into Royce and Leopoldo's battle, they bounced into the door, which swung open. The fighters didn't separate, so I felt I should let them stay in that position and moved them to another panel as stagehands fidgeted with the latch to get the Octagon gate shut again. Leopoldo and Royce remained on the fence wrestling for control for the next ninety seconds, which told me Leopoldo was strong.

I had more trouble keeping the cornermen in line during this fight than I had reffing Royce and Leopoldo. We allowed a single coach to stand on the apron to instruct his fighter, and they were situated at two opposite panels.

When the gate swung open in front of Royce's corner, Joe Son decided to leave his designated area and perched himself next to Leopoldo, now backed against the cage, to give his instructions from there.

6. After Rhodes' overexposure at UFC 2, I'd added a rule that fighters had to wear spandex or something similar under their uniforms. When he had none of his own, I loaned Leopoldo a pair of mine.

I barked at Joe Son repeatedly to get off the fence and back to his corner, but he kept sneaking back to the fighters.

Seeing what Joe Son was doing, the elderly Helio decided to inch closer to the men as well. At one point, Royce's brother Relson was even leaning over the cage screaming directions at Royce.

Disorder was taking over, and all I could do in that moment was contain it as much as I could.

Leopoldo did a good job competing with Royce, far better than the seven other opponents who had come before him at UFC 1 and 2. Leopoldo nearly tugged Royce's gi off his torso and refused to be taken down. In fact, when Royce finally managed a throw, Leopoldo took Royce's back as they hit the mat. Leopoldo lost his hook, and Royce shook himself free and reversed to top position. Leopoldo swept Royce and was on top again just as fast.

Royce wasn't as well-conditioned because of his injury. The lights, his sagging gi, and Leopoldo blanketing him got to him. Though Royce used Leopoldo's ponytail to control his head effectively, this was the first time I'd seen Royce struggle with anybody. I thought if Leopoldo hadn't had that ponytail, it might have ended differently, but Royce found an armbar and submitted Leopoldo after four minutes and forty seconds.

It was the most competitive bout I'd seen Royce in, and it set the crowd on fire. I struggled to keep order in the cage, chasing Joe Son away as he began instigating a confrontation with the Gracie corner. I wrangled both men back to the center to raise Royce's hand, but neither fighter was leaving the Octagon unscathed. Leopoldo was bleeding from a cut on his left eyebrow, while Royce, drained and in a daze, had to be propped up by his brother Relson and carried out of the arena like a lifeless marionette.

Backstage, the Gracie family gathered around Royce like a

protective cocoon. Since I was refereeing all of the night's matches again, I didn't have the time to check on him, but he later told me his family kept him on his feet and he took a shower and even sucked in some oxygen offered by one of the paramedics on standby.

When Royce reappeared two fights later for his semifinal match against Canadian Harold Howard, he wasn't the same. He was pasty and listless, though he wasn't sweating at all. I walked over to his corner and asked if he was okay.

"I can't see. I see white," he said weakly.

I called Rorion over and told him, "Your brother's not right. He shouldn't fight."

"Well, what's wrong with him?" Rorion peered through the chain link at his sibling. "He's fine. He's fine."

"No, he's not, and you need to go over and take a look at him."

Royce was exhausted, dehydrated, and certainly in no condition to fight.

Through the cage, Rorion spoke with Royce, who told his brother the same thing he'd told me. Rorion turned back to me and said, "I'm getting the alternate."

"You can't do that," I said.

Royce had already been announced after he'd entered the cage. His corner would have to throw in the towel and forfeit the fight.

Rorion and I debated this for a moment, but I was steadfast. The rules were the rules, and they couldn't be bent for anyone, including the promoter's brother. I don't think Rorion was pleased with me taking a stand like this, but he signed off on it and Royce was taken out and helped backstage, while Howard's corner flooded the cage to congratulate him.

Eliminating Royce Gracie, the winner of UFC 1 and 2, was a big deal. Leopoldo and Joe Son reentered the Octagon a few minutes later to do their victory lap, goading the audience for support.

I had a feeling this wouldn't be the last I'd see of either of them.

With Royce out of the finals for the first time ever, it was anyone's game. Truer words were never spoken. Steve Jennum, a Nebraskan police officer who entered the tournament as the second alternate after Ken Shamrock dropped out with an injury, fought Harold Howard fresh in the finals and won the $60,000 prize. Jennum took Howard down and pounded on him until he submitted less than ninety seconds into the fight, an anticlimactic finish to another night of bizarre firsts.

Ironically, I'd been introduced to Jennum a couple days before. I'd taken one look at him and thought, *Dude, what are you doing? Please don't let this guy get a fight.* Then Jennum won it all. It goes to show you what an idiot I was for judging a book by its cover. Was he the best fighter? No, but he came in and won under the rules put in front of him, so you had to applaud him for his victory.

But wasn't the UFC all about trying to find the best fighter in the world?

After watching Jennum sail into the finals full steam and injury free, Rorion decided alternates would have to fight like the rest to earn their way into the tournament without an unfair advantage.

I'd also made a mental note that night during Royce and Leopoldo's match. We couldn't let the corners have carte blanche around the Octagon ever again. Especially with moving cameramen sharing the apron's space, I had enough to concentrate on right in front of me. At the next show, we would tape off a red box on each side of the apron and the coach wouldn't be allowed to leave it for any reason during the fight.

At UFC 4 "Revenge of the Warriors," held on December 16, 1994, at the Expo Square Pavilion in Tulsa, Oklahoma, three alternate bouts yielded a trio of potential replacements that night should anyone not be able to continue. The Pavilion, which regularly held rodeo events, was packed to the gills with nearly 6,000 fans, another sellout.

UFC 4 had a few familiar faces. Kevin Rosier, the UFC 1 pizza eater, returned to fight newcomer Joe Charles. Two days before the fight, I was with him in the hotel banquet room demonstrating armbars on a bodybuilder friend he'd brought with him. Rosier had asked me for help. However, a handful of minutes does not a jiu-jitsu practitioner make. Charles tapped Rosier out with, of all things, an armbar fourteen seconds into the fight.

In the quarterfinals, Joe Son, Kimo Leopoldo's unruly manager, squeezed into the tiniest pair of red Speedo briefs he could find and entered the cage himself. I know SEG had hoped the rivalry created between Royce and Leopoldo would play out in a rematch here, but they had to settle for Leopoldo's bulbous manager. Leopoldo had been enticed by K-1, a Japanese kickboxing promotion, with the promise of more money.

Joe Son, a master of Joe Son Do, of course, was more show than substance. Returnee Keith Hackney eventually got him to the ground and introduced his fist to Joe Son's groin a few times in full view of the TV cameras. It wasn't something I would have done, but it wasn't an illegal move and certainly made for a provocative visual. Joe Son did tap out but not because the groin shots hurt him, as his cup had done a good job protecting his prized jewels; he'd just petered out when Hackney started pushing his Adam's apple through his neck shortly after the groin attack. Like all who dared enter the Octagon in those early days, maybe Joe Son had balls of steel as well.

In Royce's quarterfinal match, he choked out debut fighter Ron Van Clief with a rear-naked choke less than four minutes in. At fifty-one years old, Van Clief, a tenth dan in Chinese goju and a five-time world karate champion, was and is to this day the oldest UFC competitor to enter the Octagon.

Arizona State University Hall of Famer and three-time Olympic freestyle wrestling alternate Dan Severn also advanced to the semifinals after a thrilling display in his first bout against muay Thai striker Anthony Macias. The forty-year-old mustached, all-business Severn, the first fighter to wear wrestling shoes in the cage, caught Macias early with a perfectly executed double-leg takedown.

The display delighted commentator Jeff Blatnick, a 1984 Olympic Greco-Roman wrestling gold medalist who'd been brought in with future NBC sportscaster Bruce Beck to fill the broadcast booth with returning Jim Brown.

Severn had his way with Macias, hurling him over his head two times in the fight with violent-looking belly-to-back suplexes, before he took Macias' back and fumbled around his neck with a makeshift choke until Macias submitted.

I think what was so exciting about Severn's debut is that the fans were watching real technique, timing, and precision in his movements, and they could really see the difference.

"The Beast" made it to the finals with Royce, where he shot in on Royce and planted him exactly where Royce wanted to be: on his back. Would they ever learn?

Severn attempted to hit Royce, though I doubt he'd ever really thrown hands before; his punches were more like hesitant slaps. Severn was tough, though. There was no doubt about that.

The fight dragged on for nearly sixteen minutes before Royce submitted Severn with a triangle choke, giving Royce his third tournament victory in four UFCs.

There was one problem with UFC 4. While Royce and Severn had battled to the bitter end, SEG's allotted pay-per-view time slot had run out. Twelve minutes into the fight, subscribers' TV screens went black. Thousands missed the fight's conclusion and demanded their money back.

As a result, at UFC 5 "Return of the Beast," to be held nearly four months later back in Charlotte, North Carolina, WOW and SEG would institute yet more changes. The first was time limits: twenty minutes for the quarterfinal and semifinal matches, thirty minutes for the final bout and the first ever superfight.

The one fight that had eluded the UFC had been the rematch between Royce Gracie and Ken Shamrock, and the promotion knew it would be the most anticipated fight ever. They decided to take the reins and make it its own nontournament, stand-alone featured fight.

Time limits and a superfight weren't the only adjustments. The show was also put on a strict timetable that accounted for fighter walkouts, pre- and postfight interviews, and everything in between. Whatever couldn't be left to chance wouldn't be.

The first four UFCs had been held over thirteen months, so the schedule hadn't put much of a strain on our family at all. Elaine helped Kathy Kidd prepare for the events from our home, and we were never gone for more than a week at a time. I accrued overtime at the academy, so I could string a couple days off together or budget my vacation time to cover the missed days. Elaine's mother or sometimes my dad would watch the kids, and Elaine and I certainly looked forward to our excursions.

For UFC 5, we were heading back to Charlotte, North Carolina. The promotion wasn't exactly welcomed with open arms. Though the state had no athletic commission, the district attorney tried to argue that the event was illegal and couldn't be held there. WOW and SEG managed to talk their way around this days before the show, but the aversion was a sign of things to come. The UFC was gaining a reputation in mainstream culture, for sure, but I wouldn't have described it as a positive one with everyone.

WOW decided to add another referee to the roster at UFC 5. Rorion picked Lonnie Foster from Utah, who'd been working out with Pedro Sauer, another established Brazilian jiu-jitsu black belt instructor and a friend to the Gracie family. Foster was assigned the two preliminary bouts.

On April 7, 1995, in the first preliminary bout at UFC 5, Dave Beneteau took down Asbel Cancio, mounted him, and whaled down with the wrath of a man who'd been wronged every which way to Sunday. Cancio's face split open like a piñata, and he tapped the mat frantically, but referee Lonnie Foster was standing on the other side of them and was heinously slow to respond. Cancio must have tapped twenty times before his corner finally threw in the towel, and Foster stepped in.

Cancio flipped to his stomach, and blood just poured out of him onto the light-blue canvas.

When Foster left the cage, I said, "What happened?"

"I didn't see the tap."

I wasn't anyone to give instructions on refereeing, so I bit my tongue and walked away. Foster refereed one more prelim that night and was never asked back.

Returning from UFC 4 was alternate and future standout Guy Mezger, who was paired with a young Russian sambo master named Oleg Taktarov.

At the infamous swordfish dinner with future UFC competitors Oleg Taktarov and Guy Mezger

I'd been at Davie's office when Taktarov had come walking in, clutching a black videotape sans cover. Taktarov barely spoke a lick of English, but he had a rugged, weathered look that said he'd been around the block a time or two.

The videotape featured grainy, black-and-white footage of

Taktarov performing sambo and fighting in Russia. "I want to be a movie star," Taktarov kept repeating in broken English as we watched. I guess Taktarov figured his sambo talent and the UFC might be an avenue to get there.

He was right. Six years later, Taktarov would get his big break when director John Herzfeld, a die-hard UFC fan, would cast him in his first major film role opposite Robert De Niro in *15 Minutes*.

Davie walked Taktarov across the street to Rorion's academy to see what he could do. Pedro Sauer, the respected Brazilian jiu-jitsu black belt instructor, happened to be there, so he gave Taktarov his audition on the mat.

Afterward, Rorion turned to Davie and said, "He's no good," and walked away.

"What do you think?" Davie asked me.

"He's pretty damn good."

Aside from some rough technique here and there, Taktarov was strong and had given Sauer a good match.

Rorion didn't want to use him because Taktarov knew his way around the mat. The guy could roll, and that was that.

Taktarov didn't make me a liar at UFC 5. He swam past Ernest Verdecia in the quarters, but the returning Severn sliced Taktarov's forehead open with a knee in the semifinal match, and I had to stop the bout. Taktarov was what you'd call a bleeder. Some guys open up, and the blood just can't be stopped.

Severn advanced to the finals and took out Beneteau to become the UFC 5 tournament champion, winning $60,000 in the process.

The highly anticipated superfight between Royce Gracie and Ken Shamrock died on the vine. It was scheduled for thirty minutes, and boy, did they waste every single minute and then some. The fight actually went for thirty-one minutes, until Art Davie, of all people, jumped onto the apron to tell me through the fencing that it was time to stop it.

The fight was restarted for a five-minute overtime period, which saw Shamrock land the only serious blow of the night. Still, after a total of thirty-six minutes, the bout was deemed a draw.

The fight was simply coma inducing, but I was able to laugh in the middle of it all when Bob Shamrock, Ken's feisty adoptive father, finally grew frustrated with his son's tactics and yelled, "Well, if you're just going to lay there with him, you might as well start kissing him."

The always stoic Royce looked at the elder Shamrock and then at Ken and said, "Please don't do that."

I didn't know it at the time, but that would be the last time I'd referee Royce in the UFC, at least for a while.

The North Carolina district attorney's earlier reaction to the UFC wasn't an isolated incident. Opposition to the "barbaric" and "brutal" UFC was forming in other states as well.

Art Davie observed all of this, and I think he knew it was his cue to make a move. He went to Rorion and suggested they sell their shares of the UFC to Bob Meyrowitz and SEG on the premise that they'd just branch off and start another show from scratch on their own.

Rorion was discouraged that his vision had been tampered with anyway. He wanted to preserve the no-rules, no-time-limit vale tudo fights that had made his father, Helio, a legend in Brazil. Rorion agreed to go along with Davie's plan.

What Davie didn't tell Rorion was that he was going to sell his piece and then take a job with SEG as the UFC matchmaker for $25,000 a show. When I saw this all shake down, I felt that Rorion had been duped by Davie. He was talked into selling his share of the UFC without knowing what Davie was up to.

It was kind of surprising that Rorion had chosen to walk away. UFC 5 had sold about 300,000 pay-per-view buys—astronomical numbers for that time.

Bob Meyrowitz was the first to call me after the ink dried.

"I don't know if you know this, John, but I bought the UFC," he said in his nasally voice. "You're a big part of the show, and I want you to stay. Is this something you'll do for me?"

"Yeah, no problem, Bob."

A couple days later, I went down to Rorion's Torrance gym to work out, and he called me into his office. He had a sober look on his face.

"Meyrowitz called and requested that I stay on with the show," I said.

"What are you going to do? You can't fly two flags."

"What do you mean?"

"Well, we can't do it for a little while—that's part of the deal—but we're going to do another show, and it's going to be bigger and better. Just because they were the first doesn't mean they'll be the best. We'll do something much, much better."

All I could think about in that moment was how Rorion had always gone on about having his family to look after.

"Rorion, I've got babies to feed," I said, stealing one of the lines I'd heard him use. I wasn't making much money refereeing the shows, but with a seven-year-old, four-year-old, and one-year-old at home depending on me, every cent counted.

"Well, you can't be with them and me."

I wasn't a fan of ultimatums. "No problem." I got up, walked out the door, and never went back. I wouldn't talk to Rorion, my teacher and friend, for the next four years, until we ran into each other at a party for the Japanese promotion, Pride Fighting Championships, in Hollywood. Rorion never launched his new promotion.

There were other casualties in the shake-up as well. Kathy Kidd, who'd served as event coordinator for the first five shows, decided to jump ship and go work for Chris Peters, who launched World Combat Championship. The WCC would promote one event, which featured Renzo Gracie, Royce's cousin. Kidd married UFC matchmaker Art Davie in December of 1996. A small world, I know.

After Kidd's exit, Elaine accepted the role of UFC event coordinator, which meant she'd be running the show from UFC 6 on. She'd continue to do all the preplanning from home, which would also give me a sneak preview of the new fighters Davie and Meyrowitz would be bringing in.

UFC 6 "Clash of the Titans" rolled into the Casper Events Center in Casper, Wyoming, on July 14, 1995. It would be the first UFC without Royce, who'd obviously parted ways along with his brother Rorion. But it just so happened that there was another star waiting in the wings.

David "Tank" Abbott wasn't as much protagonist as antagonist. For every man who scoffed at the hours of training some stalwart martial artists had put into perfecting their katas and techniques without actually having been in a real fight, Tank was their antihero. Abbott actually had some previous wrestling and submission experience, though the myth was that he rolled off his barstool and into the Octagon relying on the strength of his fists and cojones and the experience of over 200 street fights. Brimming with arrogance, Abbott would resonate with a good portion of the UFC's fan base almost immediately.

I was sitting with Davie in his office the day he got the call from Dave Thomas, one of Abbott's friends and soon-to-be manager who'd been trying to get him into the show. Davie turned on the speakerphone so I could listen.

Thomas started talking about Abbott, a fighter out of Huntington Beach, California, who benched 600 pounds. "He just beat up four Samoan guys. He'll crush everybody you have."

Four UFCs in, we thought we'd already heard it all, so Davie and I were trying to hold back our snickers. Davie pointed to the phone and mouthed, "Can you believe this guy?" But playing along, Davie asked Thomas, "Where does he fight?"

"Well, he fights on the streets," Thomas stammered. "We'll go to a construction site and set up fights for him."

"Construction sites?" Davie asked. "You mean down where the bulldozers have been? In a pit down there? So he's a pit fighter."

"Oh, yeah."

I told Davie, "Sounds kind of like the character in *Every Which Way But Loose*."

Davie agreed. "So this guy is like Tank Murdock?"

"Who's Tank Murdock?"

"From the Clint Eastwood movie, that pit fighter Clint challenges." Davie drilled it home. "Tank Abbott, the pit fighter."

And that's just what the UFC called him.

In person, Abbott certainly had the bravado down. I'd met him at the after party for UFC 5 and realized the barstool story probably wasn't far off. Abbott was a drunken mess.

"These guys can't fight." He slurred the words. "Wait until they bring in a real fighter like me. I'll destroy these guys. If someone puts me in guard, I'll slam his head until his brains fall out. Only pussies fight like that. You don't fight like that in a bar where someone will stomp your head in."

Abbott reminded me of all of the guys I met who were full of themselves and talked a much better game than they played. I would soon get to see if Abbott was the real deal or just another fool I'd get the satisfaction of watching as someone made him look silly.

I didn't get that satisfaction, at least not in Abbott's first fight. He faced John Matua, who, with ten bare-knuckle victories, had been listed in the program as a first-level Kuialua, which was an ancient Hawaiian art of bone breaking. Nothing was broken here, however, other than Matua's spirit.

The 280-pound Tank steamrolled Matua with hell-bent punches and sent all 400 pounds of his opponent into the canvas in about twenty seconds after catching him with a legal headbutt. Matua was never able to recover and was put to sleep with a huge right hand. His body went rigid and his legs began to twitch, not an uncommon reaction when somebody gets his lights turned off.

Abbott mocked Matua's trembling with his own gyration, then nonchalantly walked to his corner and gave his guy a high five as if he'd just landed a three-pointer. The fans ate it up.

Abbott continued his spree by tapping out Paul Varelans in the semifinals with strikes, but he was tamed by a returning Oleg Taktarov with a rear-naked choke in a final match that went nearly eighteen minutes.

It didn't matter that Abbott had lost, though. The fans were captivated by him. The UFC had found its next star to hang its future on, but something about the sixth event concerned me.

During the semifinal match between Oleg Taktarov and Anthony Macias, I believe I saw my first fixed fight in the UFC. Both fighters had the same manager, Buddy Albin, so I think it was decided backstage that Macias would throw the match so Oleg could advance to the finals and face Tank as fresh as possible. The fight went a little too smoothly for my tastes when Macias shot in and nearly fell into the guillotine choke, which he tapped out to in twelve seconds.

The night's superfight, a rematch between Ken Shamrock and Dan Severn, was memorable to me, not because Shamrock wore purple Speedos, which he'd shown me during the backstage equipment checks. I'd thought, *You're shitting me.* No, this fight was unforgettable for its finish. After a minute and a half of clinching, Shamrock caught Severn in a guillotine choke, and I watched Severn make one last big push to escape by punching Shamrock in his groin. It backfired, though, because Shamrock was wearing a steel muay Thai cup and all Severn did was hurt his hand in the process. Severn fell to his backside and tapped out to the choke.

The promotion had also continued its great referee experiment at UFC 6. Ron Van Clief, the fifty-one-year-old competitor from UFC 4, had found his way back into the UFC as its first and only commissioner, and he'd brought with him Taimak, of *The Last Dragon* fame, to referee. The twentysomething Taimak was nice enough, but he didn't really have the constitution for this job.

Taimak officiated the preliminary bouts for UFC 6 and 7, and by the latter I think he'd seen enough when alternate Joel Sutton reached into a half-inch cut on opponent Geza Kalman's forehead and ripped it open another good three inches. That was Taimak's last trip to the Octagon.

As for Commissioner Van Clief, he began to talk to Meyrowitz about instituting additional rules. Banning throat attacks was a big one for him; he called them a killing technique. Van Clief gave his notes to Meyrowitz, and Meyrowitz came to me with them. We agreed the rule wasn't necessary at the time, because none of the fighters were utilizing that type of attack. Van Clief lasted for two shows as well.

The UFC's oldest competitor, Ron Van Clief, with commentator Jim Brown and his date

A rule we did add at this time came following the Abbott-Taktarov bout. I credit my dad with this one, because he'd taught me that what we were seeing was called fish-hooking. Years before, my dad had gotten into a fight at Dodger Stadium with a man who'd started attacking people with a box cutter. After he sliced my dad's friend across the neck and back, my dad grabbed him, picked him up, and slammed him headfirst into the seats. Then he got ahold of his mouth and fish-hooked him, splitting his face all the way up to his eye. Describing this story to Meyrowitz proved an easy way to get "no fish-hooking" added to our growing rules list.

A bright spot for UFC 6 and 7—the latter of which was held on September 8, 1995, at the Buffalo Memorial Auditorium in Buffalo, New York—was the appearance of famed boxing announcer Michael Buffer as MC for the events. Buffer was a classy guy and the best announcer, and being the avid boxing fan that I was, I thought it was a big step up for the promotion. Michael Buffer shared the Octagon with me until WCW, a pro wrestling promotion that Buffer had already been announcing for, told him he'd have to choose between the two. I don't think the money was even close, so Buffer, too, bid farewell to the Octagon.

Another man to make an appearance at UFC 7 was cageside physician Richard Istrico, who would stay on all the way through to UFC 30. Dr. Joe Estwanik, the previous cageside physician who'd also worked with the United States Olympic boxing team, had recommended Dr. Istrico to SEG. Meyrowitz liked that he came from New York, where SEG's offices were located.

Dr. Istrico jumped right in and would send the fighters out for a host of exams like CAT scans, MRIs, and stress tests. He even asked me to start getting physicals because, as he put it, "You're in there the most out of everybody," and he had no qualms telling a fighter he couldn't compete in the UFC if his medicals weren't up to snuff.

PHOTO COURTESY TOM PALMER

The view you might get from where I stand: Mark Hall vs. Harold Howard at UFC 7 "Brawl in Buffalo" (September 1995)

Though UFC 7 boasted the promotion's largest live audience to date, objections to the event were mounting. Arizona Senator John McCain, future United States presidential candidate, became the face of the anti-UFC movement when he drafted letters and sent them to the governors of every single state. Ironically, one of the first to jump on McCain's bandwagon was Senator Ben Nighthorse Campbell, who'd captained the United States judo team in the 1964 Olympic Games in Tokyo. Campbell pledged never to allow the UFC back into his state of Colorado after it hosted Ultimate Ultimate 95 in Denver. McCain's campaign would gain steam in the next year.

Meanwhile, the UFC reached its second birthday and decided to celebrate by bringing back the notable fighters for one gala night. Ultimate Ultimate 95 was meant to be a reunion of the best we'd seen in the Octagon thus far, and for the most part I thought it was. Veterans like Oleg Taktarov, Dan Severn, Tank Abbott, and Marco Ruas pulled out all the stops in their bouts.

The event also marked a big first for the UFC. Judges sat cageside to decide the fights' winners. Before the event, I'd told Meyrowitz that bringing back their standouts would lead to closely contested bouts. If a fight went the distance, it would be considered a draw, but that meant neither fighter would advance in the tournament, and nobody wanted that. Meyrowitz agreed that it was time to bring in judges.

The addition went fine for the most part, except that SEG seated all of the judges at the same table on one side of the cage. In future events, they realized the value in placing each of the three judges on a different side.

SEG also quickly abandoned the practice of showing judges on camera as they each held up a card with the name of their winner on it. Can you imagine judges doing that today? With some of the questionable decisions fans haven't agreed with, they'd probably have to run for cover after the shows.

It was a shame the UFC had brought the show back to the Mammoth Events Center. For what was supposed to be their biggest event yet, the venue was nasty. But with McCain picking up the UFC's scent and his political army joining the hunt, shoddy venues would become the least of the UFC's worries.

Elaine manning the phones in the boardroom at the UFC's first Ultimate Ultimate event (December 1995)

PHOTO COURTESY OF THE MCCARTHY FAMILY

With my best friend and fellow referee, Joe Hamilton, at his first UFC, Ultimate Ultimate 95

Having a laugh with Tank Abbott

RENEGADES

> *If you can't get rid of the skeleton in your closet,*
> *you'd best teach it to dance.*
>
> —George Bernard Shaw

From the beginning, I was shocked that people didn't just flock to the UFC and the sport that would evolve out of it. I thought every guy would love it. How could he not? It's fighting. There's nothing more pure. *People should just fall in love with this*, I thought, and when they didn't, I couldn't understand why.

Senator John McCain remained staunchly opposed to the UFC, which he described as "human cockfighting," and he became its most outspoken opponent. McCain had a sizable pulpit from which to spread his message, and he urged his senatorial peers to protect the people in their states from this "reprehensible" sideshow. A majority of them took him at his word, too, without investigating the UFC on their own.

McCain had an added motivation to see the UFC banished. He was not only a huge boxing fan; his wife was tied to one of the country's largest distributors of Anheuser-Busch, producer of Budweiser beer, a major sponsor in boxing at the time.

Though he'd sat at events where boxers had taken massive punishment and later died from it and hadn't said a word about that, McCain hit the airwaves condemning the UFC as brutal and barbaric. He also claimed there was no referee involved in UFC fights, which upset me, not because he hadn't seen *me*—and you'd have to be blind to miss me—but because it implied he'd never truly watched a UFC fight. Either that or he needed a new optometrist.

If I had to pinpoint when McCain's political pressuring began to affect the promotion, I'd say it was during the final days before UFC 8 "David vs. Goliath," which was held on February 16, 1996, in the Ruben Rodriguez Coliseum in Bayamón, Puerto Rico.

McCain was meticulous and hadn't forgotten the United States territory when he'd sent out his UFC hate mail. Puerto Rico actually had an athletic commission, but it had no purview over the UFC. The events weren't quite boxing or wrestling, and the commission had no regulations for martial arts. So at the time SEG made inquiries to host UFC 8 there, the commission told the promotion they wouldn't get involved with the event at all if it came.

When I arrived, though, it was a different story. Meyrowitz and Elaine said the commission, possibly spurred on from some last-minute phone calls from a certain senator, was having a change of heart. As fight week counted down, Meyrowitz hired a big-time Puerto Rican lawyer because it looked as if we'd have to take our battle to the courts.

When the commission opted to file an injunction against the event, SEG's lawyer got the case moved to federal court, the promotion's only chance to get a halt put on the stop order in time to put on the event.

Three days before UFC 8, I was sitting in Puerto Rico's federal court, preparing to defend the UFC. I'd already had some experience explaining the events to government officials. Whenever the UFC came rolling into a new town, the local police department usually sent a supervisor or watch commander to speak to SEG. At UFC 6 in Wyoming, I'd been elected to be the promotion's representative.

The officers had been worried there'd be rowdy fights in the crowd ignited by what was happening in the cage. Since I was an officer, SEG thought I'd be able speak their language and smooth things over.

"Look, it's not like that," I'd said. "The fans have a legitimate interest in the fighters, who are all disciplined martial artists." I'd managed to get them out the door by promising no laws would be broken in hosting the fights.

In Puerto Rico's federal court, the district argued that UFC 8 was illegal and since it didn't fall within the commission's jurisdiction, it shouldn't be allowed.

I had to sit there in the stand, questioned by both the defense and the prosecution, and explain what the UFC was. "These are all of the same sports you see in the Olympics—boxing, judo, tae kwon do, amateur wrestling. We're just combining them."

We presented the best case we could, and then all we could do was wait.

Killing time back at the hotel, UFC announcer Jeff Blatnick and I sat around discussing the name "No Holds Barred." We thought it had a negative and misleading connotation, so we started brainstorming a new name for the sport. I'd used the term "mixed martial arts" on that LAPD permit form I'd filled out to work at

UFC 2, so I threw that name into the hat. I was told later that the same term had been used in Japan for the sport, but this is the way we came up with it here in the United States.

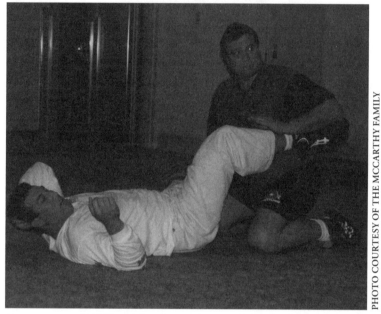

Commentator Jeff Blatnick, who made sure the name "mixed martial arts" caught on, always found time to roll and learn with me at events.

Jeff began referring to the sport as "mixed martial arts," or "MMA," on the broadcasts a couple of shows afterward, though "Ultimate Fighting" continued to be used as well. Blatnick should get the credit for popularizing the term "MMA" in the United States. It was his insistence on using it during the UFC broadcasts that finally made it catch on.

The morning of UFC 8, we got word that the courts had thrown out the injunction and we'd be allowed to hold the show that night, which was a good thing because it was sold out. About

7,000 fans packed into the sweltering, poorly ventilated venue.

I met Bruce Buffer, brother to the famous boxing announcer Michael, for the first time here. He was managing one of the fighters, Scott Ferrozzo, and convinced Meyrowitz to let him announce the only nontelevised alternate bout that night between Sam Adkins and Keith Mielke. Buffer would come back and announce the entire UFC 10 event. Except for a couple of shows here and there, he hasn't left the Octagon since.

Don Frye and Gary Goodridge also made their auspicious Octagon debuts that evening.

In a quarterfinal bout, Goodridge, a Canadian Kuk Sool Won practitioner and former arm wrestling world champion, used his own arms and legs to trap both of Paul Herrera's arms into a crucifix position on the ground when Herrera attempted a fireman's throw. With Herrera's arms tied up, he was unable to cover up and defend himself. Goodridge bashed in Herrera's left temple with his right elbow. The bout lasted merely thirteen seconds before I jumped in to save Herrera, now unconscious, but I'm sure no fighter ever forgot that attempting a fireman's throw on your opponent could end badly.

I learned a valuable lesson from this fight, too, which was to not anticipate a fight's outcome too far ahead. I'd known Herrera was a decent wrestler at the University of Nebraska, and I'd doubted Goodridge's credentials beyond his arm wrestling. This had led me to believe Herrera would control Goodridge on thc ground. As soon as I saw Herrera shoot for a single leg, I had it in my head that he'd get the takedown. I casually moved myself around the fighters to a position I felt they were heading, which was a big mistake. I wasn't near enough when Goodridge started dropping heavy elbows, and I was slow to react. I'd never do that again.

In the finals, Goodridge shed his black gi and met former Oklahoma State wrestler Don Frye, who'd gotten into the event through his old friend Dan Severn. Frye was memorable not only for his bushy *Magnum, P.I.* mustache but because he was as tough as leather in the cage and as funny as hell out of it. Goodridge made a good go at it, but Frye gained superior position to rain down punches and get the stoppage.

I wouldn't say this was the most memorable fight for me at UFC 8, though. That one happened outside the cage.

Tank Abbott, who'd become a star overnight for the promotion, was flown down to Puerto Rico to sit cageside at the event. Following his brutal knockout of John Matua at UFC 6, Abbott had been met with an eruption of cheers when he'd attended UFC 7. The UFC had then set Abbott up in a cop versus criminal match against UFC 3 winner Steve Jennum at Ultimate Ultimate, which Abbott won before getting mauled by eventual winner Dan Severn in the tournament's next round. Even with his landslide loss to Severn, fans were really into this guy, which automatically made him Bob Meyrowitz's golden child.

Sitting cageside, knocking back one vodka after another at UFC 8, Abbott recognized somebody sitting on the other side of the cage. His name was Allan Goes, a Brazilian jiu-jitsu black belt under Carlson Gracie, and he rubbed Abbott the wrong way.

Despite all his guff about not needing martial arts training, Abbott knew the deal. He'd sought out some ground instruction at a school that Goes had been working at in Orange County,

California, a few months earlier. Goes had rolled with Abbott at the school and tapped him out a few times, which was to be expected. But then, Goes did what many fighters consider disrespectful: he told people about it.

When Abbott spotted Goes across the cage, he was like a bull seeing red.

Elaine had noticed Abbott eyeballing Goes all night and told me. I hadn't thought it was that big of a deal, but Elaine knew what was coming when she saw Abbott rise, take out his false teeth, hand them to his girlfriend, and start making his way in Goes' direction. Goes saw Abbott and began moving toward him as well. The two freight trains came at each other head-on.

Luckily, Joe Hamilton, the second referee, and I were standing on the Octagon's apron during a break between fights. Joe jumped down and grabbed Abbott as they connected and spun around, while I reached for Goes and yanked him away.

"I'm going to kill you," Abbott said, as we tore the fighters as far apart as we could.

After the legal battle we'd gone through just to get the show started, this was not the event to have a brawl break out in the crowd, especially not between two fighters.

Thinking the drama had passed, I went back into the cage to referee the superfight that night between Ken Shamrock and Kimo Leopoldo. But the real fireworks were happening backstage.

When Abbott had lost his composure cageside, Elaine had gone to his girlfriend and asked why she'd kept egging Abbott on to fight Goes. Now Abbott's girlfriend was telling her boyfriend Elaine had gotten in her face.

Abbott, inebriated on alcohol and bad intentions, approached my wife and threatened to kill her.

Once I'd finished my refereeing duties and Elaine told me what had happened backstage, I dropped everything and went looking for Abbott. Ken Shamrock's crew, who loved Elaine, also joined me.

I found Abbott's manager, Dave Thomas, who apologized profusely for what Abbott had done. Everybody knew what had happened; word had spread that quickly.

I searched the hotel and anywhere else I could think of to find Abbott, but he'd flown the coop. We don't even know if he made his flight the next morning.

"We have a problem," I told Meyrowitz at the after party. "Your boy threatened my wife, and I'm not going to put up with that. Either he's gone or I'm gone. It's up to you. I don't care." Of course, I think I said it with a few more expletives included.

Meyrowitz tried to settle me down.

"Trust me, I've settled down. It's your choice, Bob."

"I'll take care of it."

But threatening Elaine was the tip of the iceberg. That was the one thing that put me over the edge, but what really bothered me was that SEG loved what Abbott represented. He was marketed as this average tough guy taking out all these trained martial arts practitioners, but I didn't buy into it. It's not that I didn't like Abbott. I did, and I thought he was smart. He was doing a great job of orchestrating his persona, but he wasn't what people thought. He had tried to train but never had the determination to put in the true effort needed to make himself better. As soon as he got with someone in the gym who could outbox him or toss him around, he would bolt. To me, that wasn't the spirit in which the UFC had been created.

SEG loved him because of the way Abbott represented that everyday man, but I looked at it a different way. To me, he wasn't good for the sport. He wasn't a true martial artist, and he went against everything we were trying to say the UFC was. His behavior played into everything our detractors were saying about us.

I knew Abbott was a big star for the UFC, but he'd threatened my wife. I wouldn't go to the shows anymore if Abbott was there. A few days later, Meyrowitz called to say he'd suspend Abbott from the show, so I agreed to stay on board. Abbott sat out UFC 9 and 10, events I knew SEG had wanted him to fight in.

In the meantime, David Isaacs, another SEG executive, continued to call Elaine to try to smooth things over. Isaacs said he'd spoken with Abbott, who'd voiced his deep regret. I told Elaine to do what she wanted to.

Finally, Elaine received a letter, supposedly from Abbott, expressing his remorse. I knew the letter wasn't from Abbott and suspected David Isaacs had written it himself. Still, Elaine decided we should all move on, and Abbott returned to the Octagon at UFC 11.

Abbott's antics aside, Meyrowitz had looked at the UFC 8 court debacle as a victory. That worried me. Meyrowitz felt so good about his legal coup in Puerto Rico that when New York cable providers became the first to pull the UFC from programming, he took out an ad in the *New York Times* that said: "Mad that you can't get your UFC? Call this number and complain." Below was the home phone number of the executive responsible. It may have been funny to him at the time, but it would come back to bite us in the ass down the line.

Though the UFC had prevailed in court and been able to put on the show, all Meyrowitz was doing was maintaining status quo. The next state could come after us just as Puerto Rico had.

March 14, 1996

Mrs. Elaine McCarthy
Unlimited Productions
438 Katella Ave., Suite M
Orange, CA 92667

Dear Elaine:

I am writing to attempt to explain and apologize for my conduct and the truly regrettable incident that recently took place in Puerto Rico.

First, I would like to tell you that although my behavior did not convey it, I hold you and your husband in very high regard. I admire the competent professional attitude that you and John exhibit at all events. I realize that you and John have extensive responsibilities proscribed by Semaphore Entertainment Group, yet you both do a commendable job nonetheless.

In view of all this, I must tell you sincerely that I am very sorry for the verbal confrontation that occurred between us in Puerto Rico. I was totally and completely at fault. Although it is no excuse, I was very distraught from the events that immediately preceded the crossing of our paths. As a result, I took a very defensive posture to what I perceived as a threat. The things I said to you were said in the heat of the moment. I did not mean anything I said to you and I truly regret any offense, harm, or trouble I caused you. In fact, I was so distraught that I cannot accurately recollect what I did say.

I would also like to apologize to your husband. I realize I put both of you in a very awkward position. I assure you I have agonized thoroughly over my behavior. This was an isolated incident and will not happen again.

Again, please accept my earnest apology.

Sincerely,

David L. "Tank" Abbott

If you believe Tank wrote this letter, I have some great beachfront property for you in Arizona.

That's exactly what Michigan did. UFC 9 "Motor City Madness," which was scheduled to take place on May 17, 1996, at the Cobo Arena in Detroit, was a lesson in the pitfalls of shortsightedness.

I'd been flown out to Detroit six weeks before the event for a press conference SEG had hosted to drum up support. Instead, the county's district attorney dragged us all back into court from that point all the way up till 4:30 p.m. the day of the show.

It was a big story in Detroit, and the press came out in droves to cover it. The battle over No Holds Barred dominated the headlines. At the first hearing, the district attorney's expert witness on Ultimate Fighting was an old-time boxing writer who'd written a book on . . . guess what. Yes, boxing.

I read the book beforehand and gave SEG's lawyer a slew of questions to ask the writer to show that he didn't have any real experience with or knowledge of MMA.

When we reconvened with the courts at the follow-up hearing the week of the show, SEG brought in Emanuel Steward, a renowned boxing trainer who was helping promote this UFC event and spoke on its behalf.

However, the DA went ahead with filing a last-minute injunction, which meant it was another race against time to get the judge to throw it out before the show was advertised to start.

The judge listened to me, Steward, and a couple other prominent local figures willing to defend the promotion.

The judge then decided he saw two similarities between boxing and Ultimate Fighting, and they were closed-fisted punches and headbutts. I don't know how he derived headbutts from boxing, but that's what he came up with. He told SEG that if they outlawed closed-handed punches and headbutts, we wouldn't be categorized as boxing and he didn't see where the state would have any jurisdiction over what we were doing, because only boxing was in the books. He'd let the show move ahead.

Standing there in court, in front of a throng of media and onlookers, Meyrowitz said, "No problem."

Outside the courthouse, I grabbed Meyrowitz. "How the fuck are we not going to have any punching in this?"

"I didn't say there wasn't going to be any punching," Meyrowitz coolly answered. "I just said I'd make it illegal. When they punch, you're going to tell them, 'That's illegal.' And you're going to have to fine them eventually. When they have to pay that fine, only God knows."

I was almost sick over Meyrowitz's decision, but the event was hours away. What could I do? I had to be there to protect the fighters, so I carefully explained the scenario to them all backstage and told them they wouldn't have to pay any fines accrued that night. Because boxing used closed-fisted punches, open-handed strikes would be interpreted as legal.

I didn't hear much fuss about it until I got to Ken Shamrock, who was scheduled to rematch Dan Severn in the superfight that night. I gave Ken the same speech I'd delivered to everyone else, but Ken had a totally different reaction.

"John, I can't do that. My father has a boys' home, and I can't set that example for those boys. I'm not going to stand there and knowingly punch illegally just because I know I won't have to pay the fine."

"Ken, you do what you gotta do. It's your choice. If you want to hit him with open hands, hit him with open hands. But I'm telling you, Dan is going to try and hit you with closed hands."

The result of this whole mess was a subpar event. During the fights, I felt like an idiot instructing the fighters to open their fists when they punched and calling out fouls left and right. And when it got to the Shamrock-Severn fight, it was thirty minutes of a whole lot of nothing, as both circled but barely laid a hand on each other. Severn, who won by split decision, later claimed that the bout was a brilliant strategic display, but I can safely agree with the fans: it was the worst fight in UFC history.

UFC 10 happened six months later on July 12, 1996, at the Fair Park Arena in Birmingham, Alabama. It was christened "The Tournament" because SEG had abandoned the elimination format at UFC 9 for single bouts but brought the tournament style back by popular demand.

UFC 10 introduced Mark Coleman, who'd placed seventh in freestyle wrestling at the 1992 Summer Olympic Games in Barcelona, Spain. Coleman was a standout from the moment he stepped onto the UFC canvas. He had the strength of a monster and could take anyone down, but nobody could do the same to him.

Determined and disciplined by years on the amateur wrestling circuit, Coleman met karate expert Moti Horenstein in a quarterfinal match, took him to the ground, and fed him a heavy serving of punches until I stopped it at two minutes, forty-three seconds.

Horenstein had been a favorite of Meyrowitz's wife, Ellen, because she thought he was so good-looking. He probably wasn't so much once Coleman got finished with him.[7]

Coleman took out Gary Goodridge in the semis en route to the finals to face Don Frye, the durable wrestler who'd won the UFC 8 tournament back in Puerto Rico. In their quarterfinal bout earlier that evening Frye, who was not a pushover, had pulverized

---

7. Horenstein's luck would continue to elude him later at UFC 14 when he'd face another All-American wrestler named Mark Kerr in his second and final UFC appearance.

Mark Hall's body like a side of beef till it was purple, and then in the semifinals he'd beaten an ever-improving Brian Johnston.

Frye-Coleman was one of the first bouts when I could clearly see that the fighters' skill levels were starting to improve. It was a war. Coleman dominated the bout with his wrestling ability, but Frye, puffy-eyed and staggering at times from exhaustion, was the epitome of toughness.

After nearly twelve minutes of scrapping that culminated with Coleman hammering down punches into Frye's guard, I intervened. Frye was bleeding, and his right eye was swollen shut. I knew he couldn't see. Coleman's family and friends, including his soon-to-be wife, Kelly, flooded the cage and flanked him.

Coleman would have so much success taking his opponents down and punching them into submission, as he had with Frye, that he'd become known as the godfather of ground-and-pound, the term given to his technique. It's a popular strategy still used today, especially by the wrestlers.

UFC 10 was one of those shows I walked away from and felt it had delivered. It was also the start of a period when wrestling took center stage in the UFC.

That December, SEG hosted its second Ultimate Ultimate event, inviting back the cream of the crop from that year, including its champions and runners-up. We returned to the Fair Park Arena in Birmingham, Alabama, the site of UFC 10.

Tank Abbott fought Cal Worsham in a quarterfinal bout, where Worsham tapped out to his punches on the ground. Worsham became incensed that Abbott had gotten in an extra lick after I'd stepped in to stop it, and I had to physically restrain him against the cage, grabbing the chain link on either side of him. As Worsham pleaded that I disqualify Abbott, I kept telling him to knock it off, giving Worsham the few extra seconds he needed to come back down to Earth. When Worsham's adrenaline dump subsided, I walked to Abbott, told him what he'd done was bullshit, and raised his hand in victory.

The show's other highlights included Tank Abbott's ruthless knockout of Steve Nelmark, who bent backward on the cage like a crash test dummy, and Don Frye's come-from-behind gut-check victory over Abbott in the finals.

Unfortunately, this night was the second time I felt I was refereeing a fixed bout. In the semifinals, Don Frye and Mark Hall met in a rematch of their UFC 10 bout. In their first encounter Frye had beaten the piss out of Hall, who'd refused to give up. Here, though, Frye ankle-locked Hall to advance to the finals without breaking a sweat.

The fight struck me as odd. Frye, a bread-and-butter wrestler and swing-for-the-fences puncher, had never won a fight by leg lock, and Hall practically fell into the submission. I also knew both fighters were managed by the same guy.

I told Meyrowitz afterward that the fight had been fake, but Meyrowitz asked me how I could think that.

UFC 11

"The Proving Ground"
September 20, 1996
Augusta-Richmond County
Civic Center
Augusta, Georgia

Bouts I Reffed:
Mark Coleman vs. Julian Sanchez
Brian Johnston vs. Reza Nasri
David "Tank" Abbott vs. Sam Adkins
Jerry Bohlander vs. Fabio Gurgel
Mark Coleman vs. Brian Johnston
Scott Ferrozzo vs. David "Tank" Abbott

I hit my forearm against Brian Johnston's nose while leaping in to stop his bout against Reza Nasri, and everyone thought I broke it, but that isn't true. "John, you hit my nose," Johnston said, and burst out yelling at the grounded Nasri because they'd exchanged words before the fight. An ill-timed camera cutaway on the pay-per-view made everyone think Johnston was having it out with me.

The main event never happened after Ferrozzo was too gassed from his first fight with Abbott to enter the finals against Coleman. With no alternates left standing, 5,000 fans were treated to Coleman suplexing protégé Kevin Randleman onto his head in an unaired wrestling exhibition. It wasn't fighting, however, and the hotheaded Randleman cursed the hostile crowd quietly, daring them to get in the cage themselves.

Rumors that Hall had thrown the fight circulated for months, until he came out and openly admitted it. Hall said Frye had offered to pay him, with the mutual manager's consent, to ensure that Frye made it to the finals as strong as he could be. Hall said he came forward only after Frye didn't settle up, though Frye denied it ever happened.

I don't know what kind of deal was struck, and I don't care what anybody says. I know what I saw.[8]

Between Ultimate Ultimate 96 and UFC 12, I finally convinced Meyrowitz and the rest of SEG to add weight divisions. Over the last few shows, I'd told them there were many great 170- to 185-pound fighters who could shine for the promotion, but no matter how talented they were they just wouldn't be able to overcome the bigger fighters.

I suggested they take a first step by splitting the UFC into two tournament divisions: heavyweight for fighters 200 pounds and over, and lightweight for those under 200. To keep the number of fights down, a preliminary round would decide the two finalists in the four-man tournament, which meant the fighters would compete in two bouts that night instead of three.

SEG decided to give it a try, though the UFC almost didn't get the chance to test out weight classes.

UFC 12 "Judgment Day" was scheduled to take place on February 7, 1997, in Niagara Falls, New York, but a day before the promotion was forced to move the entire event—fighters, cage, and all—to the Dothan Civic Center in Dothan, Alabama.

The UFC's New York story had actually begun a few months

8. Coincidentally, Tank Abbott later faced both of these questionable winners in the finals: Taktarov at UFC 6 and Frye at Ultimate Ultimate 96.

earlier, when Meyrowitz had hired a lobbyist named James D. Featherstonhaugh shortly after UFC 8 to get mixed martial arts legalized in the state. SEG's offices were located in New York, and being the center of the universe as well as the haven for boxing for many years, it seemed like a smart progression.

In less than a year, Featherstonhaugh had managed to get a bill introduced and eventually signed by Governor George Pataki that made Ultimate Fighting legal in New York for a short time. However, Meyrowitz had to make an agreement with the politicians involved with the bill to not bring the UFC to New York City and especially not to the famous Madison Square Garden, until there had been multiple events held in the state and everyone felt comfortable with it. SEG booked the upstate arena and got to work promoting the event.

In the meantime, Battlecade: Extreme Fighting, another promotion owned by New York–based movie producer Donald Zuckerman, decided it would swoop in on Madison Square Garden first. Zuckerman hadn't been part of the UFC's lobbyist movement and hadn't made any agreement to keep his show away from New York City, but when Zuckerman announced his show, it affected us all. The news attracted the attention of the press, which welcomed the scandalous headlines, as well as New York State Senator Roy Goodman, who was dead set against Ultimate Fighting.

Goodman described Ultimate Fighting as a "disgraceful, animalistic, and disgusting contest which can result in severe injuries to contestants and sets an abominable example for our youth." The press, including the influential *New York Times*, ate it up and ran story after story condemning both Battlecade and the UFC.

The uproar caused Governor Pataki to put a stay on the bill

he'd signed, and a new bill was drafted to replace it that made a complete about-face on Ultimate Fighting. While the new bill began its route through the state senate and back to the governor, SEG continued to plan UFC 12 in Niagara Falls, knowing the bill wouldn't get passed in time to shut down the show.

New York wasn't done yet, though. Floyd Patterson, a former heavyweight boxing champion and the head of the New York State Athletic Commission, had his staff draft and present a 114-page rule book to Meyrowitz that would essentially kill UFC 12 in Buffalo. The rules included mandatory use of boxing gloves and protective headgear and also banned fighters from taking their opponents down or using any ground work. It basically melded the UFC into amateur boxing.

The week of the show, Meyrowitz took his complaints to court and argued that the state had gone back on what the two parties had previously agreed upon. Then we all headed back to Niagara Falls and waited for the judge's decision, which was handed down at 2:30 p.m. the day before the show.

Since UFC 8 and 9 had survived the court's scrutiny, Meyrowitz was confident the judge would rule in the UFC's favor. However, unlike in the previous court battles, the NYSAC now had jurisdiction over Ultimate Fighting because of the first bill that Governor Pataki had signed. The judge ruled that the UFC had to follow whatever regulations the NYSAC presented to them, saying, "If you don't want to follow the rules, then don't put on a show here."

Meyrowitz was flabbergasted, but it wasn't like he hadn't had any doubts. There was an exit plan. SEG had booked a small arena in Dothan, Alabama, about ninety miles outside Montgomery earlier that week, just for this situation.

However, no other arrangements had been put in place. Elaine had to scramble to find a way to transport nearly 200 people, including 20 fighters, their corners and entourages, some media, and all of SEG's employees nearly 1,100 miles south within the next 12 hours.

Elaine rented a Boeing 757 to fly out of Buffalo and land in Montgomery, which was about a two-hour drive from the hotels and venue. She then reserved every room she could find in the area, including ones at the local Super 8 and Motel 6. The fighters would later be dispersed among the hotels, which made for a logistical nightmare when transporting them to and from the arena. In the end, I don't know how much all of this cost SEG, but I'm sure it wasn't pretty.

While Elaine made these preparations, I was sent around to the fighters' rooms to tell them they wouldn't be able to bring all of their cornermen, family members, and other guests on the plane. If people wanted to be at the show, they'd better get a car and take off now so they could make it.

At the airport, the crew added up the poundage for the Octagon, all the cameras and technical equipment necessary to produce the show, as well as the passengers and their luggage, and told SEG they were running dangerously close to the plane's limit.[9]

Hearing this, Elaine told the fighters they could now bring one guest. The rest were asked to find a way down to Alabama on their own.

Before we left, the UFC hastily held its first ever weigh-ins in Niagara Falls. Each of the lightweight competitors stood on an ordinary household scale in view of his opponents. There was no crowd and no fanfare. It was decided that the heavyweights

---

9. The Octagon was mostly made of wood, barring the fencing, and all of the structuring underneath was two-by-fours with a lot of trussing.

wouldn't have to step on the scales because you could just tell by looking that they were all over 200 pounds.

That night, with everything packed, stowed, and accounted for, we lifted off from Buffalo International Airport around 11:00. I doubt anyone got much sleep on the flight. I know I didn't. The fighters seemed surprisingly upbeat even with their opponents sitting only a few aisles away. Everyone was pulling together for a common goal: we wanted the show to happen.

We landed about four and a half hours later, and SEG's crew scattered to set up the Octagon, hang the lights, and in a few hours tend to details they usually had a few days to accomplish.

Not only would SEG have to refund the money from the tickets sold in Niagara Falls, which was substantial because it was a sell-out, but they would also have to give away all of the Dothan tickets.

I was sent to a local Dothan radio station that had been alerted to our arrival in their fair city. I invited fans to come pick up free tickets, and the station was even kind enough to whip up some T-shirts for the fans that said, "Why is the UFC in Dothan, Alabama? Because New York only allows street gangs to whip your ass."

That night, 6,000 Dothan fans were treated to a decent free show. Mark Coleman continued his reign by neck-cranking Dan Severn into submission in the night's superfight.[10] In the UFC's first lightweight tournament, Jerry Bohlander, a protégé of Ken Shamrock's Lion's Den team, defeated alternate Nick Sanzo with a crucifix neck crank. However, the night really belonged to a nineteen-year-old Brazilian named Vitor Belfort, who stunned Tra Telligman, also a Lion's Den fighter, in their heavyweight preliminary bout with the fastest hands I'd seen in the Octagon.

---

10. Prior to the bout, I asked Severn if he had any questions. Our mics picked up his statement about two trains leaving separate stations and meeting in the middle. Since UFC 6, Severn's ritual was to ask me questions about relativity or some other inane topic to get me to crack a smile. He rarely succeeded.

The UFC went to Dothan, Alabama, and all I got was this damn T-shirt. Still, it's one of my favorites.

In the finals, Belfort faced Scott Ferrozzo, who outweighed him by more than 100 pounds. Belfort stopped the flabby Ferrozzo in his tracks with his incredibly accurate fists to win the heavyweight tournament. In total, Belfort had spent two minutes, ten seconds in the cage that night. I took one look at this young, muscular athlete and knew he'd be a star.

Shaken by the drama that was UFC 12, SEG returned to safer territory at the Augusta-Richmond County Civic Center in Augusta, Georgia, for UFC 13 "The Ultimate Force" on May 30, 1997, one of the few places left where the promotion wouldn't be hassled.

UFC 13 would turn out to be a landmark event because it produced two future superstars of the sport. One was a young protégé of Abbott, Tito Ortiz, and the other was a four-time Olympic Greco-Roman wrestling alternate named Randy Couture.

Quiet and composed, the thirty-three-year-old Couture entered the heavyweight tournament on two weeks' notice and won both of his fights that evening to become the heavyweight tournament champion.

It was hard to tell what Couture would be able to do as a fighter from his initial two bouts because although both opponents had been bigger than him, neither had been particularly technical. Couture's wrestling had allowed him to control and dominate, which I'd expected. But Couture would really come into his own as a fighter in his next appearance.

That night, it was easy to recognize another fighter's potential. The tournament's one lightweight alternate, Ortiz, walked through opponent Wes Albritton in thirty-one seconds. The rest of the tournament also played out in Ortiz's favor.

In the first bracket, Lion's Den fighter Guy Mezger earned a unanimous decision against Chris Leininger to secure his spot in the final match. In the other preliminary bracket, Enson Inoue submitted Royce Alger with an armbar but took a big hit during the bout. Afterward, Inoue's eye socket swelled up when he blew his nose; he had a small crack in his orbital bone. Dr. Istrico took one look at Inoue and told him he couldn't fight the next match.

The bleached-blond Ortiz would be called to the finals, but because he was a wrestler in the NCAA collegiate system at California State University Bakersfield at the time, he wasn't allowed to accept any money for the bout, including the final prize. Ortiz had agreed to fight for free.

Mezger and Ortiz faced off in the finals, and Ortiz was doing quite well with his wrestling skills. He cradled Mezger on the ground and started kneeing him in the head, which opened large cuts on Mezger's scalp. One sliced an arterial vein, which was like striking oil: blood just started pulsing out with each heartbeat.

Feeling the heat from politicians who were calling the UFC a "barbaric bloodbath," Meyrowitz had told me before the show to scrutinize any excessive bleeding and to stop the fight if it got bad. With Mezger spouting blood like a fire hydrant, I paused the match and called in Dr. Istrico. Good old Dr. Istrico wasn't squeamish in the least. He looked at the laceration and said the fight could continue as long as the cut didn't get worse.

At the time, I was to always restart any fight standing no matter where it had been stopped. I did, which meant Ortiz lost his position on the ground. It was Mezger's gain for sure. Ortiz shot in for a takedown, and Mezger locked him in a guillotine choke, then sat back and squeezed, forcing Ortiz to tap out.

I knew after the fight that Ortiz hated me because he thought I'd taken the win away from him by restanding the bout after Dr. Istrico had checked Mezger. I'd thought Dr. Istrico would stop the fight, and I hadn't really had a choice when he'd said it could continue. For better or worse, and in this case it was definitely the latter, I had to follow the scant rules that were in place.

UFC 13 marked another turning point for the promotion, though this one would prove crippling. Senator John McCain, having been elected chairman of the Committee on Commerce, which regulated the cable industry, made sure UFC 13 was the last event to see the light of day on major cable carriers, including Time Warner, TCI, Request, Cablevision Systems, Viewer's Choice, and others. Overnight, the UFC's potential viewing audience dwindled from 30 million homes to about 5 million.

Meyrowitz had never planned for this reality. Without pay-per-view buys to sustain the promotion, he turned to the live gate revenue. But Meyrowitz had never set up the UFC to be a spectator event. He didn't give a shit about the crowd because he was a TV guy; the telecast was all that had mattered to him.

My family experienced this firsthand when my dad took my son Ron to the first Ultimate Ultimate event in December of 1995, and they sat in the front row. It's hard enough to see into the elevated cage when the fighters hit the ground, but my dad had to contend with a cameraman's ass blocking his view the entire time. My dad finally approached the cameraman and yanked him off the cage lip.

With budget costs cut, the live experience had only gotten worse since then.

What kept the UFC's small, devoted following were the fighters. After watching Royce and Brazilian jiu-jitsu dominate the first few events, fans debated when the reign of wrestlers in the UFC would ever come to an end. No one had come close to beating Mark Coleman, but Maurice Smith, a world champion kickboxer, changed that at UFC 14. Smith eventually wore the weary wrestler's legs down to unseat him with a unanimous decision nod after twenty-one minutes. It was the beginning of a wave of successful strikers to enter the UFC.

No matter what anyone tells you, the UFC was always a work in progress. There was never a time when it wasn't evolving, including in its rules. Even from UFC 1 to 2, changes had been made. Situations would arise in the cage that would make us realize certain rules had to be implemented to preserve an even playing field. Some rules we saw right away. Others took more reflection.

At Ultimate Ultimate in 1995, I'd watched Oleg Taktarov grab the fence with one hand to pull himself up and away from Marco Ruas, who was trying to take him down. He'd used the fence to change the context of the fight and ended up winning the bout. The cage was there to keep the fighters from falling out, not to aid in leverage. I went to Meyrowitz and the rest of SEG and told them grabbing the fence shouldn't be allowed, but they didn't agree with me at first. They loved what Taktarov had done and thought it was a great strategic move.

It didn't take long for certain scenarios to repeat themselves, especially if they were effective. At UFC 11, Jerry Bohlander bent the fence in his bare hands as he held on to avoid being swept by Fabio Gurgel. Then at UFC 13, Wallid Ismail took Kazuo Takahashi

UFC 14

"Showdown"
July 27, 1997
Boutwell Auditorium
Birmingham, Alabama

Bouts I Reffed:
Joe Moreira vs. Yuri Vaulin
Kevin Jackson vs. Todd Butler
Mark Kerr vs. Moti Horenstein
Dan Bobish vs. Brian Johnston
Kevin Jackson vs. Tony Fryklund
Mark Kerr vs. Dan Bobish
Maurice Smith vs. Mark Coleman

I jumped into the cage during an alternate match between Tony Fryklund and Donnie Chappell that I hadn't been reffing when Fryklund stepped on Chappell after he'd tapped out. I told Fryklund, "If you want to be a champion, you need to start acting like one."

Later, Jackson submitted Fryklund in forty-four seconds, and Fryklund pushed me away in frustration when I was helping him to his feet. In anger, I grabbed Fryklund under his arms and picked him up. I didn't think anyone had noticed until Joel Gold, the owner of the publication *Full Contact Fighter*, published a picture of Fryklund in my arms with his feet about a foot off the ground. It was not a proud moment for me. I'd lost my cool.

airborne, and Takahashi grabbed the fence the entire time so he wouldn't get dumped on the mat.

Once Meyrowitz saw this, he finally agreed to add the rule.

At Ultimate Ultimate 96, Tank Abbott scooped up Cal Worsham and tried to throw him over the top lip of the cage. That was cause for an obvious rule addition.

Some changes were much subtler. I was in the cage with the fighters up close and personal, so I was seeing details others didn't have a vantage point to notice. Once I'd get a new regulation approved by Meyrowitz, I'd pass it on to the fighters at the rule meetings, but I'd never been asked to write them all down.

Losing its pay-per-view platform had been a slow process for the UFC. Since around UFC 10, Meyrowitz had told me there was a chance of it happening and I'd wondered if that was the beginning of the end.

Just before UFC 14, Meyrowitz called. "We've got to come up with rules, John. We have to have rules. It's the only way they're going to put us back on cable. Come up with rules that look like something on paper but don't change the sport in your mind that much."

With the rules we'd already instituted, I rounded out a list of seventeen dos and don'ts for the UFC.

I didn't mind adding "no groin attacks," a tactic that didn't look good for the sport anyway. I didn't mind "no hair pulling," either, because the practice didn't derive from any legitimate combat sport.

I thought about headbutts and knew getting rid of them would be a game changer for a few of the fighters, like Mark Coleman, who dominated his fights due in no small part to his headbutts. Nixing headbutts was going to change the sport a little, but how in the world could we get away with saying they were legal when boxing had already established them as a major foul?

I added "no small joint manipulations" to the list. It wasn't a highly practiced technique, but it became a rule nonetheless.

I also added "no pressure point attacks." To me, that was a bullshit fluff rule, but it made it sound like the UFC was contemplating even the most intricate of techniques.

With the completed list, I flew with Meyrowitz to Denver to meet with Leo Hindery, the president of Time Warner Cable.

Hindery, who'd probably never seen an MMA fight in his life, was a tough customer from the start. "There's no sport you can show me where you can hit somebody in the balls," he said.

THE ORIGINAL 17

No Biting

No Eye Gouging

No Headbutting

No Hair Pulling

No Groin Attacks

No Throat Strikes

No Kicking a Downed Fighter

No Stomping a Downed Fighter

No Fish-Hooking

No Placing of the Fingers in a Cut

No Small Joint Manipulation

No Pressure Point Attacks

No Holding On to the Cage

No Throwing of an Opponent out of the Cage

No C-Clamping the Throat or Trachea

No Unsportsmanlike Conduct

Gloves Must Be Worn

Meyrowitz and I nodded and pointed to where we'd banned groin strikes.

We could counter all of Hindery's objections but one. Hindery's real problem was one man punching another man on the ground. In boxing, you'd never hit a man while he was down. There would always be a ten count and a referee would step in, and the fallen fighter would be given time to recover. Even in the movies, a man would punch another man and pick him up before he took another swing.

Taking a fight to the ground was a big component of MMA, and sitting there I realized society was not conditioned to accept that. I couldn't draw from a single existing sport where a competitor could do it.

We were wasting our breath with Hindery, which meant we were officially off the air.

THE ULTIMATE

V
IG TOP
workout top.
able in XXL
ally BIG guys.
g John,

ite, Steel,
Ash, Gold,

XL.

ET PANT
e

Posing in a catalog for Body Alive, a fitness clothing company owned by my friend Bob Donnelly

THE THIRD MAN

When one man, for whatever reason,
has the opportunity to lead an extraordinary life,
he has no right to keep it to himself.

—Jacques Cousteau

I have never considered myself a celebrity, and I don't think I ever will. I didn't become a referee to get famous. I did it because I loved the sport I saw emerging out of those early shows and wanted to be a part of it. I never imagined it would take me on the wonderful adventure it has, and I know how lucky I was to be in the right place at the right time. Still, the added attention has been something I've struggled with from day one.

The first time I was asked for an autograph was at UFC 2. I thought the fan was stupid for asking for it, and I felt stupid giving it to him. I was the referee, not a fighter. I wasn't a big deal. The fighters who got in the cage were the ones who deserved all the attention. I was just the third man, the third wheel. I thought a good referee did his job without bringing attention to himself. Period.

But at each show, fans would continue to hand me their event programs to sign or ask me to pose for photographs. After a couple shows, it dawned on me that the people coming to see the UFCs were spending their hard-earned money not just to watch some good fights but to take in the whole experience. If they approached me and wanted to take a picture or get an autograph, it was little skin off my ass. I owed it to them and the sport. If it made them feel good, who was I to deny them?

The one request I don't usually fulfill is saying, "Let's get it on," outside the cage. I've said it at the end of radio spots or for video games and for other marketing purposes I feel help propel the sport forward. I even said it when Zuffa allowed a die-hard couple to get married in the Octagon in Las Vegas the day before UFC 36. But most of the time, I politely decline. I don't like to throw around the phrase. When I say it, two fighters are about to put their lives in my hands and I'm letting them know I'm on the job, I'm paying attention, and I've got their backs.

PHOTO COURTESY OF MIKE AND LARYSSA CAMP

The first wedding ever held in the Octagon: I told the couple to "Get it on."

PHOTO COURTESY OF TOM PALMER

PHOTO COURTESY OF TOM PALMER

Above: Wallid Ismail vs. Kazuo Takahashi at UFC 12: one of the fights that led to discussions about holding the fence to control your position (February 7, 1997)

Below: Tsuyoshi Kohsaka vs. Kimo Leopoldo at UFC 16: Yes, you feel like you have a fever. (March 13, 1998)

You know you've made it when you're spoofed in *MAD*.

FROM MAD # 348 © 1996 E.C. PUBLICATIONS, INC. USED WITH PERMISSION.

Above: Fan drawings sent in to one of Japan's bigger MMA magazines: Do You Ready?

From front to back: Johnny, Brit, Ron, Elaine, and the ugly guy

Right: Raising Jerry Bohlander's hand after he armbarred Olympic wrestling gold medalist Kevin Jackson at UFC 16 "Battle in the Bayou" (March 13, 1998)

Inset: At UFC 12, I was still wondering who Vitor Belfort was after he walked through everyone that night. (February 7, 1997)

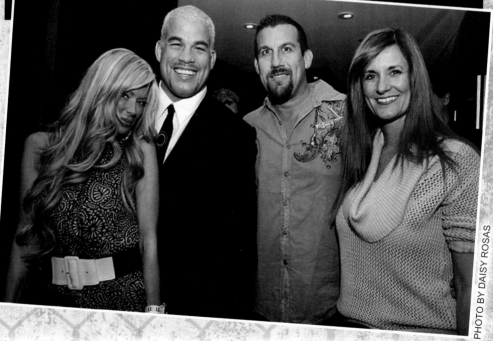

Above: With a young Tito Ortiz before he became "The Huntington Beach Bad Boy." I predicted he'd become number one. He accomplished that at UFC 25.

Below: An older Ortiz and a more wrinkled me with the two women who make us look better, Jenna Jameson and Elaine McCarthy

PHOTO COURTESY OF TOM PALMER

PHOTO COURTESY OF THE MCCARTHY FAMILY

Above: Posing next to my target at Hogan's Alley, LAPD training academy: at least they're all in the ten ring.

Below: P3 Officer John McCarthy, a little over ten years on the job

Above: Standing far enough away to make sure Akebono fell on Royce and not me (K-1 Premium Dynamite, December 31, 2004)

Below: Ringing in my fortieth birthday with my family and friends

Over the years, being an MMA referee has afforded me some interesting opportunities outside the cage. I'm continually surprised when people notice me at the airport or in the gym or on the street. I'm told I have one of those faces. I can't explain what it feels like to have people stare at you when you enter a restaurant or the movie theater before they finally ask, "Are you that referee in that fighting thing?" Most of the time, people make me laugh because they are so genuinely enthused.

It's a pleasure to be able to see fans respond to the sport firsthand. I'm a lucky guy, and I know it. I do get extra attention and always have people to talk to who love MMA as much as I do.

But it goes both ways. I have been bombarded by fans at hotels and casinos during fight weekend and had to leave my family alone so they could walk around freely without me. Nowadays, I don't leave my hotel room until it's time for the show.

I've never felt that being recognizable made me better than anyone else. I learned early on that celebrities aren't necessarily better people than the average person. Usually, they're worse off because they have the means to get away with more. When I first became a police officer in 1988, I met one of my childhood heroes. I was called to Melrose Avenue to assist another officer already on the scene. When I arrived, I saw none other than O. J. Simpson and an attractive blonde lady standing there. They'd been arguing, and she said he'd hit her, though I couldn't see any visible marks.

I stood there talking to Simpson, who had the same calm, personable voice you'd hear each week on ABC's *Monday Night Football*. He didn't hide the fact that they'd had a disagreement but said his wife had been hitting him and he'd put his hands up to defend himself.

Gene, the first officer, wanted to take Simpson to jail, but I couldn't stand by and watch this three-time American Football Conference MVP and pro football Hall of Famer get dragged away. I was twenty-four years old and impressionable. "Gene, this is O. J. Simpson. You can't take him to jail for this. Let me talk to her."

We told the Simpsons they could each go to jail for accusing the other of domestic abuse. Neither of them wanted that, so we talked it out and Gene and I eventually left. As we drove away, I felt good for saving Simpson from certain public embarrassment.

Six years later, Simpson was charged with killing his wife, Nicole, and her friend Ron Goldman on the steps of her condo. I know it wouldn't have made a difference if we'd arrested him that day, but I never forgot how I'd been swayed into thinking Simpson was somehow better than the rest of us.

I crossed paths with more celebrities as the UFC's popularity grew. In early 1997, I got an interesting call from Bob Meyrowitz that demonstrated how much the UFC had penetrated mainstream culture. "How would you like to be on *Friends?*" he asked.

"What are you talking about?"

"Do you know what *Friends* is?" Bob asked.

Of course I knew what *Friends* was. In its third season on NBC, it was one of the most watched shows on television. It was also one of Elaine's favorites.

Meyrowitz explained that the show's staff had written a premise around the UFC, in which Monica's Internet millionaire boyfriend enters the Octagon to test himself. When he mentions "the ring" to her, she mistakes it for a pending marriage proposal. I was a little surprised, given the UFC's current problems with its public perception, that a hit NBC show would want it on, but of course I said yes.

Announcer Bruce Buffer, Tank Abbott, and I were hired for the episode. We were brought onto the NBC lot to rehearse and then shoot.

Some of the actors knew about the UFC and the sport and were very welcoming. Jon Favreau, who played Monica's boyfriend and would go on to direct the blockbuster *Iron Man* films, talked about watching UFCs and liking them. Most of the other cast members were very cordial as well.

I was told that the biggest fan on the set was Matt LeBlanc but that he hadn't been available to shoot on these two days and would kick himself for missing them.

Wow, Joey Tribbiani wants to meet me, I thought. *That's pretty cool.*

Former teen actor Robby Benson directed the episode. I remembered him from a college basketball movie he'd done called *One on One*. I'd loved that movie, but I was too shy to go up to Benson and tell him that.

On the first day, the stunt coordinator approached me and said a couple of stars had questions about the UFC, so I said I'd be happy to answer them.

This tiny woman approached me, baseball cap pulled down low on her forehead. She was so petite I did a double take. "Do people die in this?" she asked, peering up.

I hadn't even realized who she was at first, and all I can tell you is that she was one of three female leads. I dove into my well-rehearsed explanation, and she listened for about thirty seconds before she turned and walked away.

It wasn't my final interaction with the woman I'll call Miss X. In the makeup room, I was told to sit next to her to prep for the episode.

Soon a production assistant came in and gently said to her, "Mr. Benson wants to work through the lunch break, so I took it upon myself to order you grilled chicken, steamed vegetables, and some pasta."

She exploded like the assistant had just run over her dog. "No, no, no. That's my time. That's my thirty minutes, and I want to go to the commissary."

"Okay, but Mr. Benson—"

"I don't care what Mr. Benson wants. That's my thirty minutes. If I want to stand out on Barham Boulevard and pick my nose, that's what I'm going to do."

The assistant nodded, walked to my chair, and gave me the same line and lunch menu. In my one Academy Award–worthy moment, I went for it. "No, no, no, no," I shrieked, startling the makeup artist. "That's my thirty minutes, and if I want to stand out—" I paused. "You know what, bud? If I said something like that, I'd be a dick. Thank you so much for the lunch. That would be great."

Miss X looked at me, daggers coming out of her eyes, and stormed out. Everybody in the makeup room applauded me, but I can tell you with the utmost confidence that she will never "friend me" on Facebook.

Now, it could have been a bad day for her, and she's probably a wonderful person the rest of the time, but her behavior always reminds me of how to not act. She'd made a hardworking man, who was simply doing his job, feel insignificant. I'd tried in my own small way to right that wrong. Nobody's above anybody else, even if they're well-known.

My second big brush with fame came from another unexpected

phone call, supposedly from a production assistant to Nicolas Cage who said the A-list actor wanted to put me in a film he was directing.

I thought one of my friends was playing a practical joke on me and said, "You're full of shit."

After many assurances, the caller said, "Could I at least deliver the script to you within the hour so you can look it over?"

"You're really going for this one, but sure, why not? Send the script over within the next sixty minutes."

When the script arrived at my house within the hour, I thought, *My friends are good.* The script looked legit. Even the Saturn Productions company listed at the bottom of the front page checked out when I searched for it online. Having watched my dad and his LAPD friends orchestrate the most elaborate jokes on each other, I had to admit this was a pretty good one.

When I started reading the script, though, I quickly realized it wasn't a prank. I'd seen real scripts. Besides appearing on *Friends*, I'd had the opportunity to work stunts and advise on the 1999 cop comedy *Blue Streak*, starring Martin Lawrence and Luke Wilson.

Looking at this script, I knew my friends weren't smart enough to come up with something this detailed.

I called the assistant back, and he asked if I'd meet Cage at his house to read for him.

The next day, on my lunch break and in my LAPD fatigues, I found myself pulling into Cage's driveway in Bel Air in my Audi TT. There was the latest model, red Ferrari 360 Spider in a line of classic cars.

Holy shit, I thought. *I don't belong here.*

Cage was a friendly guy. He told me he'd been training with Royce Gracie and had watched me since UFC 2. I fumbled through the read while Cage kept telling me I was doing great. I knew I sucked.

Afterward, he said, "I want you to do the part, but I need to check with some people before I can give you a final answer."

Later that day, I got the call. I'd been cast.

Sonny, the story of a young returning Army veteran who can't escape his seedy past, was filmed in New Orleans. They flew me down South for four days and later had me come back for another week of shooting.

The movie starred future Academy Award nominee James Franco. I played Detective Rollo, a crooked cop whose one purpose seemed to be beating up Sonny or another character every few scenes, then leaving.

In one of my scenes with Franco, I had to blindside him next to his car parked on Bourbon Street. Cage wanted me to knee Franco's stomach and face. Franco was such a good sport about it. I tried to pull it back to not hurt him, but he said, "Keep it coming," as wardrobe stuffed more and more padding under his costume.

The movie was about prostitution—something I knew a lot about—so I remember being impressed with the authenticity of it all when one of the women on set walked toward Cage to speak with him. She was wearing a rabbit fur jacket, which was all the rage with the prostitutes back in Los Angeles. She was a pretty girl, and I kept thinking she looked familiar. I realized a few seconds later that she was Cage's girlfriend, Lisa Marie Presley.

American Pie actress Mena Suvari and veteran actor Harry Dean Stanton were also in the film. Acclaimed British actress and Academy Award nominee Brenda Blethyn played Sonny's mother. I shared a van with her on the way to the set the first day of shooting.

She looked at me and started speaking in a slow New Orleans drawl. It took me a few seconds to realize she was speaking her lines and wanted me to respond with mine. She was in character and wanted me to play along. In that moment, I knew actors were a different breed altogether and I was way out of my element.

PHOTO COURTESY OF BRUCE BUFFER

On the set of NBC's *Friends*: the UFC's logo mascot, Ulti-Man, would be "softened" in a later version as the UFC tried to change its image.

One scene was particularly difficult for me because it required Franco to spit on me after I'd beaten him up. I had to stand there and take it, and I had to change my clothes between each take because Franco would get his syrupy fake blood all over me. Each time Cage yelled, "Cut," I prayed it would be the last. But we must have done that scene ten times.

During one of the takes, Cage walked up to Franco and me. "Hey, I want to put one more thing in. When he spits and before you hit him again, give him the 'kiss of death.'"

At first I thought my wife was putting Cage up to it. I don't kiss men, other than my dad or my sons, unless I'm joking around.

"Do you have a problem with this?" Cage asked.

With the set waiting for Cage to leave the shot, I nodded. "I can do it." Then at the right moment, I grabbed Franco by the ears and kissed him on the lips.

"That was awesome," Cage said. "Let's do one more take or would that be a problem?"

"Of course he has a problem," Franco said to Cage, cracking up. "I'm kissing John McCarthy!"

Imagine my relief when I got a call a few months later from the assistant. Despite everyone from Cage down to the director of photography telling me how great I was, Detective Rollo and his kiss of death were left on the cutting room floor. I'm not a religious person, but I thanked God profusely in that moment.

Acting wasn't really my thing, but I've always been grateful for the opportunities that come from being associated with the UFC and the sport. Over the years, I've been asked to play myself for films, in popular TV shows like HBO's *Entourage*, and in music videos.

Once I was even asked to record a ringtone.

I haven't accepted every offer, and some have been a little ridiculous. I've been asked to officiate weddings many times, even though I'm the furthest thing from an ordained minister. I also felt some of the offers could damage the sport's reputation.

In 2000, when pro wrestling juggernaut World Wrestling Entertainment decided to produce *WWE Tough Enough*, a reality series about training young hopefuls for the ring, they tried to incorporate real fighting. WWE hired Dan Severn and Ken Shamrock to wrestle for the organization, but when this show came around, Severn was moved to coaching. The show then morphed into having the lesser-known WWE wrestlers enter boxing matches against one another. Guess who they called to referee that circus? Though the WWE was a hugely popular and established operation, I thought affiliating myself with it in such a visible way would only confuse fans and the general public—some already thought MMA was just as fake as pro wrestling—so I politely turned down the offer.

I don't feel awkward in the cage; it's second nature. But when I'm on a TV or film set, I always feel stupid. I'm not what people think I am. I don't need the fame; I'm not that guy.

Still, it's always the greatest compliment to feel wanted and a part of something you truly love. SEG was the first company to validate what I did in the sport. After making $750 for my first event, I got a raise around UFC 7 to $1,250 for each event. Remember, at this time, athletic commissions and other regulatory bodies wouldn't give MMA a second glance, so I was hired and paid directly by the promotion.

When my role expanded to court and media appearances defending the UFC and the sport, I missed more time at the police academy. Around UFC 12, I went to Meyrowitz and told him I couldn't take any more unpaid time off. To Meyrowitz's credit, he researched what boxing referees were making for the big championship fights and offered me a $50,000 annual contract. This allowed me to continue working the events to supplement some of the income I was losing from the academy. I was also expected to review and help develop the rules and to generally speak on the sport's behalf when it was needed.

No other referee got the vote of confidence I did. My good friend Joe Hamilton refereed from the first Ultimate Ultimate event to UFC 16 before he approached Meyrowitz for a raise because he, too, was losing money taking off from the department to work the events for $500 a show. SEG told Joe they couldn't do it with him, and Joe had no choice but to leave the UFC.

Meyrowitz put a lot of trust in me to always conduct myself in ways that would help the sport. I think he knew I would take a bullet for the sport if I had to. People like that were undoubtedly needed around the promotion after Senator John McCain and Time Warner CEO Leo Hindery effectively pulled the plug on the UFC's major pay-per-view platforms.

We all marched into UFC 15 "Collision Course," on October 17, 1997, at Casino Magic in Bay St. Louis, Mississippi, with the feeling that the UFC's days were numbered. We needed only to look around to confirm our suspicions. The event was held in a tent in the casino's parking lot because there was no facility in the hotel to host it. It was a severe downgrade. Still, about 2,500 hard-core fans showed up to witness another historic night for the sport.

We had the list of rules I had drafted—the ones Hindery had rejected—and we all knew we were on the right track with them. SEG decided to try them out at UFC 15. But why stop there? The perception of bare-knuckled fighting had always plagued the UFC, so SEG also decided to try out specially designed finger-free gloves that would allow fighters to strike and grapple.

The first fighter who'd worn MMA-style gloves was Melton Bowen when he'd fought Steve Jennum in a quarterfinal bout at UFC 4. Dan Severn had experimented with an early prototype in his fight against Ken Shamrock at UFC 9, as had a few other fighters after him. However, it was definitely Tank Abbott who popularized wearing gloves inside of the Octagon. The gloves were much thinner than those used for boxing, had a small gel-like padding in the knuckle area, and left the fingers free for grabbing and completing holds and chokes. They resembled weightlifting or even cycling gloves more than anything else. They weren't necessarily designed to protect the opponent's face but to protect the fighter's knuckles and allow him to strike more.

Gloves would become an important safety addition. After the fighters tried them out at UFC 15, SEG would make them mandatory for every event, and I became heavily involved in their ongoing development.

With a set of rules and mandatory glove use now in place, this was one of the pivotal moments for the UFC. Revisionist history might try to convince you that changes like this didn't happen for another few years, but I can tell you this is when the UFC truly started feeling a sense of accountability and ran toward regulation. Many people involved with the UFC spent a lot of time and effort beginning to educate the commissions about the sport during this time without getting any credit for it.

UFC 15 was the first event to be sanctioned and regulated by a recognized governmental body, in this case the Mississippi Athletic Commission under the leadership of Billy Lyons. It was the first time I was licensed as a referee.

The most memorable fight at UFC 15 was the heavyweight bout between Brazilian phenom Vitor Belfort and four-time Olympic wrestling alternate Randy Couture, who was fresh off his heavyweight tournament win at UFC 13.

When I found out UFC matchmaker Art Davie was scheduling this fight, I told him it was stupid. "Why would you do that to the guy who just won your tournament?" I said. "Couture's a wrestler. Give him some time to learn the sport so he can fight Belfort down the road."

Throwing Couture in with Belfort, a Brazilian jiu-jitsu black belt, would lead to Couture losing by submission. It seemed to me that SEG was wasting a guy who had solid credentials and potential to be promotable later.

Davie said, "That's the point." Belfort would take out Couture, the tournament champion, and then face the winner of the heavyweight title match between Maurice Smith and Dan Severn, also on that night's card.

Davie and I were the first in a long line of doubters of Couture's talents. Little did we know Couture would go on to become one of the most decorated athletes the sport had ever seen and remain a relevant competitor into his late forties.

If Belfort was the surefire favorite, he didn't do himself any favors prior to the fight. The night before, he was a mess. He called the

UFC boardroom and asked to speak with me regarding the rules, so I went upstairs to his hotel room.

I found Belfort sitting there with his girlfriend, and he was seriously concerned.

"What's the problem?" I said.

"He's a wrestler," Belfort said. "He likes to hold, so if he's on top of me on the ground, where can he elbow?"

Belfort wasn't helpless from his back by any means, but he seemed preoccupied with what Couture could do to him—not exactly the frame of mind you'd want a competitor to be in the night before a fight.

Finally, I said, "Just go out there and do what you do best." I left his hotel room thinking, *Oh my God, this guy is going to lose.*

If there could be an exact opposite of what I'd seen in Belfort, Couture was it. When he entered the cage the next night, he was the epitome of confidence.

I walked to his corner and gave him the same speech I give all the fighters: "This is your corner, and this is where I need you to be for me to start the fight. I'm going to ask you if you're ready, and I'm going to ask your opponent if he's ready, and once I get an okay from the both of you, I'm going to tell you, 'Let's get it on.' That's your time to do your thing. Protect yourself at all times, and obey my commands, and if I tell you to stop, I need you to stop. Do you have any questions about anything?"

Couture shook his head. I returned to center cage and looked at the small entrance ramp SEG had built for the fighters. We waited. And waited. And waited. Belfort never appeared.

After about ten minutes, a UFC employee climbed onto the

Octagon's lip and whispered through the chain link, "Belfort won't come out of his dressing room."

I left the cage and went outside to the holding area, where each fighter had a camper. I climbed up into Belfort's, where his team was mulling around, but Belfort was in the bathroom. "What's wrong with him?" I said to his cornerman.

"He's having stomach problems."

Loudly enough for Belfort to hear, I told his corner, "He has two minutes to get himself in the cage, or the fight will be forfeited to Couture."

After the event, the native Brazilian would be quoted as saying in broken English that he had worms, which became the butt of many jokes at the time.

What Belfort really had was a bad case of nerves, which was understandable. The situation reminded me how vulnerable these fighters, seen as ultimate combat machines, could be.

I was certainly sensitive to Belfort's condition, but the pay-per-view was running live. The commentators were doing their best to stall, but they could say only so many times that Belfort was using mental warfare to psych Couture out.

Belfort suddenly appeared on the ramp and walked to the cage. He had no reason to be intimidated. He was the better striker and a far superior ground practitioner. Where Couture had the advantage was in the wrestling, and isn't it ironic that wrestling is where the key moments played out?

A tested wrestler on the ultracompetitive international circuit for years, Couture had mastered subtle upper body movements, which made him especially strong in the clinch. I watched him force Belfort, a formidable striker, into playing the wrestling game.

Couture softened up Belfort before taking him down and pounding out the stoppage after eight minutes. It was the first of many upsets we'd all see from Couture. And it was the first time I really understood the young Belfort's weakness: his mental game.

In the evening's other main bout, Dan Severn didn't make it to his fight with Maurice Smith for the UFC heavyweight title. A week before UFC 15, Severn had fought Kimo Leopoldo for a new promotion in Japan called Pride Fighting Championships and had hurt his hand.

Tank Abbott was called in to replace Severn, and Smith bludgeoned Abbott's legs with damaging kicks for eight minutes until Abbott called it quits.

Smith would end up defending his title against Couture at the next event, which would be held in Japan, while Pride Fighting Championships would become a significant feature on MMA's horizon.

UFC 16

"Battle in the Bayou"
March 3, 1998
Pontchartrain Center
New Orleans, Louisiana

Bouts I Reffed:
Pat Miletich vs. Townsend Saunders
Jerry Bohlander vs. Kevin Jackson
Pat Miletich vs. Chris Brennan
Tsuyoshi Kohsaka vs. Kimo Leopoldo
Frank Shamrock vs. Igor Zinoviev

Returning to Louisiana, the second state to sanction the UFC, SEG separated the fighters into three weight classes, including a lightweight division for competitors under 170 pounds. This is really when the lighter guys got off to a rip-roaring start. Mikey Burnett and Eugenio Tadeau had it out in their preliminary bout, but it was alternate Chris Brennan who would meet Pat Miletich in the finals after Burnett withdrew with a broken hand.

It was disheartening to see the athletic Russian fighter Igor Zinoviev get hurt as badly as he did by Frank Shamrock's body slam. Zinoviev sustained a broken collarbone and a separated shoulder and was knocked out cold in one fateful drop. Zinoviev never fought professionally again.

Before the UFC traveled halfway around the world for its next event, it had some housecleaning to do. Art Davie, who had been around since UFC 1 and served as the show's matchmaker, was fired for going behind Meyrowitz's back to start a new MMA promotion called Thunderdome, which never got off the ground.

Davie was replaced by John Perretti, a martial artist and movie stunt coordinator who'd worked for Battlecade: Extreme Fighting.

Meyrowitz asked me to accompany him, Abbott, and Belfort on a trip to Japan to promote UFC "Ultimate Japan," the promotion's eighteenth event, scheduled to take place two months later on December 21, 1997, inside the Yokohama Arena. It made sense to travel to a country where judo, not baseball, was the national pastime. Variations of mixed martial arts had been alive and well in Japan since the 1980s with promotions like Shooto and later Pancrase.

When we got off the plane, a few photographers were waiting to meet us. I recognized Susumu Nagao, who'd photographed every event since UFC 2. Nagao's pictures had appeared in the mainstream newspapers and magazines that covered the sport in Japan, so we were somewhat recognizable to the fans there.

Abbott made his presence known by shouting, "I am Godzillaaaaaa," at the top of his lungs for the startled commuters. Then he chased the photographers around the airport.

SEG was copromoting the event with a Japanese organization, so we met a few of their executives for dinner. I remember only one of the gentlemen's names: Mr. Koji. It took us about ten minutes to settle in while the Japanese businessmen contemplated and switched up our seating arrangement around the table, an important detail in their culture. Belfort introduced me to sushi that night.

On the second night, SEG's foreign business partners wanted to take us out on the town and spared no expense. With a restaurant on the top floor of a high-rise practically all to ourselves, we sat around a large grill while the chef cooked teppanyaki-style. The Kobe beef melted in my mouth. When asked if we wanted more, we all said yes without hesitation.

Afterward, we learned that Belfort's second helping cost about

$1,500, while Abbott and I had ordered smaller servings for the reasonable price of $750 each. Abbott also liked eating the fat, which was cut up and grilled until it was crisp, not exactly the fuel for a top-caliber athlete. I watched him scarf it down and thought, *Aw, dude, that's nasty.*

After dinner, Belfort excused himself because he had a massage scheduled, but the rest of us went to a lounge. It was a strange setup. Professionally dressed women waited on us, then sat next to us to have conversations. They weren't prostitutes, and nothing physical was going on. This was just the way the culture worked. I later got a peek at the bill, which Meyrowitz paid—$8,000 for a bunch of drinks.

The night wasn't over, though. Around 1:30 a.m., we went to a karaoke bar. Since karaoke was obviously important to our new friends, Meyrowitz asked me and Abbott if we'd get up and sing as a sign of goodwill.

Abbott, who was pretty liquored up by then, picked some freaking metalhead song and started banging around the room screaming and going nuts. He got a lot of laughs.

I sang a song by The Rolling Stones. Mick himself would have fucking cringed.

The next morning, we told Belfort over breakfast what had happened, and he was kicking himself. He thought for sure he'd missed out on something with the businesswomen at the lounge and couldn't quite grasp that it wasn't like that at all.

During the entire trip, Belfort kept trying to convince Meyrowtiz to let him, instead of Randy Couture, fight Maurice Smith for the title next. Meyrowitz wouldn't have any of it. It was quite funny to watch.

The first and last time I ever karaoked in my life: on a press tour with SEG Vice President David Isaacs and Tank Abbott in Japan

When we left Japan three days later, Abbott dumped out of his suitcase all the new "Tank" shirts he'd brought to give away and replaced them with towels and robes from the hotel. "Did you feel these things, John?" he said. "They're the softest damn things I've ever felt."

We all later returned to Yokohama, Japan, and began the week-long ritual leading up to the event. At the press conference, SEG asked me to sit at the dais in the middle between the fighters, which was something I normally wouldn't do and made me feel stupid as hell. Compared to the press reaction in the United States, the UFC seemed to be a bit of a bigger deal here in Japan. Maurice

Smith and Frank Shamrock, both with a wealth of experience fighting in Japan, knew what the crowd wanted, so they played up the charisma and trash-talking for the cameras and did a good job with it.

It wasn't all smooth sailing in the Land of the Rising Sun, though. At about 2:30 a.m. on the day of the show, I got a call in my hotel room from Meyrowitz, who was downstairs in the lobby. "John, I need you. Come down to the lobby quick."

Being a heavy sleeper, I said, "Okay," hung up, thought I must be dreaming, rolled over, and fell asleep.

Five minutes later, the phone rang again.

"Where the hell are you?" Meyrowitz asked, with a little more desperation in his voice.

I hadn't dreamt it after all.

In the lobby, Meyrowitz was standing with four Japanese men, three in suits and another in a sweat suit. I recognized the beefiest gentleman as Kazuo Takahashi, who'd fought at UFC 12 and regularly competed for the Pancrase organization. One of the other men was Mr. Ozaki, an organizer for Pancrase. When I walked up behind him, Takahashi was startled by my presence. He moved away like I was ugly, which I am, so he had every right to. But when he recognized me, he shook my hand.

UFC 17

"Redemption"
May 15, 1998
Mobile Civic Center
Mobile, Alabama

Bouts I Reffed:
Mike Van Arsdale vs. Joe Pardo
David "Tank" Abbott vs. Hugo Duarte
Dan Henderson vs. Carlos Newton
Pete Williams vs. Mark Coleman
Frank Shamrock vs. Jeremy Horn

A silent, mohawked assassin named Chuck Liddell debuted against Noe Hernandez, and they beat the piss out of each other.

Williams' come-from-behind knockout of Coleman with a kick to his face is a highlight-reel staple to this day.

I hated taking Horn out of mount on top of Shamrock, but Horn had based out and stalled. "Do something with it. You have to move. Don't just sit there," I said, but he stayed frozen. I finally stood them, and Shamrock later won by kneebar. Asked later why he didn't try anything, he said, "John, I was mounted on top of Frank Shamrock and didn't want to give him a chance to do anything to me." I just shook my head in disbelief.

SEG asked me to sit at the dais between main event fighters Randy Couture and Maurice Smith at UFC "Ultimate Japan." I felt like an idiot. (December 1997)

At first, I had no idea what was going on, but Meyrowitz was trying to subtly get me up to speed during the conversation. I was able to piece together that Mr. Ozaki wanted Meyrowitz to sign some kind of agreement to copromote the UFC in Japan from there on out. Mr. Ozaki didn't look like he was going to take no for an answer, and it was obvious Takahashi had been brought along to "encourage" a smooth process.

"This is not the way we do business," Meyrowitz said cordially and then suggested that Ozaki's lawyer draft and send a proposal to SEG for a future show.

I'd never seen anything like this, but I would come to learn that these types of strong-arm negotiations were common on the Japanese MMA scene.

Finally, Meyrowitz scribbled down something general about being willing to do business with the organization in the future and signed it.

Mr. Ozaki talked for a couple more minutes and finally left with his crew.

Meyrowitz looked at me, relieved that I'd come to his rescue.

"What the hell was that?" I asked.

"I told him I was calling our lawyer when I was really calling you. I didn't need legal advice. I needed protection!"

I was a multipurpose employee. I'm just lucky I wasn't asked to wax the floors at the SEG office, because I probably would've done that too.

The Yokohama Arena filled to capacity that night with 17,000 spectators, which was one of the promotion's better-attended efforts since UFC 7 in Buffalo. I wouldn't say the production was bigger or bolder in any way. There were a lot of Japanese employees running around busy as ants, but things weren't getting done any differently. One change that did take shape was an elevated and larger ramp for the fighters' entrances.

What was noticeably distinctive was the audience's behavior. Japanese crowds were unlike their United States counterparts. They were so into the matches but were as quiet as church mice. It was weird because I could hear the corners instructing their fighters, and they could hear whatever I said. I remember Mr. Koji getting upset because Joe Hamilton, the other referee, started the first bout of the night with the word "Hajime," which is the way you'd start a judo match.

"We don't want Hajime," Koji told me. "We want American."

I was sent to tell Joe he had to change his starting call.

Ultimate Japan was far from my crowning achievement as a referee. It's where I made my first major blunder as an official in the cage, something I've never quite gotten over because my actions affected the immediate futures of two fighters.

It all started a week before the show when dynamic collegiate wrestler Mark Kerr was scratched from the four-man heavyweight tournament. Tra Telligman was tapped to take his place against Marcus "Conan" Silveira, a Brazilian jiu-jitsu black belt and pretty aggressive striker. But two days before the show, Meyrowitz and David Isaacs approached me with yet another roster change. The Japanese promoters working with SEG had requested that a Japanese fighter named Kazushi Sakuraba be included in the heavyweight tournament. He was actually a pro wrestler who'd been in only one MMA fight—a worked match he'd lost to Kimo Leopoldo. Sakuraba wasn't even really a heavyweight.

I knew nothing about Sakuraba, but I knew Silveira was a bruiser. I protested, but Meyrowtiz and Isaacs weren't going to budge.

The last thing I remember Meyrowitz telling me was, "As soon as he's in trouble, just get him out of there. Don't let him get hurt."

That was my mentality when I walked into the fight.

In the Octagon, Silveira outweighed Sakuraba by a good forty pounds at least, but the Japanese fighter was fast and had some working knowledge of being on the ground. Silveira was out for the kill, though, and landed hard punches until he cornered Sakuraba on the fence and began to unload uppercuts and hooks. Silveira hit Sakuraba with a good right hand.

I saw the Japanese fighter fall to his knees, and thinking he'd been hurt, I jumped in to stop the fight. It was over in less than two minutes.

Sakuraba, who spoke no English, immediately protested what I'd done, as his camp gathered on the cage lip to decipher what had just happened. As I raised Silveira's hand, Sakuraba tugged at my other arm until I told him to stop.

I left the cage and jumped down to the commentators' table. "I need to see a replay," I said.

Meanwhile, Sakuraba refused to leave the cage and tried to wrestle the microphone away from Bruce Buffer to address the audience, but nobody gets Buffer's mic unless he wants them to.

In the replay, plain as day, Sakuraba took the punch and then dropped levels for a single-leg takedown. There was no debate at all. I turned to commentator Jeff Blatnick and said, "I screwed up."

Not only had I messed up Sakuraba's chance to advance in the tournament, but I'd given Silveira a victory he truly hadn't earned. I felt awful about it.

But things have a way of working out. Abbott hurt his hand in his preliminary qualifier, and Telligman, who won his heavyweight alternate bout, had broken his foot in the process. Nobody was left standing to face Silveira in the tournament finals. Meyrowitz, Isaacs, and I conferred cageside and decided the fairest thing to do would be to let Sakuraba fight Silveira again.

Sakuraba and the crowd were thrilled for a second chance, though Silveira wasn't. I think he'd gotten a good look at Sakuraba earlier and realized he was fighting a much sharper opponent than he or anyone else had anticipated. It took his head out of the game, allowing the swift Japanese pro wrestler to snag the armbar finish three minutes and forty-five seconds into their rematch.

As for the other bouts, after two overtime rounds, Randy Couture earned a hard-fought majority decision, meaning two of the judges gave him the victory and one scored it a tie, over Maurice Smith. This would be his first of many UFC heavyweight titles during his career.

In the first ever under-200-pound title bout, Frank Shamrock, the adopted younger brother of Ken Shamrock, tapped out 1992 Olympic wrestling gold medalist Kevin Jackson with an armbar in sixteen seconds. Shamrock had gotten a shot at the title out of the gate because he'd beaten Enson Inoue in a Vale Tudo Japan bout nearly three weeks prior. Shamrock had made a name for himself with almost twenty appearances in Pancrase, which had slightly different rules from the UFC's and required knee-to-ankle shin protectors and wrestling shoes.

A story floated around that Frank, who'd recently left his brother's famous Lion's Den squad to form his own team called The Alliance with Maurice Smith, had somehow intercepted the UFC contract meant for teammate Jerry Bohlander to fight Jackson. I don't know if that story holds any water, but I was there when SEG discussed the winner of Shamrock-Inoue getting the title shot, with the reasoning that the winner would attract more Japanese viewers.

Between stops in Louisiana and Alabama for UFC 17 and 18, SEG took the show to São Paulo, Brazil, home to a number of fighters on the card.

I trained and helped with the starts of two new referees, brothers Mario and Fernando Yamasaki. Both spoke English and

Portuguese, a definite plus given our surroundings. Mario and I would end up being good friends, and he stayed with the promotion, later to be added to the regular referee rotation.

The highlights of Ultimate Brazil, which took place nearly five months to the day following UFC 17, included Belfort's steamrolling of striker Wanderlei Silva in forty-four harsh seconds. Another unforgettable moment was Pedro Rizzo's rousing knockout of Tank Abbott at the eight-minute mark of their heavyweight tug-of-war. Rizzo, a quiet, likable guy, was the protégé of UFC 7 winner Marco Ruas, who'd tutored his pupil in the art of muay Thai. His potential seemed endless.

SEG added another rule to the list following UFC lightweight champion Pat Miletich's first title defense against Lion's Den scrapper Mikey Burnett. Burnett had been scheduled to meet Miletich in the finals of the lightweight tournament seven months before at UFC 16, so SEG was really anxious to make the match happen here. But Miletich grabbed Burnett's shorts to control his hips to prevent himself from being taken down. I told Meyrowitz afterward that this wasn't a jiu-jitsu match; fighters shouldn't be able to use their opponents' uniforms to control or to create advantageous positioning. Soon SEG added the rule.

Another vivid memory of Ultimate Brazil was Tito Ortiz showing

UFC 18

"Road to the Heavyweight Title"
January 8, 1999
Pontchartrain Center
New Orleans, Louisiana

Bouts I Reffed:
LaVerne Clark vs. Frank Caracci
Evan Tanner vs. Darrel Gholar
Mikey Burnett vs. Townsend Saunders
Tito Ortiz vs. Jerry Bohlander
Pedro Rizzo vs. Mark Coleman
Pat Miletich vs. Jorge Patino
Bas Rutten vs. Tsuyoshi Kohsaka

Future stars Evan Tanner and Bas Rutten made their debuts, while Tito Ortiz returned to the UFC after a brief stint as a college student at California State University Bakersfield. Fans claimed I tried to help Rutten win against Kohsaka with too many stand-ups, but it never happened. As an interesting footnote, I went back to Rutten's corner to check on him before going into overtime and heard him tell his cornermen, "Tell me when there's a minute left," because he was going to knock out Kohsaka. I laughed at the thought because it wouldn't be that easy. But with sixty seconds left, Rutten did just that. Babe Ruth couldn't have done it better.

up to the small arena with his manager at the time to pass out little trading cards he'd made of himself. It was the first time I'd seen a fighter make a concerted effort to market himself, and I was impressed by Ortiz's ingenuity and marketing savvy. He'd learned a thing or two from Tank Abbott in terms of self-promotion, but Ortiz had some legitimate fighting talent as well.

PHOTO COURTESY OF MCCARTHY FAMILY

In the Octagon with my friend and fellow referee Mario Yamasaki at UFC 20 "Battle for the Gold" (May 1999)

On the plane ride home, I stood in the back and talked to Ortiz for hours, brainstorming ways he could get himself out there more. I was surprised to learn Ortiz and Abbott had had a falling out and Ortiz believed this was the reason he hadn't been invited back to the UFC in a while.

I didn't know if Abbott was keeping Ortiz out of the show or what, but he definitely wasn't helping his former student get back in. I told Ortiz I would ask John Perretti, the new matchmaker, about him.

Ortiz would return to the next show, UFC 18, in New Orleans and defeat Jerry Bohlander.

I liked Ortiz and could see he was a good person who was willing to work hard to make it. Well ahead of his contemporaries, he had a keen understanding of the fans and treated them like gold, making time for anybody who approached him. I thought Ortiz could do something special in the sport.

The question was whether the UFC would survive long enough for that to happen.

UFC 19

"Young Guns"
March 5, 1999
Casino Magic
Bay St. Louis, Mississippi

Bouts I Reffed:
Evan Tanner vs. Valeri Ignatov
Kevin Randleman vs. Maurice Smith
Jeremy Horn vs. Chuck Liddell
Gary Goodridge vs. Andre Roberts
Tito Ortiz vs. Guy Mezger

Former Ohio State wrestling star Kevin Randleman entered the Octagon a second time but now as a fighter.

Jeremy Horn and Chuck Liddell had a classic finish at the bell, when Horn applied an arm-triangle and put the striker to sleep.

Tito Ortiz and Ken Shamrock kicked off the first great rivalry in the sport when Ortiz flipped off the Lion's Den corner following his rematch win over Guy Mezger. I had to pick up Ortiz and carry him away from Shamrock, who was leaning over the cage barking at Ortiz. Ortiz took it to a new level when he donned a T-shirt that said, "Gay Mezger Is My Bitch." I promptly told him to take it off, which he did.

The UFC crew in Japan: Elaine, me, James Werme, Maria Eveicheria, David Isaacs, and UFC owner Bob Meyrowitz

本日のご案内

自治労横浜結成50周年記念式典御席
5F
千鳥 UFCJ FIGHTERS MANAGER MEETING
4F
若菜 株式会社 CRC総合研究所様御席
4F
桜川 冬   会 様御席
4F
尾上 横浜線会 様御席
4F
口口口 社団法人日本プロテニス協会様御席
4F
口口・口口 財団法人日本自動車査定協会神奈川県支所様御席
4F

Me, Bob Meyrowitz, and Jeff Blatnick in Japan

WRITING ON THE WALL

Our greatest glory is not in never falling,
but in rising every time we fall.

—Confucius

If I had to pick one of the fights that made a huge impact on mixed martial arts, it would be the heavyweight championship bout between Bas Rutten and Kevin Randleman at UFC 20 "Battle for the Gold" on May 7, 1999, at the Boutwell Auditorium in Birmingham, Alabama.

Senator John McCain's smear campaign had cornered the UFC in the Deep South, and Alabama had no athletic commission at the time. It was the ninth UFC event in a row that wouldn't air on the major cable platforms, and viewership had taken a nosedive far below the 300,000 pay-per-view buy-rate heyday four years earlier at UFC 7. We began to refer to this time as the Dark Ages of MMA.

With millions of dollars in potential pay-per-view income gone, SEG depended on its live audiences, but we weren't even filling 5,000-seat arenas. It wasn't long before we saw the writing on the wall.

Still, amidst all the turmoil and uncertainty, this is when the sport made some of its greatest developmental strides. Necessity is indeed the mother of invention.

The Rutten-Randleman fight marked the conclusion of the promotion's "Road to the Heavyweight Title" tournament, which had been held over the last few shows to crown a new heavyweight champion. Randy Couture had won the title from Maurice Smith fair and square at Ultimate Japan, but Couture had left the promotion because of a pay cut from his previously agreed-upon contract.

Though SEG had been talking about implementing five-minute rounds between the last couple of shows, it was decided that this championship bout would remain one fifteen-minute round to be followed, as necessary, by two three-minute overtime periods.

John Perretti, the UFC's matchmaker, knew Rutten was a striker and Randleman was a wrestler. He told Meyrowitz that since Randleman would be forced to stand at the beginning of the two overtime periods, this would give Rutten a better chance to implement his striking.

None of that made sense to me since five five-minute rounds would have given Rutten even more opportunities to start from his feet. I also wasn't into the idea of them even thinking they should give one fighter an advantage over another, but I wasn't the promoter.

For the first ten minutes of the bout, Randleman, one of the most explosive wrestlers ever to enter the sport, took Rutten down at will and beat the crap out of him from top position.

Randleman broke Rutten's nose within the first five minutes, which demonstrates how lopsided the match was. I had to stop the bout momentarily and bring Rutten to the doctor to have his nose checked.

Rutten is a jocular guy, but he was pretty serious as the doctor looked him over. I'll never forget what he asked. "If I get punched again and the bone pushes farther into my brain, will it kill me?" I'm not making this up. When I told him, "No," Rutten seemed satisfied and said he could continue.

For the first ten minutes, Randleman really poured it on and dumped Rutten to the mat every time he tried to kick him. However, as the wrestler's conditioning started to peter out on him, Rutten slowly began to fight back. It went into the two overtime periods, and Rutten began to score from standing and from his back. By the end, Rutten had made a strong comeback against an exhausted Randleman.

After the twenty-one-minute fight, two of the three judges awarded the bout to Rutten.

The audience went wild when the highly controversial decision was announced. It seemed the judges had forgotten Randleman had handily dominated the first part of the bout. Perhaps watching the Dutch fighter come back and take control in the latter periods had swayed two of the three judges to award him the fight.

Mark Coleman, who'd attended Ohio State University with Randleman and was in his corner, stood on the cage's lip and nearly shook the Octagon wall from its posts as the crowd egged him on.

I had no official stance on the decision, but I knew that six minutes were not fifteen minutes. In this case, the judging system wasn't working fairly for the fighters.

Afterward, I told Meyrowitz and SEG they were asking too much of the judges to remember twenty-plus minutes of moves. If the fight were broken into five-minute rounds, the judges could weigh each one separately, write their scores during the one-minute rest periods, and hand them in for tallying at the end, just as it was done in boxing. It was agreed that three five-minute rounds would become the norm from here on out, while championship fights would be allotted five five-minute rounds.

Following the Rutten-Randleman decision, UFC commentator Jeff Blatnick and I were asked to assess what a judge should be looking for in a fight. Being an Olympic wrestler himself, Blatnick argued that Randleman had scored multiple takedowns and hadn't been credited for them.

I could see his point, though I knew we'd have to create some kind of sliding scale based on where the effective action was happening in the fight. If it stayed on its feet, the judges should be looking at striking first. If it went to the ground, they should be primarily crediting techniques there. If it was a mix of both, wherever the majority of the active bout happened should be judged first.

We also came up with four terms judges would use to score the bouts: "effective striking," "effective grappling," "aggressiveness," and "Octagon control." I wanted to add "damage" to the list of criteria, but Meyrowitz thought that sounded too harsh. However, the main problem people had with the Rutten-Randleman decision was that Rutten's face was a mess, while Randleman, other than a few small cuts on his head from Rutten's elbows, barely had a mark. Who was really the winner there?

When people ask me who won that fight, I say, "Both men did their best, and I understand the decision." I think history speaks for itself. That fight was a game changer, and it doesn't matter who I think won it.

I'll be honest, though. What I remember most about the fight was that Rutten was talking to Randleman the whole time, asking if he wanted to stand the fight up after a while because he thought it was getting too boring on the mat for the crowd. "You're on top of me, but you can't hurt me," Rutten informed Randleman almost playfully.

Randleman didn't answer him once.

The first preliminary bout of the night between Ron Waterman and Chris Condo also spoke for the times. Waterman was a competent, fit wrestler, but Condo was out of shape and far from ready to enter the Octagon. SEG was afraid Condo would get hurt, so they asked me to referee the fight, though I wasn't scheduled to.

I thought it was ridiculous. If SEG was putting me in the Octagon to save this guy's life, then he had no reason being in there in the first place.

But money was running short, which meant decent talent would start to run thin and the matchmaking would suffer.

Condo's first and last career fight lasted twenty-eight seconds before I put a stop to it.

Bob Meyrowitz knew he had to turn things around or the UFC and the sport would likely die in the United States. The UFC's only sustaining revenue was its pay-per-views. Meyrowitz went back to Leo Hindery, Time Warner Cable's CEO, and showed him the progress the UFC had made with instituting rules. Hindery told Meyrowitz that if the UFC could get the sport regulated by a major state athletic commission, he'd put it back on the larger cable platforms. What Hindery meant was that the UFC had to get sanctioned in Nevada, the one state he considered major because of Las Vegas.

This was a tall order. Marc Ratner, the Nevada State Athletic Commission's executive director, had gone on CNN's *Larry King Live* a couple years earlier and said he felt MMA wasn't a consideration for regulation in the state. Still, Meyrowitz had to make it happen somehow.

Two NSAC commissioners, Lorenzo Fertitta and Glenn Carano, as well as the commission's chief medical advisor, Flip Homansky, were invited to the next UFC in Cedar Rapids, Iowa. UFC 21 "Return of the Champions" was held on July 16, 1999, in the 8,000-seat Five Seasons Events Center. The trio sat cageside, taking in their first live MMA event. It couldn't have played out worse if Senator John McCain had planned it all himself.

In one of the middleweight bouts, Jeremy Horn weighed in right at the 200-pound limit, but his Japanese opponent Daiju Takase showed up to weigh-ins at only 169 pounds. Apparently something had been lost in translation, but both fighters agreed to continue with the bout anyway. Fighters rarely turn down bouts because of weight issues; they always want to fight because they want to get paid.

With the weight advantage, Horn took Takase down and manhandled him with elbows that opened the Japanese fighter's face. Referee Mario Yamasaki was in a no-win situation. If he stopped the fight early because Horn was mauling Takase, people would complain. But if he let it go too long, he stood the chance of upsetting the Nevada commissioners, which meant another step backward for the UFC and the sport.

He let it go till Takase was drenched in blood. It got ugly, and you could tell by their faces that Carano and Fertitta weren't happy with what they saw.

Afterward, Meyrowitz asked me and Jeff Blatnick to join him for dinner with our Nevada guests. Surprisingly, Dr. Homansky wasn't that averse to what he'd seen, but the Takase massacre was all Fertitta and Carano could talk about.

Fertitta, whose family owned a handful of Las Vegas casinos that catered to the local clientele, said he had a problem with the fighters hitting each other on the ground. He was a pure boxing proponent, so he wasn't used to the image.

I said, "You're always going to have a problem with it until you understand what you're watching on the ground." Society had trained us to believe it wasn't natural or fair to fight that way, that it was dirty fighting. In the movies, John Wayne would land a punch, but then he'd pick the guy up before knocking him down again.

"Fighting on the ground is like a chess game," I said. "It's a systematic way of moving to either defend yourself or counter your opponent's last move. The difference is that your pieces are your arms, legs, and torso positioned in various ways around your opponent's body to secure chokes and holds to get the checkmate in the end."

Fertitta wouldn't understand that until he experienced it himself. He was poised and smart and admitted he didn't understand MMA at all but that he'd like to look into the sport further.

Carano, who'd been a quarterback for the Dallas Cowboys, didn't want to hear any of it. "Those guys were trying to hurt one another," he said, which was pretty closed-minded considering his background.

I said, "If you drop back for a pass, isn't linebacker Lawrence Taylor out to bury you?"

"That's different," Carano said.

Whether he wanted to admit it or not, though, football had a combative edge. I also pointed out that a majority of our fighters shook hands, hugged, and congratulated each other after their bouts.

Carano wouldn't budge.

Ironically, years later Glenn Carano would sit in the front row at events cheering for his daughter while she blasted away on her opponents on live network TV. In 2008, Gina Carano would become one of the most popular MMA fighters on Earth.

With Fertitta willing to at least investigate the sport, I gave him the name of John Lewis, a UFC fighter and Brazilian jiu-jitsu black belt living and teaching in Las Vegas. If Fertitta was seriously interested, he could call Lewis and roll with the fighter to see what it was like for himself.

We ended the meeting, and the three commission representatives left.

I turned to Meyrowitz and said, "You're screwed."

Dr. Homansky was the only one of the three who seemed to like the sport, but he was also the only one who didn't have a vote. It wasn't going to happen right now.

The Nevada commission was far from giving the sport a chance, one of many factors spelling the UFC's impending demise. SEG had long before cut costs by scaling down the show's pageantry and using cheaper talent in the preliminary fights to save up for the main events they thought the fans would want most, much like a boxing card.

At the same time, many of the best fighters, like Mark Coleman, Vitor Belfort, and Mark Kerr, were being lured away by outrageous cash-and-carry paydays from rival promotion Pride Fighting Championships, which had deep financial backing from a TV channel and the Yakuza mob in Japan. Pride was really starting to pick up steam in terms of popularity and soon began to surpass the UFC in attendance numbers, drawing nine to ten times more spectators at some events, up to 50,000 at a time.

Pride even made a play for me, first as a referee and then as a fighter. I was contacted to possibly fight in Pride against popular pro wrestler Nobuhiko Takada, who would later become the figurehead for the organization. I priced myself out of the offer, though, by asking for $250,000. I knew if I fought, it would be the end of my reffing for the UFC.

I thought the whole thing was a bit ridiculous, anyway, especially when Pride said I'd have to throw the match so Takada won. There was no way I'd do that. The sport didn't need that type of attention.

I did approach SEG with Pride's offer to get them to compensate me when payments started to lag. Meyrowitz threatened to sue if I left for Pride, but it was all bluster.

As for the others, SEG's accountant, Steven Loeb, was highly skilled at stalling people as they came looking for their money. SEG used a production team comprised of brothers Al and Bruce Connal, and they were always three shows behind getting paid, so they had to either keep coming back to produce the shows or risk losing it all.

At one point, before they'd started paying me again, I'd called the accountant for money I was owed, and he'd asked, "Are you going to send me a bullet, too?" Apparently Tank Abbott had mailed him a bullet with the accountant's name drawn on it and a note that said, "If I don't get paid, this is what's going to happen to you."

But the biggest blow was yet to come for Elaine and me. After

UFC 21, Meyrowitz called her with bad news. "I really want you to work with me, but understand I'm under a lot of pressure here. I need you to work, but I can't pay you anymore."

We weren't completely surprised. When Elaine had started, she'd had all kinds of help running the shows, but those numbers had dwindled. Elaine had been a trooper through the decline. She would occasionally talk to me about how hard it was to get things done. She felt the fighters needed to be taken care of and respected, but the UFC was traveling to shoddy venues with limited support staff, so no one could expect much.

Meyrowitz promised Elaine he'd make it up to her when things got better, but we knew they wouldn't. The UFC was on its last leg.

I asked Elaine if she wanted me to quit, but we were paying for a house we couldn't afford, and I was still making $75,000 a year from the UFC.

Elaine left the promotion, and I stayed. Many of the fighters, managers, and cornermen had become like family to Elaine. She cared about them, and she went through a period of depression over it.

Two years later, Elaine was contacted to coordinate a new event called "Battleship," which was supposed to be held on a military carrier. It never got going, though, and Elaine wouldn't return to behind-the-scenes work in the sport for nearly ten years.

Aside from not being around the people she adored, Elaine didn't like the idea of being apart when I went to shows, especially when female fans were fairly open with their adoration. For the sake of our marriage and commitment to one another, we agreed that she would travel with me to every show. Elaine has sat cageside at most of the shows I've refereed since.

With the staff disappearing in the UFC's darkest hours, the

fighters stepped up to the plate. Their enthusiasm and passion to evolve into better fighters really kept the sport going. When the UFC lost most of its pay-per-view audience, the athletes kept the die-hard fans interested with their improvement and ingenuity in the cage.

Newspapers or TV programs wouldn't even mention MMA, but websites like *Martial Arts Worldwide Network*, *The Combat List*, *Sherdog*, and *The Underground* began to pop up to cover the sport and its fighters. It was this interest that kept the UFC alive through those lean times.

UFC 22 "Only One Can Be Champion," held on September 24, 1999, at the Lake Charles Civic Center in Lake Charles, Louisiana, promoted the most anticipated fight of its time: a middleweight championship bout between Frank Shamrock and Tito Ortiz.

Shamrock hadn't fought in the UFC for eleven months following his neck crank submission victory over John Lober at Ultimate Brazil. In that time, Ortiz had been on a tear in the UFC, taking out Lion's Den members Jerry Bohlander and Guy Mezger in their rematch. Shamrock-Ortiz, which featured the seasoned veteran versus the young rising threat, seemed to be the obvious matchup now.

Fights rarely live up to their hype, but this one delivered on so many levels. Both fighters had magnetic personalities, were in their physical primes, and were more well-rounded compared to the rest of the field. It was just the right combination for a blockbuster bout.

I had to stay on my toes because both fighters were so active. A diligent Ortiz had the edge on the champion in the first round, taking Shamrock down and pinning him against the cage to ground-and-pound him. Shamrock had an active guard, though, and responded with punches from his back.

In the second round, Shamrock kept his distance and fended off Ortiz with kicks until the wrestler slammed Shamrock to the mat.

Ortiz took Shamrock down again in the third round, but both fighters had great stamina and stayed busy. Shamrock managed to get to his feet and landed a kick and an uppercut before Ortiz took him down again. The time flew in the Octagon.

Shamrock's game plan implementation was especially impressive. Near the end of each round, with about thirty seconds left, Shamrock's cornerman Maurice Smith would alert him, and Shamrock would start attacking Ortiz with movement, punches, or anything to elevate Ortiz's heart rate and make him expend energy. By the end of each round Ortiz was just about maxed out, and at the start of the next he was never fully recovered. It was brilliant. Shamrock ran Ortiz like a racehorse, pushing a pace that finally broke Ortiz and gave Shamrock the advantage.

Shamrock was especially impressive in the fourth round. He looked as fresh as when he'd started fifteen minutes earlier, peppering Ortiz with kicks and punches for two minutes before Ortiz dumped him to the mat again. Ortiz tried to pour on elbows from top position, but Shamrock reversed and got to his feet, where he trapped Ortiz on the fence with a flurry of punches. Ortiz shot and took Shamrock down again, but Shamrock reversed a second time and bludgeoned a turtled Ortiz until I saw Ortiz tap out and stepped in to stop it. It was a commendable performance by both fighters that earned a standing ovation.

As Shamrock and Ortiz stood on either side of me for the winner's announcement, I told Ortiz, "You fought a great fight, and you'll be back a better fighter because of it."

In true Shamrock form, Frank had saved the best for last. To most everyone's surprise, he told commentator Jeff Blatnick he'd be retiring his belt in the cage that night. Then he laid his middleweight belt on the canvas and walked out the Octagon door.

I'd known ahead of time that this would be Shamrock's last fight in the UFC. He'd told me beforehand, but of course I didn't know for sure if he'd go through with it. You never know how a fighter might react after a victory or defeat. Shamrock said he'd run out of challenges in the cage, but the truth was that he felt the UFC didn't pay enough to make the training and time away from his family worthwhile. Retiring allowed him a loophole to get out of his UFC contract.

Tank Abbott also made an appearance at UFC 22, scaling the cage's wall for an impromptu prance around the Octagon that sent the crowd reeling. Abbott, in the best shape of his career, had recently signed a contract with the WCW. SEG hadn't been able to afford even their most popular fighter, so he'd gone off to pro wrestling.

For UFC 23 and 25, SEG brought the show back to Japan, yet neither event was nearly as commercially successful as the first had been. By then, Pride Fighting Championships, which boasted

UFC 23

"Ultimate Japan 2"
November 19, 1999
Tokyo Bay NK Hall
Tokyo, Japan

Bouts I Reffed:
Eugene Jackson vs. Keiichiro Yamamiya
Joe Slick vs. Jason DeLucia
Kenichi Yamamoto vs. Katsuhisa Fujii
Pedro Rizzo vs. Tsuyoshi Kohsaka
Kevin Randleman vs. Pete Williams

The final UFC to hold a tournament, this was a much smaller show than the first UFC Japan, as the venue held about 7,000 people. In their middleweight bout, Jackson hit Yamamiya so hard it knocked out his bridge. There it was with protruding teeth on the Octagon canvas, which was kind of funny if you had a warped sense of humor.

In the heavyweight headliner, Randleman got reversed by Williams and seemed to have hurt his ribs near the end of the round. Randleman lay on the mat about forty-five seconds of the one-minute break between rounds. I thought the fight would be over, but Randleman came back out for four more rounds and eventually won. Stacked up against most of the classics, it wasn't a great fight, but Randleman's resilience was impressive.

UFC 24

"First Defense"
March 10, 2000
Lake Charles Civic Center
Lake Charles, Louisiana

Bouts I Reffed:
Jens Pulver vs. David Velasquez
Bob Cook vs. Tiki Ghosn
Dave Menne vs. Fabiano Iha
Lance Gibson vs. Jermaine Andre
Tedd Williams vs. Steve Judson

You know things are bad when the heavy-weight championship fight is cancelled during the show because the champion gets knocked out backstage. Yes, Randleman was warming up in the back and slipped on some pipes strewn on the ground. He was knocked unconscious, woke up, and then started vomiting, indicating that he had a severe concussion. Dr. Istrico wouldn't let Randleman fight, which was the right thing to do, even though Randleman wanted to go out there regardless.

Dan Severn made his reffing debut when he officiated the Freeman-Adams fight. Severn, wearing a traditional black-and-white striped shirt and red wrestling shoes, did fine but never reffed in the UFC again.

elaborate fight entrances using high-tech lights, music, and video, had become king in Japan. The UFC was just an afterthought. It really hit me as I saw former UFC stars like Vitor Belfort, Mark Coleman, and Mark Kerr, all now fighting for Pride, backstage and in the audience. Pride shows were starting to attract crowds of 20,000 to 30,000 people. Meanwhile, through the fight community stories spread of American fighters bringing home wads of cash stuffed in their underwear and socks. The UFC couldn't compete with this at all.

It seemed like the ship was sinking when a ray of hope broke through. In February of 2000, the New Jersey State Athletic Control Board dipped its toe into MMA regulation by approving an MMA-style bout at a regional kickboxing show held at the Tropicana in Atlantic City, New Jersey. It was called a freestyle grappling exhibition, and the fighters could take bouts to the ground and hit with open-handed strikes. New Jersey was viewed as another leading regulatory body because of the number of boxing events it oversaw in Atlantic City, while New York was also a couple hours away. This was a big break for the sport.

On September 30, 2000, the NJSACB regulated its first MMA event on a trial basis under the leadership of Commissioner Larry

Hazzard Sr., a former Golden Gloves boxing champion and accomplished Hall of Fame boxing referee. Six MMA bouts were approved at the International Fighting Championships (IFC) event that night, but the one that really caught Hazzard's eye was a heavyweight contest between the six-feet-ten Gan McGee and a Canadian kickboxer with limited ground experience, Brad Gabriel. McGee, who'd trained with Chuck Liddell in California, took the bout to the ground and repeatedly slammed his knee into a turtled Gabriel's head until the referee called the bout. It was a type of attack that had long been admissible in MMA bouts, but Hazzard had a real issue with it.

When Meyrowitz approached the New Jersey board to hold three UFC events at the Trump Taj Mahal in Atlantic City beginning that November, Hazzard said he would allow the events to take place during a probationary period under the two conditions that knees to a downed opponent's head were made illegal and that the regulatory agency would continue to observe the sport at the next three shows. It seemed a small price to pay to get the UFC into a state as influential as New Jersey, so Meyrowitz agreed.

As a small window began to open in New Jersey, SEG also banged on the doors of Nevada, specifically Las Vegas. Sin City was the crowned jewel for combat sports. Boxing events regularly pulled in live gates in the double-digit million-dollar range.

UFC 25

"Ultimate Japan 3"
April 14, 2000
Yoyogi National Gymnasium
Tokyo, Japan

Bouts I Reffed:
LaVerne Clark vs. Koji Oishi
Ikuhisa Minowa vs. Joe Slick
Ron Waterman vs. Satoshi Honma
Sanae Kikuta vs. Eugene Jackson
Murilo Bustamante vs. Yoji Anjo
Tito Ortiz vs. Wanderlei Silva

Seeing Murilo Bustamante finally get into the UFC was a big moment for me. I had always admired his fighting and the classy way he conducted himself. The one downside was that he made short work of Yoji Anjo.

The Ortiz-Silva fight, which would determine a new middleweight champion in Frank Shamrock's place, had some good moments but overall wasn't the barn burner you'd hope for. Ortiz was really nervous about the fight, as was pretty much everyone who faced Wanderlei "the Axe Murderer" Silva, but pulled out the unanimous nod and fulfilled his own prophetic destiny to become a champion.

UFC 26

"Ultimate Field of Dreams"
June 9, 2000
Five Seasons Events Center
Cedar Rapids, Iowa

Bouts I Reffed:
Matt Hughes vs. Marcelo Aguiar
Amaury Bitetti vs. Alex Andrade
Pat Miletich vs. John Alessio
Tyrone Roberts vs. David Dodd
Kevin Randleman vs. Pedro Rizzo

In another misguided stroke of matchmaking, a young and green Alessio challenged Miletich for his lightweight title, making it into the second round before he lost by submission.

I had to disqualify Andrade for kicking Bitetti to the head three times while wearing wrestling shoes. At this point we had a rule that fighters could wear them as long as they didn't kick to the head.

As he had in New York four years earlier, Meyrowitz hired a lobbyist, Sig Rogich, to champion the sport with the Nevada State Athletic Commission and push regulation through. Right around UFC 28, SEG got word that a proposal for mixed martial arts' regulation in Nevada had been scheduled for the athletic commission's next meeting. Lorenzo Fertitta and Glenn Carano along with three additional commissioners would vote on the proposal; SEG needed the support of three.

I was flown to Las Vegas to answer any questions the commissioners had about the sport. SEG and the lobbyist figured Fertitta would support the sport because he'd now become John Lewis' jiu-jitsu student. They thought Glenn Carano would vote against it and two other commissioners would split with their votes. The fifth was a veterinarian who wasn't particularly familiar with the sport, so I was sent to meet him. With the swing vote in the balance, I did my best to persuade him to give MMA a chance, talking up its safety points, but he didn't seem to care either way.

Meyrowitz met me in Las Vegas a day before the vote. The lobbyist, who was relaying updates, said we had the three votes and would get the sport passed. However, later that night, he called back to say something had changed. One commissioner had changed his mind and was going to vote the proposal down.

Since it would be difficult to get this proposal budgeted again in a timely fashion, the lobbyist encouraged Meyrowitz to pull it from the table so they could regroup. Meyrowitz listened to the lobbyist's advice, and MMA never went to a vote the next day.

It was one in a long line of disappointing developments, but we still had the shows in New Jersey and the opportunity to convince its officials to regulate MMA. We all had to stay focused.

UFC 27

"Ultimate Bad Boyz"
September 22, 2000
Lakefront Arena
New Orleans, Louisiana

Bouts I Reffed:
Jeff Monson vs. Tim Lajcik
Ian Freeman vs. Tedd Williams
Yuki Kondo vs. Alexandre Dantas
Jeremy Horn vs. Eugene Jackson
Maurice Smith vs. Bobby Hoffman
Pedro Rizzo vs. Dan Severn

Smith hit Hoffman with so many uppercuts that Hoffman bit off about one-third of his tongue. He went in the back and tried to tear off the remaining piece still attached. Now, that was a crazy bastard.

The fight between Rizzo and Severn should never have happened. Severn, now in his midforties, had long since passed his prime and took a couple of leg kicks that ended his night in a minute and a half.

UFC 28 "High Stakes" was held on November 17, 2000, at the 5,000-seat Trump Taj Mahal in Atlantic City, New Jersey. It didn't sell out, but it was quite a good show if I do say so myself. The UFC had negotiated the return of Randy Couture in a heavyweight title bout against champion Kevin Randleman, and Couture outwrestled and ground-and-pounded him en route to a third-round stoppage. Just fifteen seconds into their lightweight bout, Jens Pulver knocked out John Lewis with a blistering left hand that broke Lewis' jaw. And Mark Hughes, the brother of future UFC welterweight champion Matt Hughes, made his one and only appearance in the Octagon with a unanimous decision victory over Alex Stiebling.

Of course, I'll never forget a mistake I made in one of the other heavyweight bouts that night. Belarusian Andrei Arlovski grabbed the cage and was able to change his direction when opponent Aaron Brink went to take him down. Arlovski, a sambo expert, quickly found the armbar, and Brink tapped out. All of this happened in just fifty-four seconds. After reviewing it, I realized I should've stopped the bout after the takedown and restarted the fighters on their feet, but I hadn't reacted quickly enough.

UFC 29 would be the promotion's last trip to Japan, though we didn't know it at the time. "Defense of the Belts" was held on December 16, 2000, at the Differ Ariake Arena in Tokyo. The arena had only 1,246 seats, so it seemed like a waste of money, but SEG was there to satisfy the contract with its Japanese copromoter.

Tito Ortiz made his first successful title defense against rising local star Yuki Kondo, who knocked Ortiz on his backside with a rarely seen flying knee. Pat Miletich defended his lightweight title against Kenichi Yamamoto as well.

However, it wasn't a banner event overall by any stretch.

Before the bouts, I sat in an empty chair next to Dana White, who managed Ortiz and Chuck Liddell. Earlier that night, Liddell had fought and beaten Jeff Monson in a light heavyweight match that had been scheduled for the previous UFC.

Though we'd never really talked, I'd met White a few shows prior and my only impression had been that he was driven. I'd been told he was trying to get Ortiz more money and was playing hardball with Meyrowitz. I knew the figure White was asking for and that he wouldn't get it because SEG couldn't afford it.

This night, White asked if I had plans after the show and if I wanted to go out to eat with him and Lorenzo Fertitta. I hadn't noticed earlier, but lo and behold, there was Fertitta sitting in the first row.

I was curious. Why would Fertitta, a Nevada commissioner, take in another UFC event, especially one in Japan? I agreed to meet them for dinner.

At first, I didn't get the connection between White the manager and Fertitta the commissioner. Though I didn't know it, they'd been high school friends. Both Fertitta and White had been studying jiu-jitsu with John Lewis in Las Vegas.

White seemed to defer a lot to Fertitta during our conversation, and he made it clear that Fertitta was his wealthy friend. The two asked me a slew of questions about the UFC, about its history and journey through politically infested waters over the last seven years. What mistakes had Meyrowitz made with the UFC? What had gone well? Who were the good fighters? Why were they leaving for Pride?

I told them that Pride had the money and that there were significant differences between MMA in the United States and in Japan, especially in the way the public viewed the sport and the type of bouts they clamored for. Japan's culture blurred the line between pro wrestling and MMA, and mismatches happened all the time. Pride, with the majority of top fighters and the bigger audiences, was the number one promotion in the world.

Trying to help the promotion, I mentioned to Fertitta and White that I'd heard Meyrowitz, awash in debt with the UFC, was looking to take on a business partner. Fertitta and White thanked me for the tip. The rest of the night, Fertitta and White never ran out of questions about the ailing business.

I didn't put two and two together until I ran into Fertitta

and White again the next day at the airport. We were booked on the same flight to the United States, and as we sat in the terminal I caught a glimpse of some paperwork. Suddenly, all these little clues added up.

When I got home, I dialed Meyrowitz's number. "Bob, are you selling the UFC?"

There was a dramatic pause.

"Yes, but you can't tell anybody yet."

A McCarthy family vacation in Lake Powell, Utah (1999)

Ushering in a new chapter for the sport: with UFC Hall of Famer Randy Couture, UFC President Dana White, and UFC owners Lorenzo and Frank Fertitta

CHAPTER 13

CHANGES

There is nothing wrong with change,
if it is in the right direction.

—Winston Churchill

Have I ever been afraid? Yeah, on more than one occasion, though it hasn't been in the Octagon with fighters charging in my direction or in the dark of night during the Los Angeles Riots with bullets whistling past me. No, the scariest moment of my life was watching my son nearly die.

My family and I were vacationing in Kauai, Hawaii, driving back to the hotel after a day on the far side of the island. The ocean was particularly choppy, and the waves were a little higher than usual. My kids wanted to go in the water again before we returned to the hotel, though, so we pulled over at the beach.

While Elaine played in the surf on the beach with Britney and Johnny, I dove in with our eleven-year-old son, Ron, who wanted to swim a little farther out and bodysurf in.

I caught a wave in myself, but when I came up again, Ron was gone. His head popped up above water a few seconds later about 100 yards out. He was stuck in a riptide, which was dragging him out to sea quickly. I told him to swim sideways, horizontally to the shoreline, as I stroked back out to him. By the time I got to him, we were about 250 yards from shore. I grabbed Ron under his arm and around his neck with one arm and paddled back in the direction of land with my other arm. But then we were both swept up in another wave, and I felt him slip out of my grasp underwater.

When I reemerged, Ron was again being towed away from me, coughing up a huge spurt of water that really alarmed me. I was probably in the best shape of my life, but when I got to him a second time, my arms were lead weights. I was dead tired, and Ron had this terrified look on his face. I knew in that moment that if I didn't do something, my son was going to drown and I wouldn't be far behind him.

"Ron, I need your help," I ordered. "You've got to swim."

Ron grabbed me, and again we stroked out of the riptide and toward the shore. We were tossed again, but this time I held on tight. We finally got close enough that I could get my feet underneath me, and I dragged him the rest of the way onto the sand.

Elaine came running to me in hysterics—but not because the sea had nearly swallowed her son and husband. In fact, Elaine had missed our near-death experience because Johnny had sat on a Portuguese man-of-war and been stung.

Ron's eyes were bloodshot, and my heart rate must have been over 200 beats a second. "That's fucking interesting," was all I could muster for Elaine.

It's a paralyzing feeling to think your child might die, something you can't understand until it's happened to you. In that moment, I didn't have any fear of dying; I just knew I had to act. Either we were both going to make it, or we were both going to die. There were no other choices.

When I teach, I tell every police recruit that fear is natural. If you don't have fear, then you're probably stupid. Everybody has fear. It's what you do when you're afraid that qualifies who and what you are. I don't think there's ever been a hero who wasn't afraid. Each one just did what was right in the right moment.

I've been shot at. I've had rounds going off near me. Was I afraid? Sure, but I've gotten smart enough to understand that running from a bullet doesn't work. It's better to attack where the bullet is coming from and end a dangerous situation. That's going to give me a better chance of survival.

Fear can be overcome by preparing as much as you can for that critical moment. That's one key factor that makes police work and MMA refereeing similar. The more knowledge and experience you have in dealing with those split-second decisions, the better you're going to react. The decisions will already be made for you.

I certainly had no fear about the UFC going out of business. Elaine and I had talked about it many times. We'd left events time and again thinking that show could be the last. I was sad about that because I loved the UFC and the sport, but I wasn't afraid.

Elaine and I had done our best to prepare for the moment when the UFC wouldn't be a part of our lives anymore. Over the last twelve years, we'd moved into eight different homes around Southern California, fixed them up ourselves, and flipped them. With Elaine's knack for interior design, we were able to make $225,000 on one sale.

So, when we'd heard two weeks before UFC 30 that brothers

Lorenzo and Frank Fertitta had purchased the UFC from Meyrowitz for $2 million, I was as braced as I could be for what was to come. Dana White, the fight manager and friend to Lorenzo, was appointed president of Zuffa Sports and Entertainment, later shortened to Zuffa LLC, and given a 10 percent share of the company.

The first time I talked to others in the industry about the purchase was on a trip to Kuwait, where I refereed a one-off event called Shidokan Jitsu: "Warriors War 1." I hadn't refereed many events outside the UFC, but this was an adventurous opportunity, so I'd accepted the assignment and was flown in with Elaine. A wealthy sheikh also brought some of the better-known fighters, including Matt Hughes, Jose "Pele" Landi-Jons and Carlos Newton, to the Middle East. Oddly, while the fighters were housed in a shit hole, Bruce Buffer, the commentators, I, and others who worked the event were put up in an upscale hotel. A few of us discussed the changes waiting for us back home, but no one really knew what to expect.

PHOTO COURTESY OF THE MCCARTHY FAMILY

In Kuwait with Bruce Buffer, Steven Quadros, Peter "Sugarfoot" Cunningham, and others

There was no guarantee that Zuffa would hire any of us who already worked with the UFC, but we didn't have much time to worry about it.

One of the first things Zuffa did was fly Elaine, James Werme, Jeff Blatnick, me, and a few other key promotion figures to Las Vegas just before UFC 30. We all stayed at Palace Station, one of the casino hotels owned by the Fertitta family, and were taken out to an Italian restaurant. There, Fertitta briefly spoke about wanting to work with all of us.

I sat next to one of Fertitta's friends, who said, "Everything the brothers touch turns to gold. They don't fail at anything." It was quite an endorsement.

Two weeks after the Zuffa buyout, UFC 30 "The Battle on the Boardwalk" would hit the Jersey shore on February 23, 2001, at the Trump Taj Mahal in Atlantic City. This would be the transitional event in which SEG passed the reins to Zuffa.

The new UFC employees followed the SEG staff around backstage and on the floor, taking notes in their one-night crash course on running an MMA event.

Even though Zuffa had only a few days to implement changes, right away you could see a difference in the live event production value. Quite a few extra staff members raced around to hang lighting or set up the fireworks display.

One of the more notable changes was Zuffa's introduction of the raised entrance ramp. A day before the show, I was walking through the arena when Lorenzo Fertitta asked me if I'd like to stop and watch a run-through of Tito Ortiz's entrance. The ramp was lined with mechanisms that would shoot fireworks and flames as Ortiz walked down it to the cage. Ortiz even had a signature song that started with a synthesizer-created voice blurting out, "Tito is in the house." It was the most elaborate UFC entrance I'd ever seen, and it sent chills up my spine.

Fertitta was a fairly reserved character, but he couldn't hide his excitement and aspirations for the UFC and the sport. He told me, "I want to be the one to pay fighters a million dollars. I don't want to be like the old UFC. They didn't make stars; they made the UFC the star."

I was all for the fighters making more money—God knows they deserved it—but I told Fertitta, "The fighters will be only as true to you as you are true to them. If someone comes along that they think is truer, they'll go to that person. They're here to make money."

The night before the event, the fighters were a little giddy, probably because of all the added frills, and decided to have some fun. Tito Ortiz, who had been managed by Dana White, decided to pull a prank on his new bosses. Ortiz had someone from his camp call White and explain in broken English that co-main event fighter Caol Uno had fallen down a hotel escalator and broken his leg. White and Fertitta nearly had side-by-side heart attacks when they heard that one. By the time they figured out what was really going on, the entire staff had had a good laugh about it.

The two championship bouts were the standout performances of UFC 30. Jens Pulver battled his way through five emotional rounds to win the bantamweight, later renamed lightweight, title over Japanese Shooto legend Caol Uno. In the main event, Ortiz slammed Evan Tanner to the canvas at the thirty-second mark, knocking him out cold.

New Jersey Commissioner Larry Hazzard was especially shaken up about the knockout and asked me if what Ortiz had done to Tanner was illegal. We discussed how the move was completely legal and went over a couple of other moments that night. This was the second UFC event that the NJSACB had allowed under the promotion's rules while they drafted their own for the state.

They were looking closely, as was Zuffa.

In light of the Tanner knockout slam, Zuffa contracted a California-based company to build a new Octagon that would have more give to protect the fighters.

I'd seen some fighters scoping out the Octagon before shows, looking for the spots with the least give. Then, when they'd pick up their opponents, they'd walk to that specific spot and slam them down to inflict the most damage.

An engineer drew up a revised schematic and rebuilt the Octagon with aluminum, eliminating the wooden struts. Extra padding was also added to both the cage posts and the Octagon floor. Zuffa was raising the bar.

There were exactly forty days until the next scheduled UFC event, so Zuffa had to work fast. The company had been created from scratch to run the UFC, so many of the employees were new to promoting. There had been some talk of certain employees crossing over to work for Zuffa, but it was clear that not everyone would be invited to join the new company.

Paula Romero, who'd taken over as event coordinator at UFC 22 after Elaine had left, wanted Zuffa to hire her for more money than she'd made with SEG. However, Zuffa had hired its own coordinator, Lisa Faircloth, to oversee the events.

James Werme, who'd served as a producer since 1995 and had been an on-air roving reporter for the last few SEG shows, was let go.

Following UFC 31, Jeff Blatnick was replaced in the booth after having commentated every event since UFC 4. I felt especially bad for Blatnick because it was clear Dana White didn't like anything about him, from his looks to his commentating skills. However, Blatnick had been integral to the sport's growth.

Frank Shamrock, the retired middleweight champion who'd sat in on the play-by-play duties for the last few events, also decided to part ways with Zuffa. There was a falling out over what exactly Shamrock would do with the promotion. I was told that Shamrock wanted to take more of a role on the business end, but Zuffa wanted the retired champion commentating only. Shamrock's and White's personalities also seemed to clash, which sped up his exit.

The commentary booth would become a revolving door of auditionees for the next few shows, until Zuffa settled on the duo of Mike Goldberg and comedian and TV actor Joe Rogan in 2002. Rogan, who'd reached national acclaim as host of NBC's *Fear Factor*, was an avid martial artist himself and had been a backstage interviewer for the UFC in its earlier days.

Joe Silva replaced John Perretti as matchmaker. From his legendary MMA tape collection, he'd sent Meyrowitz copies of fights from Japan and other countries. SEG had paid Silva in free posters and tickets for a few shows, but when they couldn't afford to do that anymore, commentator Jeff Blatnick had paid Silva to research and write up fighter bio notes Blatnick could refer to during the broadcasts. When Zuffa bought the UFC, I think it was

Blatnick who told Fertitta and White they might want to talk to Silva because of his vast fighter knowledge. John Lewis, their Brazilian jiu-jitsu teacher, was supposed to get the matchmaker job, but Zuffa took a chance and went with Silva instead.

As for me, I hoped I wasn't about to share the same fate as Blatnick, Werme, and Perretti. I'd fought hard for MMA and been through a lot of good and bad with it. The UFC wasn't perfect, but it was like one of my kids, and I'd always love it unconditionally. I was relieved when I got the call to go work UFC 31.

One more momentous development was about to happen for the sport, though. On April 3, 2001, just a month before UFC 31, Fertitta, White, Silva, Blatnick, IFC promoter Paul Smith, King of the Cage promoter Terry Trebilcock, Pride Fighting Championships representatives Yukino Kanda and Hideki Yamamoto, a few others, and I met at Commissioner Hazzard's request in Trenton, New Jersey, in a NJSACB conference room. NSAC Executive Director Marc Ratner participated by phone. We were there to discuss and agree upon a set of rules. The meeting lasted about four hours.

The board started with the UFC's current rules and discussed other hot topics like the use of elbows and knees on the ground. The board's physician weighed in on everything, giving his medical opinion of whether a move was acceptable within the realm of fighter safety. The doctor nearly had a fit over one fighter kneeing another downed fighter at the IFC show in 2000, and I think we all tried to be reasonable with his dramatics. Zuffa knew the NJSACB would have issues with certain maneuvers, so they'd prepared themselves.

The board was concerned about the slams and throws that

were acceptable in MMA, but we'd prepared a DVD that demonstrated all of these moves happening in the 1996 Olympics in the judo, Greco-Roman wrestling, and freestyle wrestling competitions. Nobody could argue with the DVD.

We also discussed weight divisions, and the board expanded the list from three to the eight main weight classes utilized in the sport today. The heavyweight division was a sticking point, though, as it started at 205.1 pounds and had no cutoff. The physician requested that the heavyweight division be capped at 265 pounds and that fighters over that mark fall into a super heavyweight division. This seemed acceptable to all of the United States promoters in the room.

The Japanese representatives from Pride, Kanda and Yamamoto, didn't say a word the whole time until the subject of clothing and shoes was brought up. On the Japanese MMA scene, gis, leggings, and wrestling shoes were widely accepted, so they wanted them kept in.

However, Commissioner Hazzard was adamantly opposed. "I don't want shoes in the ring at all," he said, even after we explained that these were the lighter wrestling shoes. "There will be no gis," he added. "The fighters will wear shorts, cups, and gloves—that's it."

I can't imagine Pride's Kanda and Yamamoto were too pleased with this. The new fighter uniform was but another detail that would make it more difficult to bring their product to the United States.

Round duration was another big issue for Pride. While the United States had officially adopted three five-minute rounds as the standard, Japanese MMA preferred a ten-minute first round, then two additional five-minute rounds to allow grapplers more time to work their game. However, the ten-five-five-round system wouldn't be allowed in New Jersey.

By the end of the meeting, Zuffa had gotten pretty much everything it had hoped for, as the NJSACB didn't veer too far from what the UFC had already been doing. No kneeing or kicking the head of a downed opponent remained in the new set of Unified Rules, while Pride would continue to allow them in Japan.

In addition, the NJSACB approved four-to-eight-ounce fighter gloves after inspecting a sample of each pair brought to the meeting. NJSACB legal counsel Nick Lembo, whom Hazzard put in charge of MMA regulation in the state, was tasked with getting down all of these rules and changes—what became known as the Unified Rules of MMA.

The sport's passage in New Jersey made me reflect on how I presented myself on the job. I'd always tried to be as professional as I could, but now I knew I had to watch my fraternization with the fighters.

From the early UFCs until now, I'd rolled and trained with them at events. My thirst for jiu-jitsu hadn't subsided when I'd left Rorion Gracie's gym in 1995. I'd continued to study with other respected Southern California black belts like Joe Moreira and Jean Jacques Machado and had worked my way up to brown belt status over the years. As we'd waited for shows, we'd all gravitated to the gyms or workout areas provided in the hotel, exchanged techniques, and goofed around. I'd rolled with anybody who'd wanted to, experiencing the moves I'd have to identify and anticipate while refereeing.

Because everyone at a UFC event shared a common passion, it would also be a normal occurrence for me and Elaine to have dinner with some of the fighters and their camps.

I understood those days were now over. It wasn't as if rolling with fighters or eating dinner with them would sway me in the cage, but I understood it was up to me to protect the image of fair officiating in the sport. That didn't mean I had to be stern or cut myself off from everyone, but my interactions had to be on a professional level only.

PHOTO COURTESY OF THE MCCARTHY FAMILY

At the surprise fortieth birthday party my wife threw me—when Chuck Liddell and Tito Ortiz were still friends

With the newly minted Unified Rules, UFC 31 "Locked & Loaded" was the third in four events to take place at the Trump Taj Mahal and the first run solely by Zuffa. I was challenged as a referee in the main event, a heavyweight title bout between UFC champion Randy Couture and Brazilian striker Pedro Rizzo. I don't like to throw the word "war" around, but there doesn't seem to be a more appropriate one to describe this twenty-five-minute battle I saw firsthand. To this day, it's one of the best fights I've ever officiated. It took a lot out of both fighters and presented multiple moments when I was on the verge of intervening.

In the first round, Couture took Rizzo down and stacked him on the fence. Couture unleashed punches and elbows into Rizzo's guard, opening up the Brazilian's face. Rizzo wasn't hard to cut because he had a lot of scar tissue on his face. I didn't stop it because Rizzo was fighting back; he was trying. I'd told the fighters that if they were at least attempting to move or slow their opponent, whether or not they were successful, I'd let it continue.

I could tell Rizzo knew where he was and his mind was still in it. He couldn't get out from underneath Couture, but he was fending off a few of the punches and staying alive. Couture kept swinging away till he'd virtually punched himself out by the end of the round.

The next round was a complete turn of the tables, primarily because Couture had used up his gas tank in the first five minutes. Rizzo started connecting some big, damaging leg kicks, which made me wonder how Couture would walk afterward.

After the second round, I went to Couture's corner and asked if he wanted to continue. I was concerned.

He and his corner said, "We're good," a few times, but that didn't change the fact that he'd gotten his ass handed to him for an entire round. I was trying to give him a way out, but he didn't take it. Certain fighters can pull it out when they have to, and Couture was that guy in this and a majority of his fights.

In the third round, Couture took Rizzo down again and

managed to control positioning for a few crucial moments to get some strength back. It really was the third round that determined the outcome of that fight because Couture was able to get back into the game.

For rounds four and five, they traded uppercuts and hooks, shot and avoided takedowns, and pretty much made each other's life miserable.

I knew the fight was close, but I thought the judges would give it to Rizzo because of the greater damage he'd inflicted over the course of the fight. However, when the scores were read, Couture was given the nod. I was fine with that and could see how the judges could have gone either way.

I think Couture might have been surprised by it, though. When I raised his hand, he looked confused.

As a small footnote, UFC 31 also marked the debut of a twenty-three-year-old Hawaiian named B. J. Penn on the undercard. Penn took down opponent Joey Gilbert and ground-and-pounded him into submission from back mount as if it were nothing. When the referee stepped in, Penn looked up with the most innocent of expressions. This was Penn's first professional fight, but you could tell his skill far exceeded that of many of the veterans on the card. Talk about a prodigy.

By UFC 32, I felt optimistic. Some encouraging changes were already happening with both Zuffa and the UFC. Fertitta had opened offices in Las Vegas and had a staff coordinating upcoming UFC events and addressing questions and concerns. Medicals and necessary paperwork were being collected and handled well ahead of the event, leaving less chance for last-minute issues.

Schedules, flights, and hotel rooms were organized and disseminated promptly. Zuffa's in-house publicity department distributed press releases with updates on each upcoming event and reached out to local and national newspapers and other media outlets to get press covering the shows. The UFC asked me to speak with too many reporters to count, but I never minded. It was an important educational process, and we all had to do our part.

Suddenly the UFC wasn't a fly-by-night operation anymore. It was obvious that the little details wouldn't fall through the cracks, but if they did someone would be there to pick them up.

However, not all of Zuffa's initial changes were successful. For instance, Zuffa dropped considerable dough for a seven-figure advertising campaign featuring fighters like Tito Ortiz, Randy Couture, Pedro Rizzo, Carlos Newton, and Jens Pulver paired with models in a handful of prominent men's magazines, including *Maxim* and *FHM*. Carmen Electra, who also starred in the ad campaign, was hired as the spokeswoman for the UFC. At a New York City press conference, when asked about her MMA experience, Electra told reporters she'd done Tae Bo. She seemed like a waste of money to me, but I thought maybe Fertitta had more experience in this than I did.

The campaign didn't even make a dent in boosting public awareness of the UFC or the sport. That was clear from the turn-out at the next event.

UFC 32 "Showdown in the Meadowlands," held at the Continental Airlines Arena, now the IZOD Center, in East Rutherford, New Jersey, was underwhelming for a number of reasons. While the event marked the UFC's return from parking lot tents and run-down community halls to a state-of-the-art venue, Zuffa shot too high, and it was virtually impossible to fill the 20,000-seat arena.

Bernie Dillon, the original chief operating officer for Zuffa, handled the arena layout and priced the tickets, which ran from $25 for the nosebleeds to $300 for cageside seats. It didn't seem super expensive, but the event sold only a few thousand tickets. Ticket pricing became an immediate issue between Dana White and Dillon, who left Zuffa after a few shows.

The real issue, in my opinion, was the weak main event, which paired Tito Ortiz against Australian grappler Elvis Sinosic. At UFC 30, Sinosic had pulled off a major upset in submitting Jeremy Horn, but he had little fighting experience in the United States and certainly wasn't ready for headlining status.

The much larger and stronger Ortiz took Sinosic down and hammered him with fists and elbows. Sinosic's forehead split open almost instantaneously, and the flaps of skin hung from his face. I try to let championship bouts play out as long as possible because there's so much at stake, but Ortiz destroyed Sinosic to the point that I had to jump in three and a half minutes into the first round.

As Zuffa tried to find its promotional legs, progress was being made in Nevada. From his time as a commissioner, Fertitta had relationships with all of the NSAC's players, and mixed martial arts was rescheduled to go to the commission for a vote.

I was flown to Reno to see Glenn Carano, the former football player who'd thought MMA was too violent for his tastes. I met him at the casino he owned there and wasn't shocked to learn he still wasn't thrilled with the sport.

After a while, when he was fed up with talking about it, he

said, "John, I'm never going to like this sport, and it's not what I consider a good athletic event, but I am friends with Lorenzo Fertitta. He believes in it, and I will vote for it."

On July 23, 2001, the Nevada State Athletic Commission voted unanimously to regulate mixed martial arts. They also adopted a set of rules nearly identical to the Unified Rules drafted in New Jersey a few months before.

It was obvious Fertitta had a lot of pull in town. Zuffa immediately secured a September 28 date for UFC 33 at the 12,000-seat Mandalay Bay Events Center on the Strip. As if that weren't enough, Zuffa also negotiated the return of the UFC's pay-per-views to iN DEMAND and all of the other leading cable providers that had jumped ship in 1997.

In six months, Zuffa had accomplished a number of the goals SEG had been chipping away at for the last few years. Things were changing fast, and I wasn't immune. MMA was now regulated by two key state bodies. As a referee, I would now report to the commissions, not the promotion, and the days of my officiating events from top to bottom were over.

MMA referees made anywhere from a few hundred to a thousand dollars per event, but I'd been on a $75,000 annual salary with SEG for all the additional work I'd done in drafting its original rules and lobbying and defending the sport in the courtrooms.

Since I'd now be hired to referee through each state commission, Fertitta told me he couldn't put me on Zuffa's payroll. Zuffa planned to hold six events a year initially, so it would have been a loss of nearly $70,000 a year for me. It wouldn't be financially feasible for me to get the time off from the police academy, so I'd have to consider giving up refereeing. It was nobody's fault. I'd been hired at a time when regulatory bodies had no interest in the sport, but now the sport was evolving.

I was touched and grateful when Zuffa figured out a way to keep me around. Since they felt I'd become fairly synonymous with the UFC, they offered me a yearly licensing contract for my name and likeness, as well as the right to use my catchphrase "Let's Get It On," which I'd trademarked through boxing referee Mills Lane in the late 1990s. I'm told Marc Ratner, the NSAC's executive director, was aware of the arrangement, though he never asked me about it. It was also understood that I'd assist the UFC in educating additional state commissions on the sport.

I was licensed as a referee in Nevada for UFC 33. When it came to combat sports, Las Vegas was considered the preeminent destination. As a young boy by my dad's side, I'd watched monumental boxing events broadcasted live from Las Vegas. Now I would be a part of it. To say it was a huge moment and victory for me would be an understatement.

UFC 33 "Victory in Vegas" was held on September 28, 2001, at the Mandalay Bay Events Center in Las Vegas. Refereeing at the event should have been more thrilling, but two weeks earlier two commercial airliners had flown into the World Trade Center buildings in New York City. As the nation mourned, we were uncertain if the show would happen at all. Many people were recommending that Zuffa reschedule, but Zuffa decided to go ahead as planned.

The other shoe dropped days later when Vitor Belfort, who was challenging Tito Ortiz for the light heavyweight title in the main event, injured his arm in a freak accident. While training in

Brazil, Belfort was pushed into a window next to the ring, sustaining a deep laceration that required surgical repair. Zuffa now had to find a new opponent to take on Ortiz. With little training time, Belarusian fighter Vladimir Matyushenko agreed to step into Belfort's headlining shoes.

It was Zuffa's third event since taking over the UFC, and the promotion spared no expense. They bought billboard ads and put the fighters and officials up in the host hotel, which was one of the nicer ones on the Strip. Just as they were at the big boxing events, the weigh-ins were opened to the public and press. Everything within Zuffa's control was managed with style.

Still, the variables of the night that couldn't be accounted for were the fights themselves. In an effort to stack the event, three five-round championship bouts were added to the card, and all three fights went their full twenty-five-minute duration as the athletes cautiously fought to not lose. This caused the pay-per-view to run over its time limit, and the broadcast cut out during the main event between Ortiz and Matyushenko.

Despite their best efforts, Zuffa had repeated the mistake SEG had made at UFC 4 in 1994. Many customers asked for refunds, and the event was considered a financial disaster. The fights weren't considered particularly interesting either. Of the eight bouts offered, six went to anticlimactic decisions.

Zuffa wasn't ready to throw in the towel just yet, though.

A few days before UFC 34, the promotion and the NSAC jointly announced another rule change at a press conference in Las Vegas. I was flown out early during fight week to speak at the podium, where I told the press that if a bout stalemated, referees would now

UFC 34

"High Voltage"
November 2, 2001
MGM Grand Garden Arena
Las Vegas, Nevada

Bouts I Reffed:
Matt Lindland vs. Phil Baroni
Josh Barnett vs. Bobby Hoffman
Matt Hughes vs. Carlos Newton
Randy Couture vs. Pedro Rizzo

The welterweight title bout fight between Newton and Hughes went down as a classic with a controversial ending. Newton had latched on a triangle choke in the first round, and Hughes countered by lifting the champion, resting him high on the cage, then slamming him down in a last-ditch effort as the choke drained Hughes of his senses. The slam knocked Newton unconscious, and he didn't come to for a good forty-five seconds. As I pushed a dazed Hughes off Newton, I noticed he was blinking to clear his vision, something I've done myself after a choke. I have both choked and been choked out too many times to count, and I've never seen anyone blink while out. Hughes was close, but only one fighter went out that night. Hughes was deemed the winner and the new welterweight champion.

be allowed to restart a fight from standing position. This new rule would speed up the action and prevent a fighter from stalling, a major issue at UFC 33.

To be honest, it was something I and the other referees had already been doing since UFC 15, but now it was a rule. If a fighter was in his opponent's guard throwing little punches now and then, it wouldn't be enough to keep him in that position. I got the drift that Zuffa wanted stand-ups to happen more because they were looking for more action in their fights.

Back at the police academy, my involvement with the UFC was getting noticed. I had to start my course by allowing the class to get their questions about the UFC out of their systems. I understood people were curious, and there wasn't anything wrong with that. Still, I wanted the cadets to concentrate on the more important materials at hand, like learning how to handle violent suspects in life-or-death situations, and they couldn't do that until they got the UFC off their brains.

When I'd started refereeing for the UFC, the LAPD hadn't said boo about it, other than asking me to get the appropriate work permits. My superiors all knew what I was doing with the UFC. Even the chief at the time, Bernard Parks, had stopped me once to talk about it. He wanted to attend a UFC, and I said I'd be happy to buy him some tickets.

So after I'd gone unnoticed for years, my LAPD superiors began to recognize me from my UFC appearances, which wasn't necessarily good for me. One thing you learn with the LAPD is that it's all about egos, and when someone thinks you have something over them, jealousy will rear its ugly head. People can be vindictive, and if they have power to use against you, sometimes they will. And if they don't have it, they might go to someone who does, which is what happened to me.

At that time, my dad was working for Safariland, which produced body armor and police duty gear. The company had asked if he could get me to model a new vest in their ads because of my visibility as a UFC referee. The company also wanted to use the slogan "Are you ready?"

I said, "Is it a favor for you, Dad, or for them?"

"For me."

"Then, of course, I'll do it."

I didn't need to apply for a work permit. I wasn't getting paid to pose in the ad. Safariland asked me to wear my badge to the shoot, but I told them I couldn't. LAPD officers were strictly forbidden to wear their badges on film, TV, or in any type of advertising, so I told them I'd get a fake one to wear.

During the shoot, I even requested that I hold a glock, which the LAPD didn't use at the time. I didn't want the department associated in any way or for them to think I might be trying to make money off them.

When I put on the vest, I asked the photographer to get the prop badge from my bag for me. As he mounted it to my bulky gear, I couldn't really see it.

When the ad came out a short time later in a police magazine, someone in the department complained that I shouldn't be allowed to pose in advertisements. When I was confronted about it, a superior asked why I hadn't filled out a work permit. I explained that I hadn't gotten paid for it, but a complaint was filed against me, and an investigation was opened to unearth my evil modeling career.

The next thing I was asked was if I'd worn my badge during the shoot. You couldn't even see the badge in the ad because it was half cut off by the gear. I told them I hadn't worn my own badge anyway but a prop one.

"It looks a lot like an LAPD badge," they said.

I insisted I'd gotten a fake one from a colleague.

I'll be damned if they didn't blow that picture up 800 times until they could read the last number on that badge. Sure enough, it matched the one on my own badge.

"You have got to be kidding me," I said when they handed me the picture.

I was accused of lying about the whole thing, and lying could've cost me my job.

My accusers treated me like one of their suspects, going after any shred of evidence they could find to prove my guilt. I was "big time" in their eyes, after all, and some of my superiors couldn't have that.

I finally told my sergeant, Andy Markel, this whole situation was bullshit and nothing more than jealousy. Andy ended up taking over the investigation and made one taped phone call to the photographer who'd shot the ad. The photographer was willing to go on the record stating that he hadn't noticed two badges in my bag and had pinned the wrong one on me, and the investigation was finally dropped.

The first batch of Zuffa-run UFC events improved on the product immeasurably. The packaging, from its advertising to its prefight videos, looked much more professional. The talent was improving quickly as well, but that didn't immediately translate into pay-per-view buys. As a train-wreck spectacle, the UFC had peaked with nearly 300,000 buys. Now a recognized sport, the UFC barely mustered 50,000 buys for its first few shows.

UFC 35 "Throwdown," on January 11, 2002, was the first held at the Mohegan Sun Arena in Uncasville, Connecticut. The main aggressor at this event was a stomach bug, which had fighters, cornermen, and even some of Zuffa's staff rushing for their toilet bowls the entire weekend.

Everyone had a theory regarding the mystery plague that pillaged UFC 35's roster. Some of the fighters blamed it on the food cooked by the hotel's restaurant, ironically named The Octagon, and a few fighters stole their personalized steak knives as payback. Some had come into town with the bug, though, so maybe it had infected the rest that way. Kevin Randleman was sick and irate at the same time, convinced the hotel had poisoned him in some master conspiracy before his big fight against Renato "Babalu" Sobral.

Luckily, I was one of the few not sick. During the event, fighters were running to the bathroom backstage. UFC middleweight champion Dave Menne was one of the sicker fighters and was throwing up till his title defense against Brazilian jiu-jitsu black belt Murilo Bustamante. A drained and depleted Menne lost the title to Bustamante on second-round punches, but the real story is that a guy who felt like he was going to die went out and fought his heart out and never complained once about the result.

UFC 36

"Worlds Collide"
March 22, 2002
MGM Grand Garden Arena
Las Vegas, Nevada

Bouts I Reffed:
Frank Mir vs. Pete Williams
Matt Hughes vs. Hayato Sakurai
Randy Couture vs. Josh Barnett

Matt Hughes delivered the best performance of his career in the Octagon, repeatedly slamming dangerous Japanese legend Hayato Sakurai into oblivion.

Randy Couture mostly controlled a much bigger and younger Josh Barnett for the first three rounds of their heavyweight championship match. But Barnett turned things around by grounding and pinning Couture against the fence, where he landed huge shots that hurt Couture until I jumped in to stop it. Afterward, Barnett tested positive for steroids and hasn't fought in the UFC since, which is a tragedy because he was and still is one of the best heavyweight fighters in the world.

Not all of the fighters got ill. In the main event, a healthy B. J. Penn challenged Jens Pulver for his lightweight crown and won the first two rounds handily. Penn secured an armbar on Pulver at the end of the second round, but just as he extended and locked it in, the bell rang. I believe two things happened in that moment: first, Pulver got pissed off over nearly getting caught; second, Penn, who was fighting for a world championship in his fourth professional bout, lost his spark because the fight literally slipped out of his hands.

I noticed a real shift in both fighters' demeanors when they came out for the third round. Though Penn had an early lead, Pulver used his newfound motivation to go after his opponent and win the final fifteen minutes to keep his title.

Fights are like that. They can turn on a dime, and a mental catalyst can be just as powerful as a landed punch or submission.

In a time of fast-paced growth, I made my second major refereeing blunder. It was at UFC 37 "High Impact" on May 10, 2002, at the CenturyTel Center in Bossier City, Louisiana. Middleweight champion Murilo Bustamante caught Olympic wrestling silver medalist Matt Lindland in a tight armbar in the first round, and I interceded when I thought I saw Lindland tapping out.

"I wasn't tapping, John," Lindland said as I separated them.

In that moment, I made another big mistake: I doubted my call.

While 8,000 vocal Louisiana fans looked on, instead of being decisive and sticking to my first call, I decided to restart the bout.

At the time, I didn't have the ability to restart the fight from the grounded position the fighters had been in; I had to stand them up and restart them from their corners. That was completely unfair to Bustamante, who'd been on the verge of winning the fight on the mat, but I did it anyway and immediately felt terrible about it.

Despite my intervention, the right man found the win that night. In the third round, Bustamante trapped Lindland's neck with a guillotine choke, and Lindland clearly tapped out this time.

When I left the cage, Elaine said something she rarely does about my refereeing: "You screwed up."

In my heart, I knew she was right.

When I reviewed the video, I saw I'd been right the first time and Lindland had tapped out. I'd been duped, but the blame was on me for caving on my original call. Referees don't always make the correct calls, but they need to stand by them in that moment no matter what. I had to make sure I never got caught up in that type of situation again.

UFC 38 "Brawl at the Hall," the promotion's first venture into

UFC 37.5

"As Real As It Gets"
June 22, 2002
Bellagio Hotel and Casino
Las Vegas, Nevada

Bouts I Reffed:
Robbie Lawler vs. Steve Berger
Benji Radach vs. Nick Serra
Chuck Liddell vs. Vitor Belfort

This six-fight event was thrown together in a week, when the UFC got the opportunity to air its first live fights on cable for FOX Sports Network's *The Best Damn Sports Show Period*. This was another big break for the UFC and the sport, but the fighters had to come through with appealing performances. Both Lawler and Liddell stepped up to the plate with victories as exciting as Zuffa could've hoped for. Held in an intimate ballroom in the Bellagio with about 2,000 fans, the event had a certain electricity not felt at the larger arena shows.

England, was held in London's 5,000-seat Royal Albert Hall. MMA had a small but loyal fan base in the United Kingdom, and a couple smaller local promotions were grooming talent. The UFC had also secured a minor TV deal in the United Kingdom to air past events, something not yet achieved in the United States.

The Royal Albert Hall was far different from any other UFC venue to date. It was essentially an opera house, with red velvet curtains and box seats on all sides. Not exactly what you'd picture when you think of fighting. I know it had never been intended to hold fights, but it really felt like the Roman days to me. A day before the show, several of us stood in the middle of the Octagon and yelled out, "Are you not entertained?" Silly, yes, but still pretty cool.

Of the matches, Ian Freeman's victory over Frank Mir was probably the most potent. Having appeared at UFC 24, 26, and 27, Freeman, a native of Sunderland, was the most recognized fighter from the United Kingdom. Freeman went into the bout knowing his father was ill, but his corner, friends, and family decided to not tell him his father had passed away the day of the event. Freeman used all of his stirring emotion to take out Mir with a flurry of first-round punches on the ground, earning his biggest career win. The crowd went nuts for him.

The event also featured the rematch of the controversial UFC 34 encounter between Matt Hughes and Carlos Newton. However, there was no doubt this time around. Hughes walked through Newton and got a fourth-round stoppage.

Many were surprised by Hughes' domination, but sometimes the fans forget that outside of the cage fighters balance complex lives just like everybody else. This was a clear case of two fighters moving in different directions. Hughes was coming into his own as a fighter and honing a style that worked for him. Newton had been in the game so long and was pursuing a medical degree and other interests at the same time. Fighting wasn't his first priority anymore.

I did attend Zuffa's after party at a trendy nightclub in London and left about a minute before the now infamous brawl broke out in the street between Lee Murray and Tito Ortiz and their drunken entourages. After that night, Zuffa decided not to host its own after parties. Fighters and alcohol didn't seem to mix too well.

Though Zuffa had now held eleven quality events in nineteen months, it didn't seem the UFC was making substantial strides. They had spent millions on a magazine ad campaign, tried to coax the mainstream press to cover them, and even taken an event halfway around the world to England. However, the pay-per-view numbers for the first eleven events under Zuffa's watch were reported to be under 100,000 buys each, with some rumored to be 30,000 or lower. It was time to try something different.

Dana White had told me a couple days before UFC 40 that Tank Abbott would be returning to fight at UFC 41, and Zuffa managed to keep the MMA press from finding out. When Abbott appeared at the top of the ramp at UFC 40 and swaggered down with his salt-and-pepper goatee and leather jacket, the audience was shocked.

UFC 39

"The Warriors Return"
September 27, 2002
Mohegan Sun Arena
Uncasville, Connecticut

Bouts I Reffed:
Gan McGee vs. Pedro Rizzo
B. J. Penn vs. Matt Serra
Ricco Rodriguez vs. Randy Couture

McGee stopped Rizzo in the first round via a nasty cut, the start of the downfall for the Brazilian striker.

Rodriguez's fifth-round victory over Couture was a tough bout to watch. Couture led early, but later Rodriguez used his size to trap him on the mat. Rodriguez then hit Couture with a legal elbow that cracked his orbital bone. It was the one time I heard Couture verbally submit in a fight.

My sons, Ron and Johnny, with former UFC welterweight champion Carlos Newton in their best Dragon Ball Z poses

Some time had passed since Abbott had been in the UFC, and I didn't have a strong opinion about his return either way. Times had changed, and the UFC was overcoming a lot of the stigma I'd felt Abbott had helped feed during his SEG days, but if it would get people to tune in, why not? I knew he wouldn't win against good fighters, and Zuffa and the audience would see that when they watched him fight.

UFC 40 "Vendetta," held on November 22, 2002, at the MGM Grand Garden Arena in Las Vegas, launched the sport's first true rivalry of the Zuffa era. The brash and outspoken Tito Ortiz took on Ken Shamrock in a flashback to their UFC 19 encounter when Ortiz had beaten Shamrock's prized student Guy Mezger and donned the "Gay Mezger Is My Bitch" T-shirt.

The bad blood built up in the days before the show. At the press conference, Shamrock uttered the now famous line, "I'm going to beat you into a living death," and kicked a chair Ortiz's way, which Dana caught midair. It was a pretty nice catch for someone who never expected a chair to come flying his way.

At the weigh-ins, I was asked to stand between these passionate showmen. I got the impression everyone else was afraid to do it. When they lunged at one another, I had to wedge between them.

The actual fight wasn't as competitive. Even though Ortiz wasn't a great striker, he managed to bash Shamrock's face until it was almost unrecognizable.

At the end of the third round, Shamrock looked my direction. "I can't see anything, John."

I walked him to his corner and told Tra Telligman, his lead cornerman, "Your fighter's having trouble seeing."

PHOTO BY SUSUMU NAGAO

Standing between Tito Ortiz and Ken Shamrock at the UFC 40 weigh-ins, a job I'm glad UFC President Dana White took over later

I wanted Shamrock's corner to have the chance to pull him out of the fight, but I had also told the ringside physician what he had said to me. It was time to get him out: the question was which way it was going to happen. Shamrock's corner called it, saving their man from any more damage. It was a great bout and an honorable ending.

The energy that night was unlike any I'd felt before. Shamrock's entrance was magic, as always, and the matchup had a "big fight" feel. Something clicked with the TV audience as well. Maybe it was the name recognition of two of the UFC's pioneers or their genuine dislike for one another, but when the pay-per-view numbers were finally tallied, UFC 40 had gotten 150,000 buys. It was Zuffa's first commercial success.

My sons were lucky enough to grow up meeting some of the sport's great stars: here with Jerry Bohlander and Ken Shamrock.

At Zuffa's second show in Las Vegas with my family. You can see Zuffa was stepping up the production value. (UFC 34 "High Voltage," November 2001)

THE HAIL MARY

We are not retreating.
We are advancing in another direction.

—General Douglas MacArthur

With Zuffa desperate to connect with new fans, Abbott would be thrown right into the fire at the promotion's next event, UFC 41 "Onslaught" on February 28, 2003, at the Boardwalk Hall in Atlantic City, New Jersey. Bringing back the now thirty-eight-year-old "barstool brawler" didn't mesh with the UFC's line that its fighters were world-class athletes trained in multiple martial arts disciplines, but Zuffa needed a hook—fast.

I wondered who they could match Abbott with so he'd have a decent chance. Randy Couture had stood up at UFC 40 to volunteer for the job, but I knew that wouldn't happen.

Instead, Frank Mir, the twenty-three-year-old grappling enthusiast, was offered Abbott first. Mir had notched back-to-back submission wins before British Ian Freeman had beaten and bloodied him to a first-round finish at UFC 38 in London. He hadn't taken Freeman's punches well at all, and that was about all Abbott had, at least for the first couple of minutes before he'd gas out.

I think the match was made because Mir had a good name but couldn't take strong punching well, which is where Abbott had the best shot. But to me, Mir was the exact type of fighter who would give Abbott problems. He was smart and would not be stupid enough to stand and trade shots with someone like Abbott.

As I suspected, Mir turned out to be a terrible matchup for Abbott. He was big and strong and managed to get Abbott down to the mat early, caught him in an omoplata shoulder lock, then reached down and applied a toe hold that cranked Abbott's ankle in a violent rotation. With no ground training to know how to get out of it, Abbott tapped out in just forty-six seconds. It was a beautiful double submission that emphasized how far the sport had progressed. However, we all realized after the fact that this wasn't a smart match if they were trying to bring back an older UFC star to gain some momentum.

Another fighter the UFC was hoping to build at UFC 41 was Ricco Rodriguez, who'd won the vacant heavyweight title over Couture five months earlier at UFC 39. However, Rodriguez wouldn't hold the belt long at all. Tim Sylvia, a six-feet-eight newcomer, came out of nowhere and knocked down Rodriguez in the first round. As soon as Sylvia hit Rodriguez, you could see the champion didn't want to stand with him anymore, but he couldn't get Sylvia down to the mat. From his back, Rodriguez tried an armbar and Sylvia lifted him up and slammed him on his head. It was the beginning of the end for Rodriguez, who never again found the success he'd achieved early in his career.

I also refereed the B. J. Penn versus Caol Uno rematch for the lightweight title vacated by Jens Pulver.[11] UFC 41's championship

---

11. Pulver had left primarily because his pay was lower than that of the heavier champions.

bout was the culmination of a four-man tournament, and the promotion was eager to get a new 155-pound champion back in the mix. But after five rounds of action, the fight was ruled a draw.

I couldn't believe one of the judges had given the fight to Uno and another had scored it a draw when Penn had clearly won. To me, it was simply a crime.

Though Abbott's drawing power had helped UFC 41 sell out the Boardwalk Hall with 11,700 spectators, things didn't bode well on the pay-per-view front. UFC 40 had been able to break through the 100,000 buy-rate ceiling, but UFC 41 was said to have dipped right back below it, where the numbers would stay for the next handful of shows.

Zuffa continued to Miami, Florida, site of UFC 42 "Sudden Impact," held on April 25, 2003, at the 16,000-seat American Airlines Arena. It was another sobering night for all of us, with only about half the venue filled with fans. Even O. J. Simpson, notorious at this point for his acquittal in his ex-wife's murder trial, was able to sneak into the arena undetected and watch the show unfettered in a sea of empty seats.

The Florida State Boxing Commission had insisted on using two of its own referees for the preliminary bouts that night. During the event, one of the local referees watched Brazilian jiu-jitsu black belt Hermes Franca dislocate Rich Crunkilton's elbow two times with a straight armlock attempt in their lightweight contest. Franca actually pointed to the dislocated elbow to let the referee know what he'd done, but that didn't work.

The referee should have been protecting Crunkilton from himself, as he wouldn't submit, but since he didn't know what he was looking at, it would've been hard to accomplish that. The commission pulled the referee from the rest of the fights he'd been assigned to that night and had me sub for him.

It wouldn't be the first or last time I'd have to sit cageside and watch a fighter's safety be compromised. Referees would accept assignments to work MMA shows when they had no idea what the fighters were doing. It upset me every time.

A bout that led to a rule change: Genki Sudo vs. Duane Ludwig at UFC 42 "Sudden Impact" (April 2003)

PHOTO BY SUSUMU NAGAO

UFC 42 led to another rule change. Japanese showman Genki Sudo was dominating his fight on the ground against striker Duane Ludwig until I halted the action in round three. I believed Ludwig was taking in too much blood and couldn't breathe properly. When a doctor deemed the fighter fit to continue, I restarted the pair from the one position I was allowed to: standing. Sudo lost the ground position he'd worked so hard to get, and Ludwig, a champion kickboxer, took full advantage, scoring with late punches and kicks to pull out a controversial split decision, even though Sudo had dominated Ludwig for a good portion of the fight before.

This didn't make sense to anybody, and fast action was taken. Both the UFC and the Nevada State Athletic Commission, which would oversee the promotion's next event, instituted a new procedure. The referee would have to remember the fighters' strategic positions before stopping a bout and bringing a fighter to the doctor for a medical opinion. If the fight continued, the referee could now restart the fighters in the position they'd been stopped in, whether standing or on the ground.

Now, when a referee thought he'd need to stop a bout for a doctor's check, he'd have to take a quick mental photo of the fighters' positions. Are they in half guard? Does he have an underhook?

UFC 43

"Meltdown"
June 6, 2003
Thomas & Mack Center
Las Vegas, Nevada

Bouts I Reffed:
Falaniko Vitale vs. Matt Lindland
Vitor Belfort vs. Marvin Eastman
Kimo Leopoldo vs. David "Tank" Abbott
Randy Couture vs. Chuck Liddell

Matt Lindland knocked himself out cold falling back for a suplex attempt in his bout with Falaniko Vitale. Lindland had felt the Octagon's floor earlier in the walk-throughs and had found a hard spot where the padding was missing. The UFC crew tried to fix the problem, but Lindland ended up hitting his head right near that spot. This would lead to even more Octagon refinements.

Vitor Belfort came back to the UFC and looked fantastic knocking out Marvin Eastman with a knee to the head that opened up the biggest cut I've ever seen in combative sports. Commentator Joe Rogan called it a "goat's vagina" during the live telecast. When I heard that later, all I could think was *What's Joe doing looking at goats' vaginas?*

We never say that we put the fighters back in their exact positions and locations; it's approximate. It's not hard for me to make these mental pictures because I understand the positions and have been in them myself repeated times. The extra effort is worthwhile because it means the Sudo-Ludwig scenario won't repeat itself.

When people had questions about the sport's regulations, Zuffa would usually call on me. Between UFC 43 and 44, I was asked to attend the 2003 Conference of the Association of Boxing Commissions (ABC) in St. Louis, Missouri, with Lorenzo Fertitta and Dana White. Comprised of a majority of the athletic commissions and other combat sports' regulatory bodies throughout North America, the ABC gathered all the people the UFC and the MMA needed to impress. MMA had been regulated in key states like New Jersey and Nevada, but quite a few more had either previously banned it or had no laws on the books to either allow or oversee it. Zuffa had gotten the UFC on the conference's weekend agenda to ask the ABC if they'd consider regulating the sport. The ABC's seal of approval could certainly open the door to more states.

Fertitta gave a PowerPoint presentation showing the economic advantages of allowing the UFC and MMA into the individual states. He also highlighted how most of the fighters were college educated and some were even Olympic-caliber athletes rather than the street thugs many thought them to be. The ABC members watched a tape of some recent UFC fights, and then the presentation was opened to a question-and-answer session, which I also participated in. The questions ranged from rules to how a state could get their officials trained if they decided to regulate an event.

Fertitta's answer regarding training was always, "John will

come and do it."

A few ABC members were interested in the sport, but the majority turned their noses up at it. A lot of these commissioners were comfortable with boxing, but you could tell they felt MMA was too new and unproven. The commission elected to not even address the question of regulating MMA without more research, so Fertitta, White, and I left St. Louis not quite empty-handed but not with what we wanted.

Zuffa sent me back to the annual ABC conferences two or three more times, and each time a few members seemed slightly more interested.

I was Zuffa's man for assignments like this, but my involvement with the promotion didn't go much further than that, which was a change for me. I'd been a part of intricate facets of the UFC since Rorion Gracie had created it. When SEG and Bob Meyrowitz bought the show, he'd call me all the time from New York City to ask for advice about specific fighters and matches.

Zuffa was different, though. They'd call me from time to time for the ABC meetings or to ask about a new official they wanted to bring in, but Fertitta, White, and their employees handled everything else. I was gradually getting pushed out of that inner circle.

I stayed pretty rational about it. I always thought of what Fertitta and White had said to me in the beginning: "Business is business, and friendship is friendship. Don't think the business doesn't come before friendship, because business is business." That's the way I felt they looked at me, and that's the way I figured they did things.

I understood the UFC was now owned by different people and that this was their show, not mine. I got paid for my job, so I didn't have anything to say about it. If they needed me for

UFC 44

"Undisputed"
September 26, 2003
Mandalay Bay Events Center
Las Vegas, Nevada

Bouts I Reffed:
Josh Thomson vs. Gerald Strebendt
Tim Sylvia vs. Gan McGee
Randy Couture vs. Tito Ortiz

The light heavyweight championship bout between Tito Ortiz and Randy Couture went the distance, and Couture started spanking Ortiz's ass in the final round for comical effect when he had him stacked and trapped on the fence. Many thought Couture was tapping out. Good thing I could easily see Ortiz had no legit hold on Couture, so I didn't intervene.

something, I'd be there. If they didn't, that was okay too.

With Zuffa at the helm, the UFC weathered the ship to a promotional milestone: its tenth anniversary. When I'd taken my place in the Octagon the first time, I wouldn't have believed the UFC would be around a decade. But here we were, 50 shows and over 400 fights later at UFC 45 "Revolution," on November 21, 2003, at the Mohegan Sun Arena in Uncasville, Connecticut. This monumental achievement for MMA wasn't recognized at all by the mainstream media, but I can tell you that many people in the arena had helped ensure the UFC's survival and realized the night's importance.

Zuffa added some nice touches to make the event special. The promotion introduced the UFC Hall of Fame and inducted its first members, the deserving Royce Gracie and Ken Shamrock. Zuffa also created a viewers' choice award for fans to vote for the UFC's ten most popular fighters of all time. Randy Couture, high off his unlikely wins over Chuck Liddell and Tito Ortiz, was voted number one and was joined by Royce Gracie, Ken Shamrock, Tank Abbott, Mark Coleman, Pat Miletich, Marco Ruas, Dan Severn, Don Frye, and Oleg Taktarov.

It's a shame that this honorable tone was fleeting.

In the fifth fight of the night, there was a miscommunication between fighter Phil Baroni and one of the other referees, Larry Landless. Baroni, a passionate middleweight from New York, had been beating the piss out of opponent Evan Tanner, until Baroni got too tired. Tanner came back and eventually mounted Baroni, where he started to unload punches and elbows on his trapped opponent.

In that tense moment, Landless asked Baroni if he wanted out.

Baroni thought the referee had asked if he was okay and answered, "Yes."

Landless jumped in to halt the fight.

Baroni was so upset that he took two swings at Landless from his back.

Swinging at an official is unacceptable in any sport, and it can be especially dangerous in combat sports. Though Landless wasn't injured, Baroni's actions caused quite an uproar.

It also led to discussions between officials about when and how they should address fighters during a bout. I'd expressed only statements, not questions, to fighters. Honestly, I'd never considered why until that night. That's when I realized you couldn't expect a guy to fight and answer questions at the same time.

The night wasn't over yet, though. In the next fight, one of the worst things that could happen to a fledgling sport happened: a riot broke out in the cage between the fighters and their camps.

Tank Abbott and Wesley "Cabbage" Correira had bad intentions from the start. They started swinging at one another in a frenzy, but as usual Abbott ran out of gas pretty fast. He'd also been cut over his eye in the first round by one of Correira's knees, and blood was dripping down his face. Abbott was exhaling so hard that he was blowing blood into Correira's face, affecting his vision as well.

I didn't believe the doctor was going to stop the fight, so I stepped in, thinking I could bring Abbott over to the doctor for a quick cleanup so he'd have a chance to see the punches coming at him. When I walked him over, I said, "The cut's not that bad. We'll clean you up and get you back in the fight."

Abbott then uttered the words no fighter ever should if he wants to keep going: "I can't see."

I warned Abbott, "If you say that to the doctor, the fight will be stopped."

But Abbott knew what he was doing. He was tired and wanted out, and going out this way allowed him to blame it on the doctor.

When the doctor recommended the fight be ended based on Abbott's comment, Abbott erupted into his defiant act, cursing the stoppage in a tantrum and stomping around the cage.

From here, things developed quickly. Correira broke out into his cabbage patch victory dance, and John Marsh, another heavyweight fighter working Abbott's corner, made a remark about it, which I didn't hear. Correira flipped Marsh off, and then Marsh threw a water bottle in the Hawaiian's direction and lunged at him. Before we all knew it, the Octagon resembled a pro wrestling battle royal.

A couple commission attendants and I grabbed Marsh and cornered him against the fence, while referee Larry Landless and others did the same with Correira. Cutman Jacob "Stitch" Duran moved to Abbott to work on the laceration, and in the chaos a disgruntled and possibly inebriated fan jumped the fence and nearly fell on Duran while trying to claw his way to Abbott. Chuck Liddell, who'd piled into the cage with a few others to break up the commotion, grabbed the overzealous Correira fan and pointed him to the Octagon door.

With the sport still struggling for acceptance with the general public in the United States, this display didn't go a long way to show how much MMA had matured. But if there's one thing that

MMA is, it's unpredictable, and you take the good and bad with that.

It was strange because I walked away from UFC 45 feeling it wasn't as big a show as I'd wanted it to be. I'm not saying Zuffa did anything wrong. I think the Hall of Fame presentation was a nice gesture, but it came down to the fights, and they didn't deliver on the level that some of the shows before, like UFC 40, had. And that's not even taking into account the referee assault and riot that had erupted in the cage.

Despite its black eyes, though, UFC 45 was still a night of celebration, a time for many of us to come together to reflect on what had been accomplished during the last ten years. The show gave Elaine and me the opportunity to see some old acquaintances we hadn't heard from in a while.

Fred Ettish, the unfortunate victim of the UFC 2 beating and ridicule that followed, attended the show. It was the first time I'd seen him since his fateful 1994 appearance, and I told him that I felt bad for the way fans had treated him. He told me he appreciated my words and was happy for me that I'd been able to stick with the sport as long as I had.

Former commentator Jeff Blatnick was also in the crowd, as well as the UFC's previous owner, Bob Meyrowitz. Zuffa had given him tickets, and it was the first time he'd attended the show since he'd sold the promotion in 2001. Dana White seated Meyrowitz cageside and made sure he was treated well.

Afterward, Elaine and I had a late dinner with Jeff and Bob. It was weird for me because I was the only one still with the UFC, and I felt guilty. Blatnick was bitter that he wasn't with the promotion anymore, and I didn't blame him. He'd spent hours drafting the UFC's rule changes with me around UFC 22 and made many other contributions to the sport.

Meyrowitz also loved the UFC and had spent a lot of money fighting to keep it afloat. He commented on what a wonderful job Zuffa was doing with the show, which was gracious of him, but I could tell he wished it was still his. He regretted selling it, even though when he'd done it, he'd really had no choice.

With the old owner's stamp of approval, the new owners kept trying to push the sport into the mainstream. UFC 46 "Super Natural," held eleven weeks later at the Mandalay Bay Events Center in Las Vegas, was the first UFC to be held over the busy Super Bowl weekend. In the main event, there was another Octagon first when Vitor Belfort cut Randy Couture's eyelid open with his glove in their main event rematch.

At the opening bell, Belfort, who was grief stricken because his sister had gone missing in Brazil a few weeks beforehand, moved across the cage and threw a blinding left hand. The punch barely grazed Couture, but I watched the wrestler clinch with Belfort and squint one eye. It was definitely a closed-fisted punch; none of Belfort's fingers had been sticking out. Belfort pushed Couture against the cage, then eased up when he felt Couture's grip loosen.

I thought Couture's upper eyelid had been flipped inside out—just like kids do to themselves sometimes—and I wondered why he didn't just reach up and flip it back the right way. The thought that he might be cut never entered my mind. There was no blood and no real indication that the punch had cut him.

Suddenly, a single trickle of blood rolled down from his eye. It was time to bring the doctor in.

Dr. Margaret Goodman needed only a few seconds to investigate. She said, "He's been cut badly along the lash line. I can't let him continue."

It had been a legal punch, so an emotional Belfort was awarded the victory and the UFC light heavyweight championship. The entire sequence played out in front of an equally confused crowd, who'd come to see a fight and felt cheated by its disappointing conclusion.

After the event, Zuffa officials approached me and asked what had happened. I explained that the fingers of the gloves were pressed together with a stitch that pinched the two pieces of material together on each side, creating the bump that had cut Couture like a razor. There was no guarantee Couture would have won the fight, but the way he'd lost it hadn't been fair. I said I'd go back to the glove manufacturer to correct the problem.

I'd been involved with the UFC's glove development since Zuffa had bought the UFC three years earlier. Shortly after the purchase, Zuffa had asked me to look into finding the safest gloves I could. I spoke to Boxergenics, the company that was producing UFC gloves at the time. I also researched and sent out e-mails to companies like Harbinger and Century, asking if they'd like to make a glove specifically for the UFC. John Ouano, of the Ouano brand, was the only one to respond, so I started working with Ouano on the design. He kept sending me samples until I knew that what I was holding in my hands was what we wanted. After UFC 46, I went back to John Ouano, and we worked on the gloves until we had a better model ready. Later, the UFC would end its relationship with Ouano to sign a deal with Century, but John Ouano was a major contributor in

UFC 47

"It's On"
April 2, 2004
Mandalay Bay Events Center
Las Vegas, Nevada

Bouts I Reffed:
Mike Kyle vs. Wes Sims
Yves Edwards vs. Hermes Franca
Chuck Liddell vs. Tito Ortiz

It got so loud during the final few seconds of Ortiz-Liddell's first round that I couldn't hear anything, including the horn to signal the round's end. Thank God I heard the ten-second clap and started my usual countdown in my head. Ortiz missed the horn as well, so when I broke them up, Ortiz thought for an instant that I'd ended the fight on him, and he pushed me in the back. I didn't feel it at the time but later was told about it and saw it on the tape. Liddell iced Ortiz in the second round with a left hook directly to the eye, which crumpled him on the fence. Afterward Ortiz claimed he'd been poked in the eye, but it was a legal punch.

UFC 48

"Payback"
June 19, 2004
Mandalay Bay Events Center
Las Vegas, Nevada

Bouts I Reffed:
Evan Tanner vs. Phil Baroni
Ken Shamrock vs. Kimo Leopoldo

Referee Herb Dean made a call referees world-wide could be proud of in the heavyweight championship bout between Mir and Sylvia. Mir snagged Sylvia in an armbar from his back and used his muay Thai cup as a fulcrum to break Sylvia's bones. Dean saw the break and stopped the fight immediately, but because of the fighters' positions and the camera angle, no one else in the arena caught it. Imagine an arena filled with 10,000 people booing you while the injured fighter walks around like he's fine: a referee's nightmare. When the crowd finally saw the break from a better angle on the big screens, they changed their minds quickly. It was a small victory for MMA referees everywhere.

●

the evolution of MMA gloves and making them safer for the fighters.[12]

As the sport evolved, the UFC continued to flounder. Around UFC 40, I'd known the promotion was struggling. By UFC 45, I knew they were having big problems. I'd hear the conversations. Everyone knew Zuffa wasn't getting what it had expected out of its investment. The UFC was back on pay-per-view, but the numbers weren't good. The company was spending a lot more money than it was making.

Remember Tito Ortiz's entrance at UFC 30? Zuffa had paid something like $50,000 for the flame and fireworks display. Double that because they also had to test the display in front of the fire marshal during a rehearsal. That was $100,000 before the fighters even entered the cage. This was money Zuffa couldn't afford anymore.

So the big ramp and the elaborate entrances were done away with, and the floor layout was reconfigured to fit in more seating. Zuffa said it was because the promotion was moving toward a more legitimate sport presentation, like that of boxing, but the real reason was to save some change.

At that time, someone at Zuffa told me the UFC was nearing $40 million in the hole and if it didn't turn around, the Fertittas wouldn't be able to put any more money into it.

12. Ouano went on to produce gloves for World Extreme Cagefighting, another promotion owned by Zuffa, as well as other promotions like King of the Cage, while glove prototypes continue to evolve and improve.

The UFC was struggling, but it wouldn't go down without a fight. Zuffa wasn't afraid to make changes when things weren't working, and I'm fairly sure this was one of the reasons it would survive this desperate time.

One change Zuffa made involved marketing the fighters and the UFC product as a whole. Zuffa had quickly realized it couldn't control what happened with fighters. Lorenzo Fertitta had told me he wanted to build stars, and the promotion certainly had boosted a few, such as Tito Ortiz, Chuck Liddell, and Randy Couture, early on. However, from the undercard up to the main event, athletes withdrew all the time due to injury. Or even worse, Zuffa could spend a lot of time and money building up a particular fighter, and at a moment's notice, he could end up leaving the promotion.

Zuffa could control the rest of the product, however. A strong brand would carry the product as the stars came and went. This way of marketing was something both SEG and Zuffa were criticized for in the beginning because it wasn't the way it was done in boxing, where fighters were the emphasis. Most of the time, the fans couldn't tell you what company was promoting a boxing event, but they could tell you who the headliner was. Yet emphasizing the UFC brand over one or two star fighters proved a wise business decision for Zuffa.

Don't get me wrong. Zuffa treated the fighters well, certainly better than I'd seen other promotions do till that point. The fighters and at least one cornerman were flown into the host towns a few days early, put up in nice hotels, and given daily stipends for food. What could anyone ask for that the promotion wasn't already providing?

Some fighters, like Randy Couture, had issues with Zuffa. He looked at things the way he looked at them. I know he always felt like Zuffa was trying to get rid of him, but I never looked at it that way. If there was one thing most of the fighters could complain about, it was the amount of money they were making, especially when others were getting much bigger paydays from Pride in Japan.

But to be able to pay the fighters more, the UFC needed to begin turning a profit. Unfortunately, the product wasn't clicking with the consumers. There was too much of a negative stigma, and the UFC wasn't reaching far outside the core fan base that had been there when Zuffa had purchased the promotion in 2001. There had to be a way to get the message to a large audience faster.

I was hopeful when Dana White told me Zuffa was working on landing a reality show on one of the TV networks. He wasn't thrilled about it; he'd dreamed that, like boxing, the UFC would get its own live weekly fight night show. White told me Fertitta was the one who wanted to do the reality show because he'd allowed a producer to shoot a series called *American Casino* at one of his Las Vegas properties and had seen firsthand what the exposure could do for business.

It wouldn't be cheap. Zuffa would have to pay for all of the show's production costs to get the show on Spike TV, an up-and-coming cable network that catered to men and the only one that would agree to allow MMA on the airwaves. This would be a big opportunity for the UFC and the sport. White asked me to be a part of the show.

"I want you to come in and talk to the fighters about being a part of the UFC," White said.

I told him that wouldn't be a problem. That part of my involvement on the show never materialized, but I didn't mind. I thought anything that could bring attention to the fighters and the sport was worth trying, so I was content supporting the show in any way they needed me to.

The way White explained it to me, they were going to bring a bunch of fighters together and have them compete for a UFC contract. I didn't know how they were going to do it, and I wasn't privy to any of the development talks, but it quickly became obvious to me that the reality show was Zuffa's Hail Mary. If it didn't work, this would be it for the UFC.

About a year and a handful of events later, filming for *The Ultimate Fighter* began. Zuffa flew me to Las Vegas, and I reported to the set, which was a warehouse a few blocks off the Strip converted into the UFC Training Center.

The gym always appeared much bigger on the show than it was in person, but they did a nice job with it. There was a heavy bag area, a small ring, and, of course, an Octagon identical to the ones used at UFC events. Photographs of fighters in every stage of their banged-up glory hung throughout the hallways. The gym had production offices for Spike TV and Pilgrim Productions, which had produced *American Casino* and pitched *The Ultimate Fighter* (*TUF*) to the cable network with Zuffa.

I usually got changed in a spare office, then reported to the set. I was concerned about the fights and nothing else. Spike TV would usually shoot a single fight in one day. The Nevada commission, led by Executive Director Marc Ratner, was present to oversee the bouts.

Prior to entering the competition, the fighters signed UFC

contracts as thick as phone books and were cut off from the rest of the world for the shoot's duration in a house miles off the Strip.

Some of the fighters I knew, and some I'd never seen before. The fight I really remember from that first season was between Kenny Florian and Chris Leben. Florian, a lightweight fighting up at middleweight to participate on the show, was getting tossed and pushed around until he managed to cut Leben's forehead open with a standing elbow. I let the fight go for a bit until I had no choice but to bring the doctor in to check the cut, and he promptly stopped the fight. I felt bad for Leben because he was winning before one elbow took him out of advancing into the finals. Florian, a huge underdog, met Sanchez in the middleweight final, but lost.

For the next eight weeks, I made many one-day trips to Las Vegas, and each week the fighters in the gym were whittled down. The atmosphere of the fights was always strange because there wasn't an audience to cheer them on. You had the judges, the inspectors, the EMT workers, White, sometimes Lorenzo Fertitta, sometimes his brother Frank and maybe a few guests here and there sitting around the cage, but that was it. During that first season, the fighters who lost would leave the house immediately afterward and be taken to a separate location. By the end, there'd be two guys fighting and maybe twenty people, including the production team, watching them.

Nobody really asked me for the fight results when I'd get home because the show wasn't on anyone's radar yet. I wouldn't have been able to tell them anyway. The entire cast and crew signed confidentiality agreements.

The Ultimate Fighter reality show debuted on January 17, 2005, airing at 11:00 p.m. following one of the World Wrestling Entertainment (WWE) programs, as Spike TV was trying to get a strong lead-in.

I remember watching it alone at home and thinking, *Holy Christ, they have a guy pissing on another guy's bed.* My dad called me afterward and asked why the UFC was letting that happen on TV. But I knew young guys were going to eat it up. I knew the show's bad boy Chris Leben was one of the toughest kids in there, and I'd originally picked him to make it to the finals.

We were told that the show needed to get a 1.0 rating to get off to a good start and keep its spot on the cable network. The first show drew a 1.2 and seemed to gain a little more of an audience each week. By the end of the season, the show was being called a success.

UFC 49

"Unfinished Business"
August 21, 2004
MGM Grand Garden Arena
Las Vegas, Nevada

Bouts I Reffed:
Justin Eilers vs. Mike Kyle
Randy Couture vs. Vitor Belfort

Eilers made his UFC debut with a great knockout win over Kyle.

Couture demonstrated once again that he was Belfort's Kryptonite, pulverizing the Brazilian for three straight rounds. Belfort was so downtrodden after the third round that he didn't even stand to go back to his corner. I asked if he was all right and told him he had to get up and go back to his corner, which he did, but the realization that he couldn't stop what Couture was doing had already set in, and the bout was called shortly after.

The first season of *The Ultimate Fighter* culminated with a live finale four months later at the Cox Pavilion on the University of Nevada, Las Vegas campus. The venue held about 2,500 people, and the UFC still had to give away tickets to fill it. That was about to change.

All sixteen fighters featured on the show were paired up again and given fights. Forrest Griffin, a former police officer from Georgia, and Stephan Bonnar, a Carlson Gracie Jiu-Jitsu student from Chicago, fought a three-round stand-up tug-of-war in the finals. I got to watch this one from my seat while Herb Dean refereed.

Griffin earned the unanimous decision to take the first *Ultimate Fighter* title and a six-figure contract with the promotion.

The UFC was so impressed with both fighters, however, that Bonnar also got a contract. I thought it was a classy thing for the UFC to do. Bonnar had left his heart in the cage, and there shouldn't have been a loser after such a compelling fight.

I refereed the main event, a light heavyweight bout between Ken Shamrock and UFC newcomer Rich Franklin. Standing in the center of the Octagon, I wondered how this fight could top the previous one. It didn't, but it's still one of the fights I get asked about the most. Shamrock and Franklin traded punches for a bit until, out of nowhere, Shamrock slipped. He kind of jumped down and went for Franklin's leg. Shamrock had a good lock on Franklin's leg and torqued it, but Franklin worked his way out of it. Franklin then pounded the piss out of Shamrock, and I had to step in to stop it.

I've been asked about Shamrock's slip many times. I admit I thought it looked odd in the moment, but I've seen fighters do stranger things during fights. I've been asked outright if I think Shamrock threw the fight, but I don't. First of all, Shamrock was the star of that fight and the favorite to win. I honestly think he was trying to drop levels. The leg lock that followed was real, as was the beating he took at the hands of Franklin afterward. It wouldn't have done Shamrock any good to throw the fight.

After Zuffa had taken over the UFC in 2001, I'd never seen a worked fight in the Octagon. I knew that was something Fertitta and White would have no part of. For one, Fertitta could lose his Las Vegas casino license for any involvement in fixing a fight that had gambling lines placed on it. People also have to remember that not every UFC fight will be a barn burner, and sometimes they can be downright boring. What separates MMA from pro wrestling is that MMA is real. Promoters can't make every fight a Griffin-Bonnar epic, and they certainly can't control the outcome. That's mostly up to the fighters.

After UFC 51, my next assignment came from the other side of the world.

Scott Coker, then working with the Japanese kickboxing promotion K-1, called to ask if I'd like to referee a special MMA fight between sumo legend Akebono, whose real name is Chad Rowan, and Royce Gracie at "Dynamite," K-1's annual New Year's Eve show.

Out of loyalty and respect, I went to Dana and asked for his blessing. At the time, the Japanese MMA scene was still killing the UFC in attendance. I told Dana I'd get paid $5,000 to referee the fight, which was actually appealing to him.

"For $5,000? Yeah, you can go do it," he said. "Take them for all the fucking money you can."

I also thought this would be the last time I'd get to referee a Royce Gracie fight, and I wanted to be there. I thought it was a silly matchup, though, and felt sorry for Akebono. In 1993, he'd been the first foreign-born wrestler to become yoko-zuna, the highest rank one could achieve in the sumo system.

UFC 50

"The War of '04"
October 22, 2004
Boardwalk Hall
Atlantic City, New Jersey

Bouts I Reffed:
Evan Tanner vs. Robbie Lawler
Matt Hughes vs. Georges St. Pierre
Tito Ortiz vs. Patrick Cote

I noticed that the younger, less experienced St. Pierre wouldn't look at Hughes in their stare down, which told me he was intimidated. St. Pierre performed well until he made a beginner's mistake trying to hold on to a Kimura from the bottom without having control of his opponent's legs or body. Hughes capitalized by spinning around for the armbar, nailing the tapout with a second left on the clock.

A rubber match between Ortiz and Mezger fell apart when something happened to Mezger in training. Cote, a young and fairly green fighter, stepped in against Ortiz in the main event on short notice. Personally, I would have loved to see Ortiz and Mezger go at it one more time to close the book on that rivalry.

UFC 51

"Super Saturday"
February 5, 2005
Mandalay Bay Events Center
Las Vegas, Nevada

Bouts I Reffed:
Nick Diaz vs. Drew Fickett
Andrei Arlovski vs. Tim Sylvia
Tito Ortiz vs. Vitor Belfort

Diaz, whose style I'd admired from afar, liked to call his opponents "bitch" during fights. Every time he connected, he started saying things like, "Oh, that hurts. Come on, bitch, fight." I'd had other fighters curse in the cage, but Diaz took it to another level. I finally warned him to stop or I'd take points. Cursing an opponent is listed as a foul in the Unified Rules. Regardless, Diaz still easily stopped opponent Drew Fickett with strikes in the first round for the victory.

Ortiz and Belfort finally met in the main event, a bout that had originally been scheduled to happen back at the ill-fated UFC 33. A treat to see up close, Belfort broke Ortiz's nose in the first round and almost finished him in the second, but heart and guts kept Ortiz going. Ortiz got a split decision nod.

He was a major reason the sport flourished on TV in Japan in the 1990s, and he'd been in over 1,000 matches, becoming a grand champion many times over. Now the Japanese were making a freak show out of him. I didn't worry so much about his safety; I just felt that his honor and pride would get damaged in the fight.

The 500-pound Akebono was athletic for his size, but he wasn't a real fighter. He could hardly move his body weight once he hit the ground. On top of that, he wasn't especially strong.

The match reminded me of the fight I'd refereed at UFC 3 some ten years before between the 600-plus-pound Emanuel Yarbrough and Keith Hackney. The difference here was that Royce wouldn't be able to hurt Akebono by punching him; he'd submit him.

Elaine and I flew to Osaka, Japan, and Royce approached me right away in the hotel. I hadn't talked to him in many years, since he and Rorion had broken away from SEG back before UFC 6. Royce said, "I told them I wouldn't do this fight unless you refereed it."

I hadn't known Royce had specifically requested me, and it felt good to hear. By this time, Royce had branched out on his own from Rorion as well, so there were no ill feelings on either side.

The fight itself lasted a little more than two minutes. Akebono rushed Royce at the bell and literally fell on him, but Royce, wearing only his gi pants, escaped and got back to his feet. Royce then pulled Akebono into his guard and trapped him in an omoplata shoulder lock. The trapped sumo wrestler couldn't free himself, but the pressure on his shoulder wasn't enough to make Akebono tap out, so Royce submitted him with a wristlock on top of that. The usually silent Japanese crowd, 50,000 strong, exploded into cheers.

Back home in the United States, Zuffa was winning some minor battles in its war to legitimize MMA. Around UFC 46 and 47, fan interest seemed to pick up a little with the introduction of the Couture-Liddell rivalry in the light heavyweight division.

The second true rivalry of the Zuffa era had been born out of chance. Couture, coming off two losses in the heavyweight division, had agreed to drop down a weight division and fight Liddell for the interim light heavyweight title after champion Tito Ortiz had turned down the matchup due to an injury. In reality, Ortiz hadn't wanted to fight Liddell because he'd had a lot of problems sparring with him in the past. So while Ortiz had stayed out of the Octagon tending to injuries, movie roles, and other commitments, Couture had slid into the role as headliner against Liddell at UFC 43.

Most people hadn't given the nearly forty-year-old Couture a chance against Liddell. I'd known Liddell would have to avoid the clinch, where Couture would surely try to trap him, and I'd thought he would tag Couture before he could get ahold of him. I was wrong. Couture outstruck Liddell and got a third-round stoppage in one of the most surprising fights ever in the UFC.

Their rematch at UFC 52 on April 16, 2005, at the MGM Grand Garden Arena in Las Vegas, was something different. In reaction to their first bout, most people now thought Liddell couldn't beat Couture, though at this point Liddell had been on one hell of a run and had even taken out Ortiz at UFC 47 along the way. There was a real swing in public opinion for this fight, and the buildup from both appearing as coaches on *The Ultimate Fighter* made it even more interesting.

PHOTO BY LINDA HAMILTON PHOTOGRAPHY
WWW.LINDAHAMILTONPHOTO.COM

Outside our home in Agua Dulce with our English bulldog Tapout

Backstage, Liddell was his usual low-key self, but he was ready to go.

Couture is always easy in the locker room, smiling and joking. He never really shows a chink in the armor if he's carrying in any problems. This night wasn't any different.

I left both locker rooms unable to predict anything but that it would be a great fight.

It was. The rematch attracted over 12,000 paying fans for a $2.5 million gate, a record for Zuffa at the time. Liddell had his revenge, tagging Couture when he overcommitted to a punch and lost his balance along the fence. Couture was knocked out for the first time in his career, and I was right there to put a stop to any further beating from Liddell.

No matter who won, it was a great ending to the show. It was now clear that the UFC and the sport were heading into a brighter future.

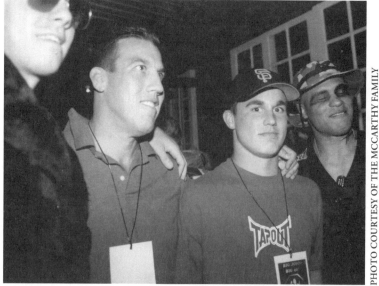

"Skyscrape," me, Ron, and the one and only Charles "Mask" Lewis

The actual first row seating at a show in Kuwait with manager extraordinaire Monte Cox

THE ART OF THE CALL

They say that seeing is believing,
but if you believe it, you will see it!

—Charles "Mask" Lewis Jr.

The most difficult thing about being a mixed martial arts referee is striving for that perfect bout where the fighters do everything right and you do everything right in response. It's no different than sinking a long putt in golf: you'll hit it now and then but not every time.

This job is all about stopping the fight at just the right second. I always think of a fight as a triangle with its point at the top. I can't stop the fight on the right side, where the bout hasn't completely played out and fans might feel it's early, or the left side, where I'm letting a fighter take more damage than he should.

I aim for just the right point in time and sometimes hit it perfectly. I can't overemphasize how important that can be in certain fights. A handful of seconds can determine whether a fighter will be able to leave the cage under his own power. I never felt this more than at UFC 64 "Unstoppable" on October 14, 2006, at the Mandalay Bay Events Center in Las Vegas, when middleweight champion and former Ohio math teacher Rich Franklin defended his title against Brazilian striker Anderson Silva.

Zuffa had tried for years to bring Silva into the promotion, and when he had finally signed, the former Chute Boxe fighter had annihilated brawler Chris Leben on his feet in forty-nine seconds in his Octagon debut nearly four months earlier.

We all knew the combination of Silva's speed and accuracy with punches could make him dangerous, but none of us were quite prepared for the way he would handle Franklin.

When Franklin and Silva clinched, I could see right away that Franklin couldn't get out of the Brazilian's plumb, a grip in which Silva locked his hands behind Franklin's neck to keep him close. Now, this was the champion of the world at the time, so you couldn't say he hadn't been taught this. In the heat of the moment, Franklin just didn't respond with an effective countermove. What he'd been taught and what had worked for him in the past weren't working against the skill level Silva brought to the cage. I think Franklin thought he would be able to muscle his way out of it, but when he tried to weave his hands inside to replumb and establish the dominant position, Silva's hold was too tight.

Franklin took some huge knee shots to his midsection while he stood helpless in Silva's grip. Maybe when you're watching from the outside, a knee to the body doesn't seem like a big deal. Trust me, it's a big deal. It knocks the life right out of you.

Every time Franklin wiggled free from Silva's grip, Silva would just clamp it back on. After a while, I didn't even look at Silva; I just kept moving to every angle so I wouldn't lose sight of Franklin's face.

They always say a fighter has a puncher's chance, but in instances like these, it's just a saying. Now it becomes a matter of when a referee can get the fighter out because he's overwhelmed and can't protect himself.

That was my job that night. It just happened that it was for the middleweight championship of the world, and nobody had expected a domination like that. I hit the triangle perfectly that night at that point when Franklin went down from a final knee that crushed his nose into his face. Three minutes into the bout, I called it off. If I'd let it go longer, who knows what else Franklin would have left with besides a broken nose.

The right moment isn't always so clear, and sometimes I've let bouts go longer than I should have. It's never on purpose; I always worry about a fighter taking too much damage. But it's never an exact science because no two fights are alike.

A bout I think I let go too long was at UFC 63 "Hughes vs. Penn" on September 23, 2006, at the Honda Center in Anaheim. Rashad Evans took on Jason Lambert, and I read that fight all wrong. I gave Lambert too much credit and Evans not enough.

Evans, the winner of season two of *The Ultimate Fighter*, mounted Lambert and began throwing down strikes. Lambert was trying to fire back, but he was absorbing too many shots. He got hurt and went out cold before I registered that it was time to step in. I shouldn't have let it go that far.

As soon as I walked out of that cage, I was thinking about that fight. I constantly dissect fights like this to figure out where I screwed up, where I should have stopped them, and why I didn't. I never stop thinking about them.

Every time I run into Lambert, I think of this fight. Even though I've refereed Lambert in fights where he's had great victories, none of those come to mind. Rashad Evans does.

I don't like to see any athlete get hurt or embarrassed in front of his family, friends, and fans because I stopped a bout too early or too late.

When I step into the cage in search of that perfect fight, I always tell myself to be in the moment. I block everything else out. No cameraman tells me where to stand or to get out of the way, though a few brave ones have tried. I stand where I have the optimum vantage point, and no one else determines where that is.

Most people think they could referee as they sit on their couches and are fed multiple camera angles one after the other. But they really have no idea what it's like to be the person inside the cage with the fighters. Every bout a referee walks into can be the one that goes desperately wrong.

Everyone on the outside—every fan watching in the arena or from home—has an interest in watching the fight, but that's as far as it goes. If something goes wrong, they can walk away. They don't know what it's like to be the one with two lives in his hands.

I'm always looking for which fighter is starting to win the fight and which one is starting to receive more damage. I've learned to stand on the open side of the weaker fighter, where I'll be able to read them the fastest. I have a signal for doctors when they enter the cage to let them know if I think the fight should be stopped, though it's always their final decision.

The last thing a referee thinks about in the cage is the fans. If the crowd boos, the crowd boos. Entertaining the audience is not in a referee's job description, but protecting the fighter is. Everything else is a distraction.

A referee can't get caught up in the distractions, including his own fears. *Am I going to make the right call? Will I screw up?* These are valid questions, but they can't dictate my actions. What I have to do is slow things down. I have criteria to follow, and when the time comes I do what I'm supposed to do.

A referee has to try to be selfless. The media always says a good referee is the one you don't even notice in the cage. Personally, I don't care whether I'm on TV or in a ballroom refereeing a match where nobody sees me. As long as it's a good, competitive fight, I'm happy.

Still, just like the fighters, almost every referee wants to do the big fights. Some beg to be in the main event on TV, but they're not there for the right reasons. When they finally get that fight and feel the pressure, many of them freeze.

I guess one of the greatest fears a referee can have is looking stupid getting hit or even knocked out in the cage. I've never thought about that once in there. In this line of work, you're going to get hit. All the time, I see referees go in for a stoppage and turn their heads or stick their butts into the fighters and fall on them to avoid getting hit. A referee shouldn't be concerned about getting hurt. He should be making sure the fighter he's stopping the bout to protect doesn't get hit again. If he gets hit in the process, then he's done the right thing. I know the job I signed up for, and I just try to protect my chin.

I also always tell myself that things won't go the way I want them to. Weird things can happen in a fight, so I have to be ready for anything. In my eighteen years of officiating, I've seen a lot, but I'm positive I still haven't seen it all. I've been in the Octagon when fighters have farted, and I've had to keep a straight face. I've listened to full-blown conversations between fighters as they beat the piss out of one another. I've been there midfight when the arena's lights have gone out, leaving me in the pitch black with two fighters grappling at my feet. I've been there when fighters have accidentally soiled their shorts, but everybody had to keep going.

Being a referee isn't always fun or comfortable. I've had to tell fighters to take a shower before bouts because they smelled so bad I believed they'd have an unfair advantage.

A referee won't always be popular. Everyone will have an opinion about the job I do, whether good or bad. If I have to make a decision or stop the fight for some reason, half the fans will think I did the right thing and the other will think I sucked. Journalists will sometimes write about me, and I'll wish that for once in their lives they could really just get a clue or be in a referee's shoes in that flash of a second in the cage. I've had to learn to take critiques in stride. I'll never make everybody happy.

What makes it all rewarding is the relationships I've gained. I don't know if it's because the rest of the world has always seemed to be against it, but mixed martial arts has always felt like a family to me. I see the managers, agents, cornermen, cutmen, and fighters at show after show and know we all share a common bond.

I cherish my friendships with people like Monte Cox, still the most understatedly powerful manager and one of the funniest SOBs in the business. I met Cox around UFC 13, when he asked me for an autograph for his son. Cox would go on to manage three UFC champions simultaneously and oversee the careers of some of the most famous fighters from Pat Miletich's camp, like Matt Hughes and Jens Pulver. I enjoyed talking with Cox about the fighters and potential matchups over our meals at the shows. I didn't always agree with him, but he has a great knack for telling his funny fighter stories. Cox would do just about anything for his fighters. He's even let some of them live with him and his family while they've gotten their starts.

Cutmen like Leon Tabbs and Jacob "Stitch" Duran, fight coordinator Burt Watson, Nevada State Athletic Commission Representative Colleen Murphy, and others are the real people of the sport, the ones who go above and beyond behind the scenes to make it as great as it is. And then, of course, there are the fighters.

I don't have a favorite fighter. I like them all. I'm not saying that to be impartial. They're all different, but they all have the balls to step up and do what others are afraid to. What most people don't understand is the fear involved with going out there. It's not so much a fear of the fight but of failure. You're putting yourself out there for everyone to judge you.

When you're an NFL player and you go out on the field with the rest of your team, you can hide. There's a chance you'll be exposed in that play you don't get right, but most of the game, you're shielded among the rest of your team.

In fighting, there's no hiding. All eyes are on you and your opponent. When you're out there in the cage, with the lights blaring and the crowd cheering and camera bulbs flashing, it's incredibly stressful. Fighters are surrounded by all these people—trainers, family members, teammates, cornermen, and fans—expecting so much and judging their skill based on this one fight. "You're only as good as your last fight," as the popular saying goes.

It's how fighters handle the pressure that gives me so much respect for them. It also tells me a lot about who they are. I get to see a lot of this firsthand backstage. Some fighters are laughing and joking as if they've almost forgotten they're about to go out in front of thousands to show what they've got. Then there are the ones throwing up, not communicating, or standing still while their minds are going a thousand miles an hour. If I could bet on the sport, I'd be a rich man. I can't tell you how many times I've left the locker rooms knowing exactly which fighter would win.

Not a lot of people can climb into the cage and lay it all on the line. That's what makes fighters special. They can.

Maybe because of their hazardous choice of occupation, fighters often have great senses of humor. A lot of them are pranksters, which is something I can appreciate, of course. I've had some funny moments with fighters over the years, but I think Scott Smith, a middleweight from California who's fought for both the UFC and Strikeforce, got me the best.

I was making my usual rounds backstage one night when Smith told me he had a problem. I don't remember if he was fighting or cornering a teammate that night, but he looked concerned, and my natural response was to help him if I could.

"I think I have a hernia," Smith told me, "but I don't want to show the doctors."

With an entire roomful of cornermen standing around, Smith walked me to the side for a little privacy. There, he pulled out the waistline of his pants and motioned for me to take a peek.

"What do you think?" he asked seriously.

I looked down to see he'd positioned one of his testicles to protrude from his shorts at its maximum density.

The room erupted in laughter. I'd fallen right into it, and, yeah, it was a good one.

Sometimes it's hard for fans to grasp that fighters are people too. Being around them so much, I really get a sense of who they are, especially after watching them grow up in the cage over years of shows. I'm a referee, and I'm impartial when I step into the cage, but I've certainly been touched by fighters and others who have traveled through the sport, some right alongside me.

I was deeply affected by the death of former UFC middleweight champion Evan Tanner, who succumbed to heat exposure while in a California desert in September of 2008. Elaine and I had both watched the quiet but intellectual Tanner struggle with alcoholism when we'd first met him at UFC 18. Tanner would drink heavily at the after parties, sometimes to the point that he wouldn't remember what he'd done.

One night, Tanner got especially inebriated, picked up Elaine, put her on his shoulder, and refused to put her down. Then he fell and dropped Elaine on her head. We weren't sure he remembered it until he brought it up in an interview years later while talking about his alcoholism and how embarrassed he was that he'd done that to her. Tanner apologized to Elaine shortly after that.

Still, Tanner was a self-made fighter and a darn good one at that. A loner by nature, he learned jiu-jitsu by watching videos, before later joining the formidable Team Quest with Randy Couture, Matt Lindland, and Dan Henderson in Oregon. We watched Tanner win the UFC middleweight title against David Terrell at UFC 51 only to lose it four months later. Tanner's journey to a UFC championship title was unique, which is why I think many people were inspired by him. His first teacher was his VHS player, but that didn't stop him from becoming a champion.

I was also impacted when Charles Lewis Jr., a clothing entrepreneur of the famous Tapout brand, died in a car accident in 2009. Lewis, known as "Mask" because he always wore colorful superhero-like makeup, championed the sport and preached its merits as he sold his Tapout T-shirts from the trunk of his car in event parking lots.

Lewis was an incredibly giving person and became quite close to my family. My youngest son wore Tapout wristbands for nearly a year straight until we ordered him to take them off because they were so filthy, and I know my daughter had a crush on Lewis for quite some time. I even named one of my English bulldogs Tapout. At events, I always knew when Lewis and the Tapout crew were approaching because he'd yell, "Biiiig Joooohn!" from across the crowded room. It always embarrassed me, but I knew I had a true friend in Lewis.

Speaking at Lewis' memorial was one of the hardest things I've ever done. My friend had been too young and full of life to be gone.

In their own ways, Tanner and Lewis touched many lives in the sport. They both used the same simple term: "Believe." When I think about the way they both incorporated it in their lives, it tells me a lot. Every time I see that word, I think of these two people. It brings a smile to my face and reminds me, *Just believe. Don't let people put limits on you. Do what you need to do how you need to do it.*

One of the most uplifting fighters I ever got to be around was Justin Eilers, a former Iowa State middle linebacker who'd been recruited to UFC champion Pat Miletich's Iowa powerhouse gym by his roommate and former UFC lightweight champion Jens Pulver. Eilers was a good athlete and a free spirit and could strike up a friendly conversation with practically anybody.

I had a running joke with Eilers about an incident when he'd gotten a little too intoxicated and wound up making out with a transvestite in a club, something his Miletich teammates ruthlessly ridiculed him for. I would always come into Eilers' locker room and go over the rules and procedures before the fight in my usual serious manner. I'd finish with the same question I ask every fighter: "Do you have anything else you want to go over or any questions at all?" Once I got the "No, I'm good," from fighters, I'd leave the locker room. But with Justin, I always had just one more question: "Justin, if it's a girl from the waist up, does that make it okay?"

He'd always start cussing at me and then laugh, the prefight tension broken. "I'm telling you, she had some of the best tits I've ever seen," he'd say.

At UFC 53 "Heavy Hitters," held on June 4, 2005, at the Boardwalk Hall in Atlantic City, New Jersey, Eilers challenged Andrei Arlovski for his heavyweight title. I had to stop the fight prematurely when Eilers fell to the ground cradling his leg. He'd blown out his knee.

It would be the last fight I'd have the privilege to referee him in. The day after Christmas in 2008, Eilers was shot and killed by his stepfather, an ex-sheriff, during a dispute at a family gathering. It was another senseless loss for the MMA world.

Tanner, Lewis, and Eilers all contributed to the sport in their own way. Their individual efforts helped propel the sport to new heights in mid-2005.

On the heels of Couture-Liddell II, UFC 53 was the show where I felt the atmosphere changing at the events. The strangest thing I noticed was that fans were now packing the arena way ahead of the start of the show.

UFC 54

"Boiling Point"
August 20, 2005
MGM Grand Garden Arena
Las Vegas, Nevada

Bouts I Reffed:
Chuck Liddell vs. Jeremy Horn

Now that Liddell was the UFC light heavyweight champion, Liddell got to avenge one of two career defeats to Horn, who'd choked him unconscious with an arm-triangle at UFC 13 in March of 1999. It was a hard fight to watch as Liddell hit Horn with incredibly hard punches. Remember: in the cage, I can hear and feel how heavy some of the punches and kicks are and the wheezing of an athlete who can't breathe correctly. Horn put up a great fight but got knocked down a few times. When Horn advised me that he couldn't see the punches coming anymore, I stopped the fight.

When Forrest Griffin, who was fresh off his win over Stephan Bonnar at *The Ultimate Fighter* finale two months earlier in Las Vegas, made his entrance, he was practically accosted by crazy fans trying to touch him as he made his way to the cage. When Griffin won his fight against Canadian Bill Mahood, the crowd blew the top off the place. Griffin got the kind of reception reserved for Tito Ortiz, Randy Couture, and Chuck Liddell—fighters who had toiled in the UFC for years.

It was clear right then and there that the reality show had already impacted the UFC's popularity. The promotion often refers to the series as its Trojan horse because it was the vehicle they used to bring mixed martial arts to the uninitiated masses. It wasn't the live fight show Dana White had envisioned to do the job, but the public's obsession with reality TV couldn't have come at a better time for the sport. The story goes that Spike TV head Brian Diamond struck a handshake deal with White and Fertitta for the second season of *TUF* and more live *Fight Night* events in the alleyway behind the Cox Pavilion only minutes after Griffin and Bonnar had knocked the tar out of each other.

Griffin-Bonnar became a "watercooler fight," the one talked about in offices across the country Monday morning. The ratings were the sport's highest to date in the United States, with 2.6 million viewers tuning in. The finale was the highest-rated program on both cable and broadcast TV that night for men ages eighteen through thirty-four, which is the coveted demographic for advertisers. Here at UFC 53, more than four years and $40 million later, Zuffa's purchase of the UFC looked like it might finally turn out to be a worthwhile investment.

Zuffa used its big break to its best possible advantage. When the second season of *The Ultimate Fighter* debuted on Spike TV that August, UFC welterweight champion Matt Hughes and middleweight titleholder Rich Franklin were cast as the new coaches. What better way to familiarize fans with their champions than to have them broadcasted into millions of homes each week?

I returned to referee some of the fights on the show, and when it concluded in November to steady ratings, both Hughes and Franklin had already been assigned to headline UFC 56 against their respective challengers two weeks later. Zuffa had momentum, and it wasn't stopping now.

UFC 55

"Fury"
October 7, 2005
Mohegan Sun Arena
Uncasville, Connecticut

Bouts I Reffed:
Marcio Cruz vs. Keigo Kunihara
Joe Riggs vs. Chris Lytle
Andrei Arlovski vs. Paul Buentello

Buentello rushed in throwing a jab–right hand combo that Arlovski dropped under while launching his own counter overhand right. Luckily I was on the side where I could see the effect on Buentello, who clearly went out when Arlovski connected. Buentello fell forward onto Arlovski, who was bent forward from ducking. Buentello slid off Arlovski and hit the canvas, which woke him up. The crowd booed until the replay, which clearly showed that Buentello had been knocked out. Buentello came to, asked me what had happened, then complained. However, Buentello's wife thanked me afterward for stopping the fight and protecting her husband. Nothing could have made me feel better about the job I had just done.

At UFC 57 "Liddell vs. Couture 3" on February 4, 2006, at the Mandalay Bay Events Center in Las Vegas, I got to referee the third and final bout between the two stars and *TUF* season one coaches. Their exposure on the show had made Liddell and Couture Zuffa's most recognizable fighters, and they each had a win over the other, so the rubber match made perfect sense.

At the top of the bout, I thought Couture was fighting really smart. He got hit with a big shot that busted up his nose, which

UFC 56

"Full Force"
November 19, 2005
MGM Grand Garden Arena
Las Vegas, Nevada

Bouts I Reffed:
Thiago Alves vs. Ansar Chalangov
Matt Hughes vs. Joe Riggs
Rich Franklin vs. Nate Quarry

Franklin-Quarry ended in spectacular fashion for the crowd when Quarry fell back like a stiff tree from Franklin's last punch, but I wasn't happy with the outcome. I'm not saying I cared who won or lost, but Quarry took substantial damage and was out there trying to survive as much as he was trying to win. The fans were thrilled because they had a dramatic and definitive ending to the fight, but I knew it was over before that punch ever landed. I just wasn't able to protect Quarry from that final blow.

was bleeding a lot, but after much effort he took Liddell down in the last thirty seconds.

It went into the second round, but Liddell caught Couture again in the first two minutes. Couture went down and tried to flail his arms and legs to keep Liddell off him, but Liddell connected again.

I watched Couture's arms fall and his head bounce against the canvas. He came to from the impact as I was coming in. Liddell could have caused more damage if I hadn't stepped in.

I was pleased with this stoppage, even after Couture told the press he hadn't felt out of it at any point. Fighters who've been knocked out often claim they weren't, so I don't ever take it personally. They don't know what's happened because they've lost that little piece of time. The two most popular lines for fighters during these times are "What happened?" and "Why is my opponent putting on his shirt?"

Throughout 2005, the UFC's future seemed to get steadily brighter. In August, Spike TV debuted *Ultimate Fight Night*, later rebranded *UFC Fight Night*, a two-hour live fight show featuring the previous *TUF* season's fighters, which would serve as the lead-in to the reality show's next season debut.

I don't think the pay-per-view numbers took off that year. Zuffa never released the buy numbers, though Lorenzo Fertitta or Dana White would sometimes share them with me.

However, the live crowds were consistently growing, and it

would take me a bit longer to leave the arena, as I'd be asked for a few more autographs and pictures each time.

UFC 59 "Reality Check," held on April 15, 2006, at the Arrowhead Pond in Anaheim was a bittersweet moment for me. On the bright side, it was the first UFC ever held in my home state. After fifteen years of traveling across the country and the globe to referee fights, I had to get in my car and drive only one hour south this time.

I'd spoken before the California State Athletic Commission at its public meetings in the months prior as it locked down its own set of regulations to oversee the sport in the Golden State. I defended the Unified Rules already widely utilized stateside, much to the chagrin of Pride Fighting Championships' executives from Japan, who were also in attendance to try to get some of their own rules recognized in the key state.

I never had a problem with Pride or their rules, but it had taken California five years to finally approve MMA's legalization with a four-to-one vote. Pride's requests would hold up the regulation process for another six months to a year. To me, that was crap. I figured they should let the legalization go through entirely, then attempt to put in an addendum that allowed for what they were asking. I have heard some people say that I fought to keep Pride out of the United States, but that's not true. I was just fighting to get MMA going here as fast as possible.

UFC 58

"USA vs. Canada"
March 4, 2006
Mandalay Bay Events Center
Las Vegas, Nevada

Bouts I Reffed:
Nate Marquardt vs. Joe Doerksen
Rich Franklin vs. David Loiseau

Franklin-Loiseau was highly anticipated, as Loiseau was a talented striker who liked to throw spinning back kicks, flying knees, and landed elbows that cut and incapacitated quality opponents. But it was Franklin, an unorthodox southpaw, who put a beatdown on the French Canadian.

Between rounds, I heard Franklin tell his cornerman Jorge Gurgel his hand was broken (he also broke a foot). Gurgel looked straight at Franklin and said, "Just keep hitting him with it, and it will go numb."

What people didn't know was Loiseau was having problems with his management that were sapping his focus. I'd noticed Loiseau's tension and anxiety in the locker room beforehand, then watched Franklin bludgeon his face over five rounds until he resembled the Elephant Man.

Ironically, UFC 59 marked the first UFC when I wasn't assigned to the main event fight. This wasn't a really big deal for me, but it upset Elaine because she knew why the commission had decided not to assign me.

About a month prior, I'd been offered the main event bout in a Strikeforce show, which would be the first regulated MMA event in the state. The commission was kind about it. Executive Officer Armando Garcia said I'd earned the honor of officiating the fight for all I'd done in the sport.

However, I felt I needed to turn down the assignment.

I had a personal issue with the fight because it paired former UFC champion Frank Shamrock against Cesar Gracie, a Brazilian jiu-jitsu black belt who'd never entered an MMA fight in his life. I told the commission if this were a boxing match, they never would have approved it. The commission and Gracie went to great lengths to prove Gracie had a record of fourteen wins and zero losses back in Brazil. However, I knew he was just a grappler, a good grappler, but not a person who'd been under the pressure of performing in an MMA match in front of thousands of people the way Shamrock had. When a grappler who's never been hit in a real fight gets struck in the face and he's not used to it, things can go bad for him quickly.

The proof was in the pudding. Shamrock needed one punch to crumble Gracie for a twenty-second finish. I'm glad it didn't go longer, because I didn't want to see Gracie get seriously hurt.

But since I didn't support the fight that the CSAC's executive officer had approved, I sat out a UFC main event for the first time.

Honestly, I preferred the bouts I was assigned to at UFC 59 because they were evenly matched. Tito Ortiz and Forrest Griffin went to a split decision. It was also great to have my family with me for part of fight week. My dad and children sat together in the audience, something we couldn't swing often at the out-of-state shows.

MMA's passage in California was a coup for many more in the sport as well. A number of fighters and their camps lived in the Golden State, so it was a hotbed market that the UFC didn't hesitate to tap into. Following the success of UFC 59 in Anaheim, which drew 13,000 paying customers, UFC 60 "Hughes vs. Gracie" was scheduled for the 20,000-seat STAPLES Center in Los Angeles.

In the main event, UFC welterweight champion Matt Hughes faced a returning Royce Gracie in a special nontitle bout. Royce had taken a few fights overseas but hadn't competed in the Octagon since UFC 5 in April of 1995.

I had mixed feelings about it. I knew why the UFC was making the bout: to illustrate the difference between the UFC now and the UFC then and to pump Hughes up as this unbeatable star who wrecks past champions. Businesswise, it was a smart move. The name Royce Gracie still drew a lot of interest from the casual fan who didn't buy all of the pay-per-views. Royce had done so much in helping to create the sport and had carried himself in such a respectful and noble manner, and people were interested in seeing him return to the house he'd built.

There was no doubt in my mind that Royce absolutely felt he could win, but I just didn't see it. Obviously Royce had his jiu-jitsu, but Hughes wasn't one of the befuddled fighters Royce had met at the early shows. Like any other fighter of this time, Hughes knew jiu-jitsu and was damn good at it.

On top of that, they were completely different guys physically. Hughes was powerful and could grind his opponents down, while Royce's wiry figure required that he achieve positional leverage to overtake his opponent.

I felt Royce couldn't hurt Hughes standing up, and if Hughes wanted to keep it on its feet, he could. Royce wouldn't be able to take the former collegiate wrestler down unless he hurt him standing, and that wasn't likely to happen. In other words, Hughes could take the fight wherever he wanted to.

It broke my heart when Hughes flattened out Royce hard and crushed his face into the canvas. It wasn't that I cared who won or lost. I simply felt bad that in the end, just as with 99 percent of fighters who compete till the age of forty or beyond, Royce was on the receiving end and there was nothing he could do to stop it.

Royce dragged himself back up to his knees, but Hughes muscled him flat onto his stomach and started hitting the sides of his head. Royce had nothing for Hughes. I told Royce the same thing I tell all fighters: "Move. Get out." All I was looking for was for Royce to try and move himself out of the horrible position he was in.

But Royce just lay there taking shots, each one denting his pride a little bit more than the last. I knew Royce's wife and kids were sitting in the front row, so when it was obvious Royce couldn't come back, I promptly jumped in.

As I stood center cage with Hughes on my one side and Royce on the other, I spoke to my former teacher. "You're a warrior. You did good, and you should be proud."

I could see one of Royce's kids crying cageside, and that resonated with me on a raw level. I felt terrible inside.

One of the only good things to come out of Royce's UFC return was that I'd gotten to see Royce's father, Helio Gracie, another time when I'd given my prefight talk to the fighters. I'd always had a special place in my heart for Helio, the father of the sport. The relationship Helio had with his sons reminded me of the great respect I have for my own father.

"All of this is because of you," I told him, "and I want you to know how much I appreciate you and everything you did to make this possible."

In his nineties but still as vivacious as ever, Helio answered me through his translator, and I'll never forget what he said. "Everything that I have done with jiu-jitsu, you have done with this sport. You are the best there ever was or ever will be. I am proud of who you are and what you have done."

It would be the last time I'd get to speak with the sport's patriarch. In January of 2009, he passed away. He was ninety-five.

Zuffa continued on with UFC 61 "Bitter Rivals," held July 8, 2006, at the Mandalay Bay Events Center in Las Vegas, Nevada. I officiated two fights on the card, including a spirited lightweight contest between Yves Edwards and Joe "Daddy" Stevenson. I'd always thought highly of Edwards and Stevenson, and their bout was competitive. Stevenson took Edwards down and planted him against the cage. Edwards was protecting himself until Stevenson reached back and acted like he was going to set up a leg lock. Edwards responded by sitting up toward Stevenson, who timed a perfect elbow that connected with the side of Edwards' head. It created a small one-inch laceration but cut a vein that started spraying the mat and the fighters.

Dr. David Watson, one of the best cageside physicians in MMA, wasn't squeamish about blood; only the cut and its location mattered. He always said he wasn't worried about a fighter bleeding to death from a cut in the cage, but this fight may have changed his mind. After thirty seconds, the canvas had a bloodstain like a crime scene, but Watson examined Edwards and let the bout continue for another minute until the bell.

As Edwards went back to his corner, Dr. Watson came into the cage to look at him again and then walked to me. "You need to stop the fight."

I said, "Okay, but why'd you change your mind in one minute?" The fighter's face was now clean, and the blood was out of his eyes.

"I would guess he's lost about 400 cc of blood at this point; if he loses 500 cc, I'll be giving him a transfusion."

I didn't doubt Dr. Watson's wisdom and promptly waived off the fight.

Six weeks later we all returned to the same venue for UFC 62 "Liddell vs. Sobral," held August 26, 2006. There was some controversy in a lightweight bout I officiated between Hermes Franca and Jamie Varner, when I stopped the fight in the second round to take a point away from Varner for timidity—something I've rarely had to do in recent years.

After winning the first and possibly the second round, Varner gassed out fast and was actually running away from Franca in an attempt to steal time and not engage in the fight. After I warned Varner, Franca turned up the heat in the final moments, which prompted Varner to backpedal again. He was tired and spit out his mouthpiece, either in an attempt to kill time on the clock or get a clearer airway. I stopped the fight and took a point away. Franca ended up winning the fight with a guillotine choke, but I was criticized for slowing down the fight for the point deduction. However, if Franca hadn't caught the last-minute submission, that point would have made the bout a draw—a much fairer outcome in a bout where one fighter was trying to stall to his advantage.

In the main event, Chuck Liddell defended his light heavy-weight title against Renato "Babalu" Sobral in a rematch of their UFC 40 bout when Liddell had knocked out Babalu with a beautiful left shin kick to the face. Babalu started the bout calm, but Liddell quickly connected, and that pissed off Babalu. Fighters usually can't fight mad because they make stupid mistakes and their opponents usually capitalize. Babalu went after Liddell and left an opening for a right uppercut, which sent the Brazilian down. Liddell followed up with more punches, and Babalu was holding onto Liddell, but there was nobody home. I put myself between Liddell and the prone Babalu, but Babalu thought the fight was still going and his training took over. He found a leg and grabbed it; however, the leg belonged to me. Babalu tried to take me down as I kept telling him the fight was over, but his mind was too scrambled to understand what he was doing. I realized if I didn't do something I'd have a fighter on top of me. I under-hooked his arm, forced him over, then moved to mount where I was finally able to get control of Babalu, who was snorting and gasping for air. Just one more thing to add to the list. Fighter tried to take me down—check.

PHOTO BY LORETTA HUNT

Teaching my first COMMAND referee course
(December 2007)

Coaching my son and the Canyon Cowboys in
the Pac Youth Football League

ALL IN THE TIMING

> *You can fool the whole world down the highway of*
> *years, and take pats on the back as you pass.*
> *But your final reward will be heartache and*
> *tears if you've cheated the man in the glass.*
>
> —Peter "Dale" Wimbrow Sr.

Heading into 2007, I had no idea I was entering what would be my fourteenth and final year as an MMA referee. This wasn't necessarily a bad thing; the sport was evolving, and so were the people within it.

It had been my dream back since my powerlifting days to open my own gym, but I'd gone into police work instead. Back then, I hadn't thought to open an MMA gym. The sport hadn't existed in the United States at that point. However, over the years I'd soaked in every detail I could about the combat sports gyms I'd walked into.

I'd been in everything from filthy boxing gyms that smelled like the inside of a never-washed jockstrap to tidier karate dojos filled with kids in their white, pressed gis. Rorion Gracie's school was the nicest gym I'd ever been to. The mats were kept clean, and it even had a juice bar, but it was limited to Brazilian jiu-jitsu classes.

As I watched mixed martial arts evolve and grow over the years, my dream shifted to opening a facility where a fighter could get all the necessary instruction, equipment, and experience to compete and excel in the sport.

Dana White, who had opened a couple gyms in Boston and Las Vegas prior to getting involved with the UFC, gave me some advice. First, he said I was an idiot for wanting to open a gym because all they did was lose money, but he helped me nonetheless by hooking me up with equipment distributors, like Ringside, who gave me discounts that kept some of my initial costs down. White also gave me a few of the thirty-foot canvases that covered the Octagon floor—bloodstains and all—from some past events.[13] I hung these pieces of MMA history on the gym walls.

I also ran the gym's name, Big John McCarthy's Ultimate Training Academy, past Dana to make sure I had his blessing. Elaine and I found a warehouse on an industrial road a few minutes from our house, and we filled it with a cage, a ring, an ample mat area for grappling, and weightlifting and cardio equipment.

People who know me understand that when I do something, I like to do it right. Billionaire Donald Trump says if you're thinking of something, you might as well think big. So BJMUTA, which Elaine and I opened in Valencia, California, in September of 2006, lived up to its name. At 16,000 square feet, it was three times the size of most MMA gyms. The best part was that it was all mine to run the way I wanted.

The plan was to get the gym on its feet so I could eventually

13. The Octagon's canvas is replaced at each event with new sponsors' decals.

retire from the police department. My time with the LAPD had run its course, and although I hated a lot of politics in the department, I loved a lot of the people who worked there, which made it fun. But I knew once I left the police force, the gym would be a place where I could find my next team.

I also liked the idea of opening my own gym because I'd be able to train anytime. With my police job and my UFC assignments, it was difficult to get to a gym to take a jiu-jitsu class or hit the weights. I was still a brown belt in jiu-jitsu, and every time I watched a fighter line up a crafty submission in the cage, I missed being able to do the same.

In reality, though, I ended up working out less once the gym finally opened. Every time I'd walk in there, somebody, whether an instructor or a student or a friend who'd stopped by to visit, would need to talk to me. Sometimes I was tempted to sneak off to the gym down the street so I'd be left alone during my own workouts.

At the start, owning a gym was a bit of a strain because I was still teaching at the LAPD. In 2000, the training academy had been moved to a nasty patch of Earth located in the hottest part of the San Fernando Valley. It was a lot closer to where we now lived, but I'd still be out my door at 4:30 every morning, teach the cadets,

---

UFC 65

"Bad Intentions"
November 18, 2006
Arco Arena
Sacramento, California

Bouts I Reffed:
Antoni Hardonk vs. Sherman Pendergarst
Tim Sylvia vs. Jeff Monson
Matt Hughes vs. George St. Pierre

Hughes had been a dominant champion and had already defeated the rising French Canadian star with a first-round armbar at UFC 51 in 2005. This time around St. Pierre's gaze never left the Illinois wrestler's eyes. St. Pierre confidently attacked Hughes with a variety of stand-up techniques performed to perfection. St. Pierre's footwork was beautiful, like a master painter throwing colors on a canvas, each new hue making the portrait that much better. St. Pierre clipped Hughes with a flurry, and he went down, but the bell sounded before the younger fighter could finish the job. In the second round, Hughes tried to figure out what to do with his lightning-fast opponent. Then, St. Pierre landed a left high kick that dropped the champion and finished him with ground punches. It was an electrifying performance by St. Pierre.

UFC 66

"Liddell vs. Ortiz"
December 30, 2006
MGM Grand Garden Arena
Las Vegas, Nevada

Bouts I Reffed:
Thiago Alves vs. Tony DeSouza
Keith Jardine vs. Forrest Griffin

Jardine-Griffin was a competitive fight until Jardine landed a clean right hand that knocked Griffin down. When Griffin couldn't recover, I put an end to it so he wouldn't get hurt more. Griffin came to his senses and broke down crying on the telecast as the cameras chased him around the cage to get his reaction.

What most people don't understand is that fighters are just like you and me: they work hard and put everything they have into something, and when they come up short, it can be a serious letdown. Losing a fight could be the difference between being able to pay your bills or not.

then head to the gym around 3:00 or 4:00 in the afternoon to stay until it closed that evening. I hired instructors in all the disciplines, from Brazilian jiu-jitsu to boxing, and helped teach a nighttime MMA class where the fighters could put it all together. Afterward, I stayed around mopping the mats and cleaning up for the next day and wouldn't get home until midnight or later. Then I was up a few hours later to do it all over again. In the beginning, if I wanted to have my own gym, this is what had to be done.

Despite the rigorous schedule, I was delighted to be grappling again. A couple months after the gym's opening, my Brazilian jiu-jitsu instructors Lou Salseda, Mike Ortiz, Todd White, and Felicia Oh jointly awarded me my black belt.

In late December, Zuffa promoted the rematch between former light heavyweight champion Tito Ortiz and his rival Chuck Liddell at UFC 66 over the New Year's weekend in Las Vegas. The show was said to have gotten 1.05 million pay-per-view buys. It was the first time the promotion had broken the 1 million barrier, and the event garnered nearly twice as many purchases as the previous installment had.

Ortiz lasted into the third round with Liddell this time, but the outcome was still in the Iceman's favor.

At $50 a pop and with Zuffa supposedly receiving half of that amount for each buy, the promotion would have made over $26 million in pay-per-view dollars alone. Not a bad day's work in anyone's book.

With profits like that seemingly possible, in 2007 the market began to flood with new promotions, clothing companies, and other MMA-related businesses that sold everything from gear to mats to cages. It seemed everyone with money thought they could get into the business to make a buck or two, and why not? Zuffa made it look much easier than it really was. Some new MMA businesses did find success, while others weren't as lucky.

A new group called the World Fighting Alliance was one of the first to realize promoting fights isn't as elementary as putting a big-named card together. After a handful of shows hosted in nearly empty arenas, the UFC swooped in on the promotion in turmoil and bought out a bunch of the WFA's more attractive fighter contracts.

UFC 67 "All or Nothing," held on February 3, 2007, at the Mandalay Bay Events Center in Las Vegas, was a big night for Dana White and the UFC, as it marked the debut of a couple of those key WFA fighter acquisitions. Quinton "Rampage" Jackson had been with Japan's Pride Fighting Championships before switching over to the WFA. Lyoto Machida was also under a WFA contract and, although he wasn't as well-known as Jackson, people who knew the sport were banking on the unbeaten Japanese-Brazilian contender as the future of fighting. Both passed their Octagon debuts with flying colors.

The other big name White was waiting to unleash was Mirko "Cro Cop" Filipovic, the Croatian knockout artist who had defected from Pride just as the foreign promotion stumbled in Japan because of a magazine article linking it to the Yakuza mob. Filipovic went for the bigger payday the UFC was now able to offer, and his first opponent would be the lesser skilled brawler Eddie Sanchez.

NSAC Executive Director Keith Kizer told me I'd originally been scheduled to referee this fight but had been removed because of comments I'd made about the match to other NSAC officials on the set of *The Ultimate Fighter* weeks before. I'd said it wasn't a matter of who'd win but of which row Cro Cop's lethal left high kick would launch Sanchez's head into. It may not have been the right thing to say, but to me there was little doubt that Sanchez was being sent in for nothing more than to fill Cro Cop's highlight reel.

I don't blame Kizer for taking me off of the fight. In fact, I thank him for it. I got to referee two more evenly matched bouts, including a rematch between Quinton "Rampage" Jackson and kickboxer Marvin Eastman.

In 2000, I'd watched their first fight at a King of the Cage show at the Soboba Casino in Southern California. The fight was a war. Jackson absorbed three hard head kicks from Eastman and kept coming forward. I was amazed by his chin as much as anything. Afterward, I told Jackson, a wrestler with a penchant for stand-up brawls, he had a great future if he kept working hard.

The rematch at UFC 67 was a well-paced affair. Eastman, a Las Vegas prison guard by day, would fight anyone, anywhere, anytime and was stopped only after Jackson nailed him with a knee and follow-up punches. Jackson's win set him up nicely for a rematch with UFC light heavyweight champion Chuck Liddell.

Now that the Las Vegas shows were drawing healthy attendance numbers with some consistency, it was time again to take the show on the road. UFC 68 "The Uprising" on March 3, 2007, was scheduled to coincide with the Arnold Sports Festival weekend at the Nationwide Arena in Columbus, Ohio.

The Arnold Sports Festival is an annual fitness and bodybuilding expo started by Arnold Schwarzenegger that hosts many kinds of competition, from Arnold Classic bodybuilding to table tennis to archery. The festival also attracts over 175,000 sports fans, who can meander through aisles of sports-related product booths and meet their favorite athletes. It was a great opportunity for MMA to get exposure alongside some other popular niche sports.

The Arnolds takes place during the first week of March every year. In 2007 that week, a monster snowstorm was gripping the Midwest, which would make travel to Columbus a challenge for most of us.

The only recurring dream I've ever had about the UFC is one in which I'm frantically trying to get to a show and miss it, disappointing the promotion and the people who depend on me to be there. I've never been able to let myself be late to an appointment or event because, to me, that would be disrespecting the people I'm working with. I just have to get there, and that's that. Not being able to is my nightmare, and UFC 68 would be the show where it came to life in excruciating detail.

It started in Las Vegas three nights before UFC 68. I got on a plane with Elaine to Minneapolis and then on to Moline, Iowa. At the time, Elaine had opened her own interior design business and agreed to help manager Monte Cox furnish and decorate his new house in Bettendorf, Iowa. From Moline, we'd fly into Columbus for the show.

The plane was late getting into Minneapolis, and while we

were taxiing in, I watched from my window as our next flight, to Moline, departed without us. We spent the night at the airport, and the next morning I was in line to get us on the earliest flight. But the weather seemed to be worsening by the minute, and I was now beginning to worry that I wouldn't get to Columbus in time.

Screw Moline, I thought, *and screw whatever Elaine was going to do for Monte.*

We booked a flight to Columbus, but the snow was falling heavily. The TVs in the airport blared news of the approaching storm.

Finally, we boarded the plane to Columbus only to sit on the tarmac for three and a half hours as workers deiced the plane and the pilots waited for a break in the bad weather. After another hour, the head pilot's voice came over the intercom and told us the storm was just too strong. Then the pilot pulled the plane back into the terminal.

I wasn't in a good mood. At the counter, the attendant told me she'd booked a new flight for us, this one from Minneapolis to Chicago, then to Philadelphia, then back to Detroit, and finally to Columbus.

I looked at her as if she were crazy. "How in the hell can you say you'll fly me to four different cities when you can't fly me to one right now?"

I asked for our luggage back and told Elaine to go to the rental car agency. While we'd been on the tarmac, she'd already called to rent a vehicle with four-wheel drive and a GPS.

We were talking about 650 miles to Columbus, so there wasn't a minute to waste. By the time we had the rental keys, our luggage was still on the plane, so we took off without it. Of course, we got a call thirty minutes into the drive. Our luggage was available, so I went back for it. By now, we were in the heart of a blizzard.

We called Monte, who told us he'd also be driving to UFC 68 and that the weather was fine where he was, so we headed south toward him and the great state of Iowa.

At first, we shared the highway with snowplows. After a while, all I could see was our car and white. We were the only ones stupid enough to be out. I could barely see five feet in front of me as snow whisked past the windshield. It looked like we were hitting warp speed in *Star Trek*.

When we made it to the bottom of Minnesota, we may as well have arrived at the end of the world. Highway patrol had closed the interstate, and there was nowhere left to go. Elaine and I pulled in to a truck stop, which had a convenience store, gas, and a Wendy's.

I was getting more and more irate at the thought that I might miss the show. I called UFC coordinator Burt Watson and left a message. "We're stuck at the end of the fucking Earth and trying to make our way to Columbus."

Elaine was waiting in line at the Wendy's counter when I walked in. She started laughing, which struck me as odd, and told me to look at the guy flipping the burgers. I turned around and saw the clone of one of my favorite movie characters, Fat Bastard. This guy had to be five feet four at most and 380 pounds at least with huge red chops running down the sides of his face. If I weren't so mad about getting stuck at this twilight zone gas stop, I would've laughed.

With the highways closing all around us, Elaine asked some truckers if they knew of any roads that would be open heading toward Iowa. They gave us a new route to take but said the roads would probably be a mess.

We had no other options. We had to keep moving.

When I couldn't see the road in front of me anymore, I started to follow the light poles as a guide. I was hauling ass because I didn't want to get stuck. Cars were abandoned in ditches off to the side. I felt bad because I was taking my wife's life into my own hands, and I apologized for getting her into this mess.

I drove through the night. Everything had turned white: the roads, the sky, the car, my knuckles.

I don't know how we did it, but we made it to Moline. I dropped off the rental car at the airport, and Monte picked us up and drove us the rest of the way so I could get some rest.

We arrived in Columbus the morning of the show, where a light snow was dusting the city streets. It had taken us sixteen hours to get here. We'd missed the weigh-ins for the first time ever, but I'd made it, which was the most important thing to me.

If I hadn't, yes, the commission would have handed my fight assignments to another referee and the show would have gone on. But that wasn't the point for me. What mattered was that I was where I'd said I'd be and wasn't letting the promotion, the fighters, or the sport down.

Besides my traveling drama, there was another behind-the-scenes issue that made UFC 68 stand out for me.

When I'd heard the main event would match former champion Randy Couture against current heavyweight champion Tim Sylvia, my first thought was that they might assign me that fight. Under different circumstances, this wouldn't have been a big deal, but Couture had retired for an entire year and we'd actually sparked a friendship. Our families had spent time together, and Couture and I had enjoyed quad riding and other outings in the past few months. I hadn't thought he'd come out of retirement.

I called Ohio Athletic Commission head Bernie Profato right away to tell him that if he wanted to exclude me from the fight, I understood. I didn't want any speculation that I'd give an unfair advantage to one fighter. Profato agreed and said he'd assign me to different fights.

I was surprised a few days later when Profato called me back. "I told them what you said, John, but Sylvia's camp wants you to do the fight."

I thought about it a moment and agreed to referee if both sides and the commission approved. Yes, I had a relationship with Couture that extended outside the cage, but I also had a longstanding relationship with Sylvia's manager, Monte Cox. I'd assumed both camps believed this wouldn't affect my judgment in the Octagon, but it had been my responsibility to at least put it out there.

I'm glad I got to officiate the bout. Today it's considered one of the sport's greatest. Many in the industry were concerned for Couture's well-being heading in. Aging fighters usually don't fare well, and this one had taken a year off from a constantly evolving sport full of young guns.

We would all come to understand that Couture was the exception to the rule. The forty-three-year-old dropped the six-feet-eight Sylvia out of the gate with an overhand right.

After the punch, Sylvia spent the next twenty-five minutes either fending Couture off his back or chasing him around the cage trying to land a punch. As Couture bobbed and weaved out of the way to win each round, the crowd's enthusiasm crescendoed. It was as if everyone held their breath until the entire crowd counted down the last ten seconds. When the bell finally sounded, everyone let it out all at once. The cheers for Couture, the symbol of underdog perseverance, were deafening.

The event broke a North American attendance record for an MMA event with 19,079 spectators, and it was one of the most electrifying nights I've ever refereed.

Zuffa followed up with its next pay-per-view event a month later. UFC 69 "Shootout" was held on April 7, 2007, at the Toyota Center in Houston, Texas, in the UFC's first visit to the Lone Star State.

For days before the event, the Texas fans clogged the fighters' hotel lobby with their Sharpies, posters, and cameras. And it wasn't just the fighters they were interested in.

The day of the show while I was eating with Elaine in the hotel's restaurant, fans were gathering three deep at the entrance. I had to go back to my room, pack my gear, and get to the arena, but with so many fans around I knew it would take too long to get across the hotel to the elevators—and you know I hate being late for anything.

I asked the restaurant manager if there was any other way to get upstairs, and he ushered us through the kitchen to the service elevators.

The door opened, and Dana White popped out. We flashed each other knowing smiles.

The UFC was taking off in a big way. Two years after the debut of *The Ultimate Fighter* on Spike TV, Zuffa had nearly doubled its number of events per year, going from ten to nineteen. Zuffa had also purchased the World Extreme Cagefighting promotion in December of 2006 and made a deal to air events on the sportscentric Versus channel, so we were assigned to those events as well. In another coup that shook the sport's very foundation, Zuffa also bought Pride Fighting Championships, the UFC's longtime superior competitor for a rumored $65 million dollars. With Pride, Zuffa acquired practically all of the world's greatest fighters other than the ones they already employed.

There was now a major UFC pay-per-view event every month with a few *UFC Fight Night*s and *Ultimate Fighter* finales sprinkled in on free TV. Celebrities like Dwayne "The Rock" Johnson, George Clooney, Cindy Crawford, Kevin James, and Shaquille O'Neal showed up Octagon-side in droves. It always surprised me when a celebrity approached. One of my favorites to meet was Michael Clarke Duncan of *The Green Mile* fame. Like me, he'd studied jiu-jitsu at the Gracies' Torrance academy. He ended up holding Elaine's mini terrier, Yoda, whom she'd snuck into the arena in her bag. That night Duncan left the show with his girlfriend chewing on his ear about getting a dog just like Yoda. All I can say is sorry, Michael.

The United States market seemed well on its way, so Zuffa turned its attention to the virtually untapped United Kingdom, which had shown an appetite for the sport with regional promotions like Cage Rage and Cage Warriors Fighting Championship in the years before. Though Zuffa said it wouldn't go where the sport wasn't regulated by an independent government-recognized agency, they made an exception for the United Kingdom. Zuffa had opened an office in London about six months before, and I think they realized if they waited for an existing agency to regulate it, they'd be waiting awhile.

UFC 70 "Nations Collide" was to be the promotion's first event in the United Kingdom as well as its first event outside the

United States since UFC 38 in London in 2002. With no regulatory agency to oversee it, the UFC would be hiring referees, judges, and other officials on its own. The flight was ten hours from Los Angeles, so I asked if Zuffa could fly me business-class. This is when the wheels began to fall off the wagon.

Under my contract with SEG, it had actually been agreed that I'd be flown first-class to all the international UFC events, but I'd always told SEG that it could purchase two coach seats together for me because that was cheaper. After Elaine had stopped working for the UFC, we'd paid for her seat ourselves. I didn't think asking for a single business-class seat in place of the two economy seats was outrageous, and I wasn't by any means making this an ultimatum.

My request wasn't so much a question of privilege; it was more about functionality. I know most people say travel is exciting, but I hate stuffing my six-feet-four, 275-pound self into a seat and pouring out onto the person next to me for ten awkward hours. And I'd be lying if I didn't say people recognized me and wanted to strike up a conversation when all I wanted to do was get some sleep.

The UFC employee I spoke to about it promised to take my request to Dana White and get back to me.

A week later, I got a call. It was Mark Ratner, the former head of the Nevada State Athletic Commission, who was now working for Zuffa as its vice president of regulatory affairs and would be assigning the officials for the show. "John, what's this about you asking for a first-class ticket to Manchester?"

"I didn't ask for a first-class ticket. I asked for a business-class seat. It's a long freaking way. I'm not expecting it, but if you can do it, I'd really appreciate it."

"Maybe I heard it wrong. Let me talk to everyone, and I'll get

PHOTO BY SUSUMU NAGAO

PHOTO BY SUSUMU NAGAO

Above: UFC 40 "Vendetta," the event that made me believe the sport was here to stay: Tito Ortiz vs. Ken Shamrock (November 22, 2002)

Below: When a fighter gets knocked out, I just want him to come back so I know he's okay: Ricco Rodriguez vs. Tim Sylvia at UFC 41. (February 28, 2003)

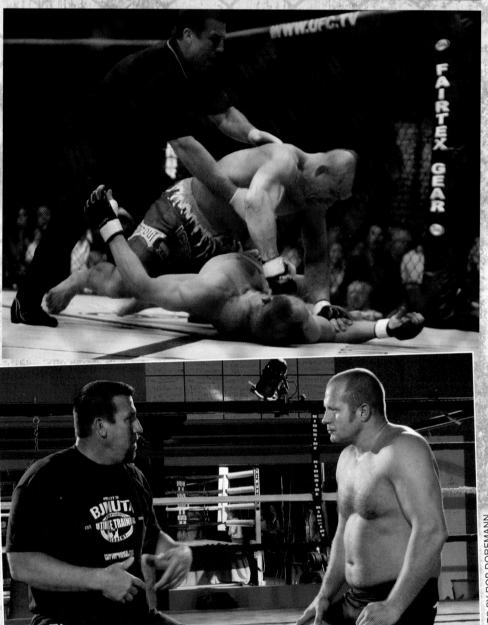

PHOTO BY SUSUMU NAGAO

PHOTO BY ROB DORFMANN

Above: The type of punch we refs try to prevent: Chuck Liddell vs. Randy Couture at UFC 52 (April 16, 2005)

Below: Telling Fedor I'm coming for his belt—okay, maybe not. On the set of National Geographic's *Fight Science* at BJMUTA in Valencia, California

PHOTO BY CHARLES PENNER / COMBATCAPTURED.COM

PHOTO BY CHARLES PENNER / COMBATCAPTURED.COM

Above: Injuries can happen in the blink of an eye. I came in a beat later on this elbow dislocation at Pure Fighting Championships 3. (October 16, 2009)

Below: Reffing my first World Boxing Council title bout in Canada

PHOTO BY DAVE MANDEL

Above: The video game version . . .

Below: . . . and how it really went down: Fedor Emelianenko vs. Brett Rogers at
Strikeforce/M-1 Global "Fedor vs. Rogers" (November 7, 2009)

Above: The day of my police retirement with my family at the academy's rock garden in Elysian Park, California

Below: Going over the rules with Fabricio "Vai Cavalo" Werdum before he submitted Fedor Emelianenko at Strikeforce/M-1 Global "Fedor vs. Werdum" (June 26, 2010)

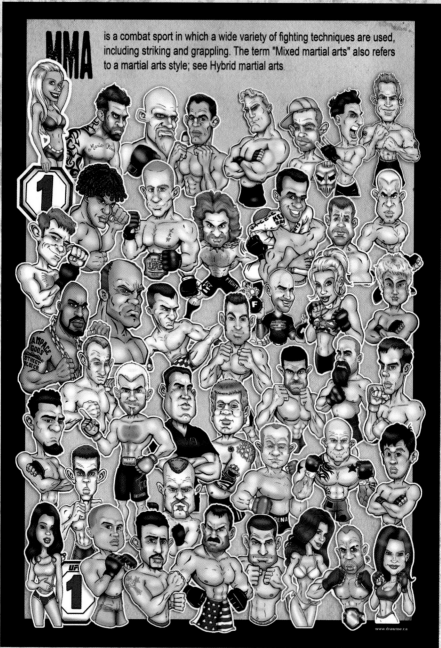

MMA is a combat sport in which a wide variety of fighting techniques are used, including striking and grappling. The term "Mixed martial arts" also refers to a martial arts style; see Hybrid martial arts.

ARTWORK COURTESY OF LYLE DOUCETTE

Above: Can you guess which of these fighters I haven't reffed?

Opposite page: Staying on my toes in Strikeforce's light heavyweight title bout between Rafael "Feijao" Cavalcante and Muhammed "King Mo" Lawal (August 21, 2010)

Last page: Pausing for the national anthem at UFC 23 "Ultimate Japan 2" (November 19, 1999)

Answer: Excluding the Octagon girls and Dana White, I've never reffed for Antonio Rodrigo Nogueira, Igor Vovchanchyn, Julie Kedzie, Takanori Gomi, Aleksander Emelianenko, Marcelo Garcia, and Mauricio "Shogun" Rua.

back to you."

I didn't hear from Zuffa until I got a text from Dana White a few days after that: "What the fuck is up with you?"

We were on the phone a few minutes later, with White asking who the fuck I thought I was asking for a first-class ticket.

I understood his anger over what he'd been told, but the information had been incorrect. As I'd explained to Ratner, I told Dana I'd never demanded a first-class ticket. "Look, Joe Rogan and Bruce Buffer told me you fly them first-class, and I wasn't even asking for that. I just asked if it was possible to get a business-class seat so I could stretch out on a ten-hour flight."

"I don't fly them first-class," Dana said. "They upgrade themselves."

"I'll just take a regular ticket," I said. I hadn't meant for it to become such a big deal.

But to Dana, I guess it had become just that. "No, I think I'll take Mario Yamasaki."

The bull in me answered, "Well, take Mario then."

It wasn't that Dana hadn't fulfilled my request. I would have flown whatever way they'd wanted me to. I guess it was the way it was all handled that irked me. It seemed like a big miscommunication, and it shouldn't have turned out that way.

In fourteen years, I'd never skipped a UFC event. Even when my son Ron had graduated from high school, I'd missed his big day to fly to Connecticut for UFC 55 in 2005. I'd felt it was my responsibility to be there and I owed it to the UFC and Zuffa. Now I was going to miss UFC 70 over a lousy plane ticket.

While heavyweight Gabriel Gonzaga was shocking everyone by knocking kickboxer Mirko "Cro Cop" Filipovic out cold with a high kick at UFC 70 on April 21, 2007, in Manchester, England, I was with my wife at our cabin in Bear Lake, Utah, shoveling snow. The ice and snow got the worst of it.

As it turned out, the UFC wasn't pleased either. Though UFC 70 had filled the Manchester Evening News Arena with 15,000 rabid United Kingdom fans, Zuffa had been concerned about a couple of questionable referee calls.

The next day, Dana and Ratner called to ask if I could come speak with them about what had happened. Dana offered to have me flown in, but I wasn't anywhere near an airport that could do this, so I said I'd drive from Utah to Las Vegas. We agreed to meet Monday at 11:30 a.m., which meant I'd have to leave the cabin at 3:00 a.m. to make the eight-hour drive.

I was there on time, as I always am. I hadn't been to the Zuffa offices in a while. A security guard was stationed outside, and I had to give him my name to check in. Things were getting very businesslike.

Dana didn't show up for another hour, so by the time he'd ushered me into his office with Ratner, I was a little perturbed. I know Dana had just flown back from England the day before, but I'd gotten up before the crack of dawn and driven eight hours straight because he'd asked me to be there at a certain time. Again, it was a matter of respect. I respected Dana, but I was getting the feeling I was becoming more of a pain in the ass than an asset to him.

As he's known to do, Dana got right to the point. "We can't have this happen again. This is crazy that this kind of stuff happens."

I think Dana was referring to both the officiating he'd seen in England and the fact that I hadn't gone on the trip. Dana told me I was the best referee there was and I had to be at all the shows from here on out.

Ratner suggested I get involved with training other referees, and I told them that was great, but there wasn't enough time in the day for me to do all that and still work my police academy job. If they wanted me to do some training for them, I'd have to retire from the LAPD.

However, it was agreed that it wasn't Zuffa or any other promotion's place to facilitate training programs for officials. It was really the responsibility of athletic commissions to make sure the people they hired were prepared.

Before I left, I brought up the issue of the plane ticket and reiterated to both of them that I'd never asked anyone for a first-class ticket.

"Well, that's not what I was told," Dana said.

I'm sure when I walked out, Dana and Ratner thought everything was great and back to normal, but I have to admit, at the time, it wasn't for me.

It was completely my hang-up, but I felt like I was being kicked in the nuts by the sport, or at least by its evolution. I wanted things to be like they were in the past, but that wouldn't happen. The referee's role was changing, and because I'd been around the longest of all the officials, it affected me most. I'd started at a time when athletic commissions wouldn't have given mixed martial arts a second glance. Now the commissions were controlling every aspect of regulating the shows.

For instance, I'd handled the fighters' gloves for just about every UFC event for the last fourteen years. In my hotel room,

I would gently knead each pair myself before rolling them up so they'd keep their stretch, and then I'd bring them to the weigh-ins.

Once there, I'd sit at a table backstage, and each fighter would try them on until he found the right size to mold to his hands. Then, I'd have him initial a roll sheet with his size listed next to his name so I knew which size to bring the next time he fought.

I'd repeated this ritual since UFC 15, which was when gloves had become mandatory, until one of the commissions had decided they'd handle the responsibility themselves. Shortly after that, the Nevada State Athletic Commission asked the referees and judges not to attend the weigh-ins so we wouldn't form a biased opinion of the fighters prior to their bouts.

These had been smaller changes I'd learned to live with. But what really bothered me, which would get me into hot water later, was the trend of some commissions assigning more and more inexperienced referees and judges. Boxing officials who'd previously shunned MMA saw all the buzz surrounding it and suddenly wanted in on the party, but the majority of them couldn't tell an armbar from a heelhook. How can you know when to restand two fighters locked on the ground or evaluate their progress when you don't really know what you're watching? I was seeing fighters working hard to move to dominant positions, setting up submissions, only to be stopped and stood by referees who had no idea one of the fighters could be on the verge of ending the fight.

This wasn't a case of ego for me; I'd always known more referees would enter the sport. But if you're a race car driver, would you rather be in the pits or on the track, especially when you can get the car around without crashing it?

Official Bout Order as of 09/13/07

UFC 76
Honda Center
Anaheim, CA
Saturday September 22, 2007

9th Draft

Prelims

*Blue corner walks first
Blue Corner

Red Corner

Lightweight Bout 3 Rounds

Michihiro Omigawa ⑤

⑤ Matt Wiman

Heavyweight Bout 3 Rounds

Scott Junk XL

XL Christian Wellisch

Lightweight Bout 3 Rounds

Diego Saraiva Ⓜ

Ⓛ Jeremy Stephens

Welterweight Bout 3 Rounds

Anthony Johnson XL

Ⓛ Rich Clementi

Main Card

Lightweight Bout 3 Rounds

Thiago Tavares Ⓜ

⑤ Tyson Griffin

Light Heavyweight Bout 3 Rounds

Kazuhiro Nakamura

Lyoto Machida
XXL

Ⓜ Jon Fitch

Diego Sanchez

Welterweight Bout 3 Rounds

Mauricio "Shogun" Rua

XL Forrest Griffin

Light Heavyweight Bout 3 Rounds

Keith Jardine 2/0

XL Chuck Liddell

Light Heavyweight Bout 3 Rounds

ALL BOUTS LIVE AND SUBJECT TO CHANGE

Since UFC 15, I'd handed out the fighters' gloves and kept track of their sizes.

Change is inevitable, but that doesn't necessarily mean you enjoy it, especially when you feel you're being pushed away from what you love. The last time I'd left the Zuffa offices in Las Vegas, as I'd walked out, I'd looked around at the army of employees bustling about preparing for a handful of upcoming events, and I hadn't recognized any of them. I think it was in that moment that I felt I wasn't really a part of the UFC anymore.

I tried to bury these ominous thoughts and concentrate on what I could control: my own performance in the cage.

At UFC 71 "Liddell vs. Jackson" on May 26, 2007, at the MGM Grand Garden Arena in Las Vegas, it was my backstage routine that made the difference. That night, as always, I went over the basics with each fighter I'd be refereeing, and it was a good thing I did. Among the points, I said, "If you're caught in a submission and scream out in pain, it's the same as a tap, and the fight will be stopped."

In his lightweight bout against Din Thomas, newcomer Jeremy Stephens was doing well until he got caught in a deep armbar submission. He tried working his way out and finally screamed as Thomas hyperextended his elbow joint.

I immediately stopped the fight, and the first words out of Stephens' mouth were "I did not tap."

When I reminded him of what we'd covered backstage, he deflated like a balloon.

I also officiated the headlining championship rematch between Chuck Liddell and Quinton "Rampage" Jackson that night, which had had one hell of a buildup for a bout that wouldn't leave the first round. Liddell came in with a left hook to the body but left Jackson an opening to land a counter-right hook flush on his chin. The punch dropped Liddell, and Jackson went in for the kill, hitting the champion unconscious with one punch and back into consciousness with the next.

I had already moved in to stop the fight when I saw Liddell go out.

It was the first time Liddell had been whipped in three years, and it snapped the cool California fighter's seven-fight win streak. Not coincidentally, the last fighter Liddell had lost to had been Jackson himself, who'd brutally taken the UFC fighter out in a 2004 Pride grand prix tournament in Japan.

The day after UFC 71, I received a call from John Hackleman, Liddell's coach since before his start in MMA, who thanked me for protecting Liddell. He said he'd been climbing up on the apron to stop the fight when I'd done it. That was a phone call I very much appreciated.

For UFC 72 "Victory," we traveled to Belfast, Northern Ireland, for the first time. Elaine came with me, as always, but this time there was no question about my plane ticket. I did what Dana had suggested and upgraded myself to business class for the trip. It hurt paying $1,000 for the upgrade, but in the air it was worth' every penny.

My hectic schedule continued till something had to give. I'd given up coaching the local high school football team to referee more shows and open the gym. But each time I would add something to my life, something would have to fall to the wayside.

Elaine had wanted me to quit the police department for quite a while. I'd turned down a lot of opportunities in MMA already because I didn't have the time. More opportunities for TV and movie appearances cropped up, and though I didn't seek them out, I certainly didn't mind the extra money to support my family.

The UFC had about thirty events a year now, and I'd eaten up all my personal and vacation time. Elaine reasoned that the sport had grown immensely in the last couple years, and between the gym, appearances, and requests from commissions for me to teach their officials, I could now make a living off of MMA. I know Elaine was also worried about the pace I was keeping; no one could keep it up forever.

My tolerance for some aspects of the LAPD and its politics had long been gone, but I'd always looked at the job as our safety net. If everything else went to hell, I'd still have a steady paycheck and medical insurance from the department. I also loved teaching new recruits, but the job was taking up about 70 percent of my life.

I wrestled with this decision for a while and eventually came to the decision that it was time to take another step in my life. Now, after twenty-two years of service, I'd say good-bye to the LAPD.

At the same time, I was falling under immense scrutiny in the fight community. I'd been working with athletic commissions since UFC 15, but I'd always felt like I was a part of the UFC and was obligated to them. In the sport's early years, it hadn't been a problem because there hadn't been many promotions outside of the UFC to referee anyway. When Zuffa had taken over, they'd always given me the schedule months ahead so I could juggle my paid time off or vacations days.

When athletic commissions had begun to call to assign me to other promotions outside the UFC, sometimes on short notice, it would often conflict with my LAPD schedule. I couldn't accept all of the assignments. Eventually, word got back to me that some commissions thought I was a prima donna who thought I was too good to work any show besides the UFC. Honestly, I would have loved to do the other events, but some of those other promotions had caused problems with the UFC and had basically become their enemy, and I didn't want to do anything that caused a problem. Whatever I did, I was going to piss off either the UFC or the commissions. It was really a no-win situation.

If circumstances could have stayed the same, it would have been fine, but some commissions said if I didn't work the other shows they asked me to, I wouldn't be working the UFC when it came to their state. After hearing that, I felt it wouldn't be long before the UFC told me they couldn't bring me along at all.

I understood the commissions' stance, and I didn't blame the UFC either. Zuffa had been generous in coming up with a solution to keep me on when it had swooped in and purchased the UFC. It wasn't anybody's fault that the sport had evolved, changing my role, over the years.

As I did when faced with many of life's big decisions, I went

UFC 74

"Respect"
August 25, 2007
Mandalay Bay Events Center
Las Vegas, Nevada

Bouts I Reffed:
Frank Mir vs. Antoni Hardonk
Joe Stevenson vs. Kurt Pellegrino
Georges St. Pierre vs. Josh Koscheck

In the second round, St. Pierre caught Koscheck in a topside Kimura that Koscheck defended by grabbing ahold of his own shorts. "He is holding onto his shorts," said St. Pierre, which I advised him was legal. You cannot grab your opponent's shorts, but you are allowed to grab your own.

St. Pierre didn't know how to successfully break the grip, but his trainer Greg Jackson gave him the proper instruction between rounds on pushing the hand down first before trying to pull up. It was a beautiful moment to me. I was watching one of the top fighters in the world learning his craft.

With a minute left and with St. Pierre on top of Koscheck, the bottom fighter started congratulating him on his win. St. Pierre stopped and gave Koscheck a curious look and then a huge elbow to the face.

to my dad for advice.

"You've been loyal to them, and the UFC's been loyal to you," he said. "They don't owe you anything, and you don't owe them anything."

Of all my reasons, politics was the biggest one that led me to retire from refereeing. I wasn't leaving because I didn't enjoy refereeing. I still loved it, but I was stuck. I was in a no-win situation and felt I couldn't make everyone happy.

My dad gave me one last bit of advice. "Walk away from it but only if it's what you want to do."

I knew this wasn't what I really wanted, but I felt I had no choice. Elaine quietly started to put out feelers to some media outlets to see if someone might want to use me as a commentator or an analyst. I never wanted to be a commentator; it was merely something I could do to stay involved with the sport I loved.

Meanwhile, the UFC, with no knowledge of my own inner struggle, continued to pump out shows to a widening audience. At UFC 75 "Champion vs. Champion" on September 8, 2007, at O2 Arena in London, England, I was reminded how human fighters really are, ironically by one of the most feared athletes in the sport.

Croatian striker Mirko "Cro Cop" Filipovic's streak of brutal stoppages in Japan had conjured up words like "invincible" and "unbeatable." That is, until Fedor Emelianenko exploited a chink in Filipovic's armor when they met in Pride Fighting Championships in August of 2005. While everyone else did all they could to stay away from Filipovic's now legendary left high kick, the sambo expert Emelianenko decided to not only stand with the former K-1 fighter but go after him and make him back up. This strategy gave Cro Cop fits, as he was never able to set his feet to kick and couldn't gain a comfort zone moving backward.

Once a fighter uncovers a flaw or a weakness in another, other fighters are like swarming sharks quick to exploit the same.

By UFC 75 in 2007, Filipovic was losing his indestructible aura. Brazilian jiu-jitsu black belt Gabriel Gonzaga had knocked him out months before at UFC 70 by stunning him with his own left high kick.

Filipovic was in desperate need of a win, and the UFC matched him against French kickboxer Cheick Kongo to ensure a stand-up battle from two fighters who likely wouldn't be looking for the takedown.

Though Kongo is one of the most physically imposing fighters in MMA with a body that could be used as an anatomy chart, he was hesitant to engage at the top of his bout with Filipovic. This is called giving respect to your opponent's skills, and it had Kongo's corner screaming at him to not back away. Slowly but surely, though, Kongo began to land powerful body blows that hurt Filipovic.

By the end of the first round, it was clear Kongo now believed what he wasn't too sure of before the fight started: he belonged in the cage with Filipovic, and he could win. I watched Kongo's confidence soar as he started to dictate the pace of the second round. Several times during the fight Kongo threw knees that Filipovic

UFC 76

"Knockout"
September 22, 2007
Honda Center
Anaheim, California

Bouts I Reffed:
Jeremy Stephens vs. Diego Saraiva
Lyoto Machida vs. Kazuhiro Nakamura
Keith Jardine vs. Chuck Liddell

When you name your show "Knockout," you'd better do your best to deliver. Zuffa tried by pairing former UFC light heavyweight champion Chuck Liddell against fellow striker Keith Jardine. If Liddell was known for his unorthodox counterpunching style, Jardine was—times five. Jardine tore up Liddell's body with beautiful kicks from a variety of angles and took a decision most never predicted. Neither fighter held anything back, and it was an honor to be in the cage with two athletes willing to lay it on the line for both themselves and the fans.

reacted to as if he'd been hit in the groin, but I paid close attention to where the shots landed and didn't stop the action.

In the third round, as Kongo clinched with his opponent, he started throwing knees again, one of which hit Cro Cop low. I called time to allow Filipovic to recover from the low blow. He crouched on the fence.

"It's not the low blow," a pained Filipovic answered, looking up at me. "I just can't do this anymore. John, do you think I am too old for this anymore?"

I covered the microphone on my shirt. This was a vulnerable moment for one of the most feared fighters on the planet, and I'm sure he didn't realize I was wired for the world to hear him doubting himself.

"You're not too old. You just need to believe in yourself and go back to what you're good at. Get yourself right before we restart. Or if you don't want to restart, I'll get you out."

It was nobody's business what was said between Filipovic and me, but cageside commentator Joe Rogan was sitting close enough to hear some of the conversation and relay what he'd heard. That's the only reason I would share this now.

Fighters have told me things I've never told anyone else. I want fighters to know they can trust me in the cage, and that includes keeping some of our conversations private.

By October, I was having my own private conversations with The Fight Network, a two-year-old Toronto-based cable channel that broadcasted boxing, MMA, and pro wrestling content twenty-four hours a day across Canada. The channel wasn't available in the United States yet, but it hoped to bridge that gap shortly. What I liked about The Fight Network was that it covered as many combat sports events as it could from the UFC down to the smaller promotions, so this was a way for me to still be a part of the sport. The Fight Network reminded me of ESPN when it had launched years before, and there was something intriguing about getting in on the ground floor.

On November 6, 2007, I verbally agreed to join the company full-time as an on-air analyst and commentator, signaling the end of my fourteen-year career as a referee.

We kept the news under wraps for weeks. I wanted to tell a few key people in the industry on my own. I still felt a great sense of loyalty to the UFC and wanted to speak to Lorenzo Fertitta alone, if only to thank him for what he'd done for me and MMA over the past six years.

Just before I committed to the The Fight Network, I headed to the U.S. Bank Arena in Cincinnati, Ohio, for UFC 77 "Hostile Territory," to be held on October 20, 2007. While we prepared for the event, Fertitta pulled me aside and asked if I remembered the conversation we'd had six years before at UFC 30 in New Jersey about paying fighters millions of dollars. "I never realized that would be the start of all my troubles," said Fertitta, who'd been hit with the very public resignation of disgruntled heavyweight champion Randy Couture over a contract dispute the month before. The UFC was getting popular and, in turn, the fighters were expecting a larger share in the profits.

I didn't share with Fertitta then that this would be my last

UFC pay-per-view as a referee. Only a couple friends knew of my plans, and I conducted myself as I would any other given night.

But visible to the astute eye, I took a slight pause before delivering what I thought would be my last "Let's get it on" to start a UFC pay-per-view. I savored that moment.

After I'd left Dana White's office a few months earlier, I'd thought about the state of officiating in the sport. Rather than continue to complain to my wife every time I saw an inexperienced referee make a bad call, I decided to do something about it. I pored over fight tapes and prepared a curriculum to begin teaching others how to properly referee mixed martial arts fights. For years, Elaine had received inquiries about a course from all over the world. I thought if anyone was going to teach it, why not me?

On December 1, 2007, I held my first COMMAND (Certification of Officials for Mixed Martial Arts National Development) course in Valencia, California. I'd feared we wouldn't get a single person to sign up, but the first run had twenty-one attendees, some from as far away as Brazil and Australia. A few of the students had already been refereeing for years in their states; others never had. One guy said he'd sat in the front row of the first Ultimate Ultimate in 1995 in Denver, Colorado. All of them had a passion for MMA, which was obvious from their questions and willingness to be there.

My dad even made it up for the day and watched from the back of the hotel conference room as I went through my PowerPoint presentation. There was so much to get through that we went well past the allotted time, so we ordered pizza for the class and stayed until midnight. Not a single person complained.

The course lasted two days and included hands-on instruction, with my fighters demonstrating techniques in the cage at my gym, and final-day testing. Of that inaugural class of twenty-one participants, only four passed. I didn't mind the low pass rate at all. I knew it was a difficult test. I'd made it that way to flag any weak areas because I wanted each student to leave as prepared as possible.

The regulations and rules could be learned, but what I really wanted to impart above everything else was that referees should be decisive. "When you make a decision, go with it," I told them. "Don't hem and haw before or after the call. It doesn't mean in the end someone won't say you're wrong. If you say it's right, it's right at the time. If you waver, you'll always be in a position to make more mistakes. Trust your instinct." It was a lesson I'd learned in the cage.

I'd never had the benefit of learning MMA refereeing from anybody. Everything I'd picked up had come from seeing what had worked and what hadn't over the last fourteen years. But if I'd had someone teach me, this was one of the more crucial lessons I would have wanted.

A week after my first COMMAND course, I refereed my last fight at *The Ultimate Fighter 6* finale at the Palms Casino and Resort in Las Vegas. A friend and I had tried to calculate how many fights I'd officiated since 1994. We came up with 535 bouts, give or take one or two I may have forgotten.

The Fight Network began to publicize my retirement from officiating and my move to full-time analysis and commentary. They'd had a conference call for me earlier that week with the media, and I'd chattered on about this great new opportunity to offer insight into fights for the fans. I'd told everyone how excited I was, but inside I'd been scared and felt like a fool for having a conference call to announce my retirement from refereeing. I'd wanted to just walk away and not make any fuss about the whole situation, but my new employer had wanted to use this opportunity to get publicity for the channel. The whole time, I wondered if leaving was the right decision.

I didn't want my final night as a referee to change anything for the fighters I was there to protect, and I certainly didn't want any extra attention. I was completely relieved when Lorenzo, Dana, and the rest of the Zuffa staff approached me backstage between bouts and privately presented me with an Audemars Piguet watch with an Octagon-shaped face. I certainly appreciated the gesture. It was something they definitely didn't have to do, and it showed just how classy they could be.

I refereed the main event that night, a bout between hungry light-weights Roger Huerta and Clay Guida. As he'd done with almost all of his opponents before him, Guida drilled Huerta into the mat with takedown after takedown and pulled well ahead on the scorecards. But in the third round, Huerta, who'd been tossed around and pretty much abused the entire fight, caught Guida with a knee as he bull-rushed in with his head down. Huerta got the rear-naked choke submission shortly afterward to punctuate a highly emotional and entertaining come-from-behind win.

It was a perfect fight for me to end my career with.

Afterward, The Fight Network hosted a retirement party for me in one of the hotel's famous suites upstairs. Dana and Lorenzo didn't attend, but there was a great turnout from fighters, including Matt Hughes, Tito Ortiz, Forrest Griffin, Urijah Faber, and many others. Many were kind enough to give me a validating word.

When he'd heard I'd be hanging up my black uniform, Royce

Gracie, who was in the Philippines at the time and couldn't attend, had sent a message to be read for the other guests. UFC announcer Bruce Buffer did the honors. "We are a dying breed, John, but it was fun while it lasted. Good luck, my friend. Wish you all the best in life and future endeavors. Your friend, Royce."

PHOTO BY DAISY ROSAS

At my retirement party: standing between Stephan Bonnar and Forrest Griffin, the two guys who turned the sport around with one fight (December 2007)

A few nights later, back at home in California, I got a phone message from Dana White. The UFC president sounded like he was out enjoying a cocktail or two, but I still got a kick out it. "John, you are the fucking best," an excitable White said. "I fucking love you, man."

A picture that says it all about this sport: Fedor Emelianenko vs. Andrei Arlovski, Affliction "Day of Reckoning" (January 2009)

LET'S GET IT ON!

The journey is the reward.

—Chinese proverb

It only took me a day to realize I'd jumped off a cliff I should never have been standing on.

The morning after my retirement match at *The Ultimate Fighter 6*, I sat in Las Vegas with my new bosses at The Fight Network to take a meeting with M-1 Global, a Russian-based fight promotion that had recently teamed up with American partners, including longtime manager and promoter Monte Cox. As a management team, M-1 Global also controlled the business dealings of Fedor Emelianenko, who was considered the world's greatest heavyweight. After turning down a lucrative offer for Emelianenko to fight in the UFC, M-1 had instead decided to start its own North American fight promotion using Emelianenko as its poster boy.

As the new executive of strategic planning for the channel, I had been the one to bring the two groups together when TFN expressed interest in airing M-1 events. However, one of my bosses turned the entire point of the meeting around and asked M-1 to invest in the network.

Oh my God, I thought, as I sat there listening. *I gave up doing what I loved for this?* It wasn't a promising start to the next chapter in my MMA career.

A week later, Elaine and I flew to Montreal for my debut as a cageside commentator at TKO 31 at the Centre Bell. Elaine was excited for me, but I was completely clueless about commentating. I'd been interviewed about the sport countless times over the years, but this was different and I felt like I was being thrown to the wolves.

Sitting on the other side of the chain-link fence felt foreign. I wanted to be the guy on the inside making the decisions, but it wasn't what I'd been hired for. I certainly wasn't what you'd call a natural in this new role, and I felt unprepared. Still, I figured I would work, try to get better, and be the best I could be at it.

My broadcast partner, Mauro Ranallo, on the other hand, was a savant at spewing out rapid-fire descriptions that made sense. From the start, Ranallo and TFN executives were encouraging, though I look back now and know I was horrible that first night. Ranallo helpfully told me how to follow his setups and play-by-play analyses.

In the end it was a fun night, but I had a long way to go.

As I moved from commentating duties to shooting promos in the studio, I realized just how hard my new role would be. If you watch TV broadcasts, the announcers have teleprompter screens displaying their scripts, but a start-up company like TFN didn't have a teleprompter. It was no bother for Ranallo, who could study his script in hand for less than a minute, then jump in front of the camera without looking down at his notes once. For me, though, it was one of those "You expect me to do that?" moments.

If I'm being asked questions about something I know well, that's simple. But when I stood there with someone feeding me lines I'd never say, I realized I was in the wrong world.

I also understood that I'd been hired for my notoriety in the sport and that a big facet of my job would be to promote the channel. However, I didn't care much for the spotlight at all.

I'd never refereed because I wanted people to see me, and I'd never fancied myself a commentator or on-camera talent. You have to love what you're doing to be good at it. That's where I got it wrong.

My former life as a referee and my new one as an on-air analyst became muddled fairly quickly. I knew TFN had hired me for my officiating and general historical knowledge of the sport, and questions pertaining to this would usually be directed my way. This I expected with the job. What I never anticipated was that the channel would use my expertise as a bargaining chip.

In March, ProElite, another start-up company that began promoting its EliteXC events on Showtime in 2007, approached me to referee its next main event featuring Kevin "Kimbo Slice" Ferguson against British fighter James Thompson that May in New Jersey. What was special about this show was that it was going to be the first live MMA event on a major broadcast network, airing on CBS.

One TFN executive wanted me to do it to push the channel, as if I could wear the network's logo on my referee shirt. Of course, this was a ridiculous notion. I was no longer a referee and knew jumping between officiating and broadcasting would be a conflict of interest. In fact, when I'd previously let the Nevada State Athletic Commission know of my career change, they'd pointed this out to me. I told ProElite I appreciated the opportunity but wouldn't take the assignment.

The Fight Network came up with other ways to use my visibility. In April, the channel ran a contest where the winner would get two front row seats with me at UFC 83 in Montreal.

It was an odd situation because the UFC wasn't on good terms with The Fight Network, as the channel had aired the ending of the Randy Couture–Gabriel Gonzaga headliner at UFC 74 without Zuffa's permission.[14] When Zuffa found out, it pulled all of TFN's press credentials and access to its events.

Even though this had happened before I'd joined TFN, I spoke to Dana to see if he'd reinstate them. I knew the chances were slim. Zuffa took this kind of thing seriously, as they should. A Zuffa employee even asked why I'd gone to work for "scumbags," saying that what TFN had done was like going into his house and raping his wife.

I told the TFN executives they needed to meet with Zuffa in person and apologize for the error. However, TFN didn't take it seriously, and in the end it cost them big-time. Unable to secure press access to UFC 83, TFN tried to sneak into the event by renting the sports bar inside the Bell Centre, where Ranallo, Randy Couture (who'd been hired by TFN before me), and I hosted our prefight and postfight shows.

After the preshow, I met the contest winner and his girlfriend so we could all watch the main card together. I immediately felt bad for this nice couple, as our seats turned out to be about fifty rows up—the lousiest view I've ever had for an MMA event. The worst thing about it was that fans kept approaching me for autographs during the fights. It got so bad that the venue posted security

14. The UFC regularly released footage to media outlets the night of the fights, but that footage never contained the main event's outcome, ensuring pay-per-view sales through replays.

guards at each end of my row. When each fight ended, the guards would let the fans into our row, and I stood there taking pictures the entire time. I felt bad for everyone sitting behind us, but I felt even worse for the couple. They were good sports for sure.

Besides promotional events like these, a couple media tours, one weekly appearance on the network's radio show with Ranallo, and some radio interviews on other stations to promote the network, I wasn't given much more to do during my employment with TFN.

I guess the silver lining was that I had more time to develop and refine the curriculum for COMMAND. I pored over fight footage, jotted notes, and continued to add to my PowerPoint presentation. Elaine and I began to host the three-day courses at our own gym, and I was surprised and grateful each time they'd fill up with eager students.

PHOTO BY LORETTA HUNT

Graduation day for my son Ron from the Los Angeles County Sheriff's Department: three generations of law enforcement

I also got to spend more time with my family. My two eldest children were now out of high school, and I proudly watched my son Ron graduate with the Los Angeles County Sheriff's Department Class 370 that April.

Still, this wasn't what I'd signed up for with TFN. I'd taken the job partly because TFN had reminded me of ESPN when it had first launched, and we all saw what ESPN had grown into. Though I wasn't a fan of professional wrestling, I thought the idea of a twenty-four-hour combat sports network was a good one.

My greatest concern was that TFN wouldn't have enough work for me, and I knew I needed to stay busy. I'd opened the gym, but that was now up and running on its own, so I could commit the time to the channel. I offered to go up to the Toronto headquarters anytime they needed me, but I was assured there would be plenty for me to do in the States.

Instead, I sat around my office and kept calling to see if anything was happening. I was always told there was a lot coming up or the plans to create a satellite studio in California were moving forward or the channel was just about to break into the United States market, so I waited.

I wanted TFN to succeed, but I couldn't do much from my gym in Valencia. I started to get the impression that they didn't have the money to move into the next phase of expansion I'd been brought on to be a part of.

I didn't like sitting around doing nothing. If you told me I could either have all the money I need for the rest of my life and not work, or work for the rest of my life and earn enough to make ends meet, I'd take the latter. I know that may seem crazy, but I honestly believe staying busy helps in keeping you productive and alive. I see people who retire and stop doing everything, and they just dry up and die. I had to stay busy.

Although TFN continued to underutilize me, there was plenty of activity in the rest of the fight community. With the success of *The Ultimate Fighter* and the UFC's rising popularity, I was approached by a couple of fledgling fight promotions interested in hiring me. One of them was going to be started by Affliction Clothing, a trendy designer brand that had sponsored many fighters, rock stars, and other sports figures with much success. Affliction had had a falling out with Zuffa over its sponsorship deal, so Affliction had decided to promote its own events and offered me the position of president of Affliction Entertainment.

It was a phenomenal offer with an incredible salary, but in the end I just didn't believe the business plan was well thought out, so I didn't accept.

However, this led to conversations between the new promotion and TFN, and by July the network had exclusive Canadian rights to air Affliction's first event from Anaheim, California. As part of the deal, I was loaned out to Affliction as its color commentator alongside NFL reporter and TV host Jay Glazer and former UFC fighter Frank Trigg. Along with color commentary, I was asked to do the in-ring interviews with the night's winners after their bouts.

Affliction "Banned" was a grandiose pay-per-view event with an astronomical $3 million dollar–plus fighter payroll to match.[15] In the main event, Emelianenko swarmed former UFC heavyweight champion Tim Sylvia with punches and submitted his much larger opponent in only thirty-six seconds.

After the quick finish, I found myself where I usually am at these events, standing between two fighters—except this time I had a microphone in my hand. Randy Couture, who'd announced his resignation from the UFC months before in order to pursue a

---

15. Though Affliction's cards were stacked, paying the fighters this much wasn't sustainable. The promotion would do one more show and cancel a third just days before.

bout with Emelianenko, had stepped into the ring for a brief, respectful exchange with him. At the time, this was the biggest fight that could happen in the sport, so having these two standing next to one another blew the top off the Honda Center that night.

Though my job description in the sport had changed dramatically, I was still being asked to participate in some athletic commission functions. Prior to "Banned," members of the Association of Boxing Commissions had invited me to be a part of a committee that would review and propose revisions to the existing MMA regulations. The committee presented its findings two weeks before the Affliction show at the annual ABC meeting in Montreal. Part of that presentation had included the introduction of additional weight divisions outside of the eight already widely utilized, which the ABC members voted on and passed by majority.

UFC President Dana White came out shortly after the vote and said his organization wouldn't acknowledge the additional weight classes. He also pointed to me as the author of the controversial amendment, saying I was trying to change the rules of the sport.

In reality, my name had appeared on the revised MMA guidelines packet along with other names, but I wasn't the one who'd written in that particular amendment.

In fact, I was in agreement with Dana. I thought adding more weight divisions would dilute the sport, as I thought it had in boxing. During the committee's review period, I'd suggested only one additional weight class, between light heavyweight and heavyweight. I felt the disparity between the two divisions left fighters who weighed 220 to 230 pounds in a quandary. They had to either gain weight to keep up with some of the bigger behemoths or cut sometimes unrealistic amounts to get under 205 for the light heavyweight class. I suggested a cruiserweight division, or whatever they wanted to call it, for fighters weighing 205 to 230 pounds, and then heavyweight could be limited to 231 to 265 pounds.

No athletic commission would ever consider putting 145-pound champion José Aldo against 205-pound champion Jon Jones, but that was basically what they were doing when they matched someone like Randy Couture against Brock Lesnar, because the weight differential was the same. When you know a fighter like Lesnar weighs in at 265 pounds but by fight night is up to somewhere about 285 pounds, while Couture remains the same 220 pounds he weighed in at the day before, we're talking a 65-pound difference.

I'd voiced my concerns to the other committee members about the other proposed weight classes I'd thought were unnecessary, but it was decided that the amendment for six additional weight divisions would stay in and be presented for a vote anyway.

After Dana came out at a press conference basically blaming me for these rule changes, I probably could have offered this information to clear things up. However, that would have meant throwing some committee members under the bus, and I didn't feel that would be in anyone's best interest.

Publicly, this is where people say things got uncomfortable between me and the UFC. Honestly, though, my relationship with Dana and the UFC had begun to unravel some months before.

As I mentioned, TFN booked me for many radio interviews to promote the channel. During one of those interviews for a Toronto radio station, one of the three hosts started talking about the UFC when Zuffa took it over from SEG. The radio host described how

Dana White bought this "diamond in the rough," ran toward regulation with the state athletic commissions, and changed the rules to make the sport safe.

Some MMA websites called this version of MMA's history the "Zuffa Myth." It really wasn't a myth but a shortened version of what had transpired over time. When Zuffa bought the company, they did run toward regulation, just as they were stating. The problem was that major media outlets only heard this part of the story and didn't investigate things any further. If they had, they would have seen that the UFC's previous owners had begun working with athletic commissions since UFC 15.

It's a fact that the UFC and MMA were first regulated in Mississippi back at UFC 15, long before Zuffa or Dana White owned the promotion. I told the host that UFC 16 and 17 had been sanctioned and regulated by state athletic commissions and that UFC 28 had been sanctioned by Larry Hazzard and the New Jersey State Athletic Control Board in 2000. Again, all of this happened before Zuffa bought the UFC and was the result of the concerted effort of many people behind the scenes who cared very much for the sport.

I then explained how the rules of the sport had evolved over the years and that finally in April of 2001 the NJSACB had brought together many promoters, including Dana White, Lorenzo Fertitta, Paul Smith of the IFC, Marc Ratner of the NSAC, and representatives from Japan's Dream Stage Entertainment (which promoted Pride Fighting Championships), to write down a set of regulations everyone could use.

"This is not what Dana says," the radio host repeatedly stated throughout my tutorial.

I guess I could have backed down and not bitten, but I'd finally had enough and said, "Well, if that's what Dana's telling you, then Dana is lying to you."

It was stupid of me to say it that way and to fall into the trap the radio host was hoping I would. I didn't think Dana was lying about anything. He'd just quickly abbreviated everything into one statement, and they'd taken it as fact.

The news got back to Zuffa fast. About two weeks later, I received a phone call from the UFC's majority owner, Lorenzo Fertitta, who asked me about the interview. I told him what was said and that the radio host was trying to say things that weren't true. I told him I gave them the facts and that if people asked me about the sport or the UFC, I'd always tell the truth, plain and simple. I didn't tell Lorenzo this in an adversarial manner; I had and still have enormous respect for him as a businessman and a person. I simply wasn't going to condense, alter, or cover up the sport's true history.

After that conversation, I knew my relationship with the UFC had changed forever. I was raised to hit back harder when someone hit me. It might be a great way for a kid or for an adult destined for jail to handle things, but the civilized world is made up of much smarter people than me.

When the UFC pulled away from me, one of the smarter people who tried to advise me was Marc Ratner, who'd retired from the Nevada State Athletic Commission and taken a job as Zuffa's vice president of regulatory affairs. I've always admired and respected Marc as an even-tempered man able to complete just about any task because of how smart he is. I appreciated that Marc never gave up on me.

Corey Schafer, who heads up an MMA and kickboxing sanctioning body called the ISKA, is another one of those guys who's smarter than me. Corey showed me that just because someone says something about you doesn't mean you have to react immediately. He taught me to be smart and look at what I'd done that could have brought about this response, analyze it, and then figure out how to make it right for everyone. I have to admit I'm still working on it, but I hope to someday live up to Corey's example.

It's taken me a long time to be able to say this, but I now take full responsibility for what happened between me and Zuffa.

●

Being an analyst for TFN wasn't easy for me. After every questionable referee stoppage or judges' decision, my phone would ring off the hook with reporters looking for comments. As a referee, I'd tried not to speak judgmentally about my colleagues. But I wasn't a referee anymore. I was hired and paid to give my opinions and impressions and was expected to do my job. Doing this without upsetting some people proved difficult.

I also figured that if I spoke truthfully, maybe it would improve things. But when I suggested that some officials were being assigned to MMA events they were vastly under-qualified for, it alienated me with a few athletic commissions.

My time away from refereeing was probably one of the harder periods of my life. I'd cut something out that I'd really enjoyed and taken pride in. I would sit at home and watch events and get angry when a referee would get a call wrong or not remember a rule correctly.

In the fall of 2009, I started to think about returning to refereeing.

Then I began to talk to Elaine about it. I knew it wouldn't be easy to return, but the more I thought about it, the more I felt it was where I truly belonged.

The Fight Network made it a much easier decision for me in the end. The channel went through a drastic change in leadership, and its cash flow issues only mounted. My paychecks were delayed, then stopped coming altogether. In October of 2009, I resigned from the company.

I owe a debt of gratitude to the California State Athletic Commission for taking me back into the fold as quickly as they did. My return engagement to the cage came at Strikeforce "Destruction" on November 21, 2008, at the HP Pavilion in San Jose, California.

I don't mean to sound cliché, but it felt like I'd never left. The other referees, judges, and backstage officials all welcomed me back with enthusiasm as I went about my regular routine that night before the fights started. Everyone seemed genuinely happy to have me around again, which was a good feeling.

Strikeforce was a Bay Area promotion that used a lot of local talent, so I didn't know every fighter. In the locker rooms, I took a knee to go over the rules with each fighter stretching and warming up on the mat. I tried to make them feel at ease, as I'd always done. If a fighter was nervous and made a joke, I'd come right back with humor. If he seemed a little in awe of the situation, I talked to him until I felt he'd absorbed the instructions.

Then I walked out into the arena and did my job. It wasn't different from the hundreds of nights I'd refereed before, except for one thing: after one of the bouts, as I went to raise the fighter's hand, he turned and gave me a big hug. It was totally unexpected.

I felt better already.

The welcome back I got in California wasn't felt everywhere. It became clear over the next few months that the UFC preferred I not referee at their events. When Zuffa took the show abroad and could bring along any officials it wanted, the UFC didn't call me, which was really no surprise.

There wasn't much I could do but be grateful for the assignments I did get and perform them as well as I could. Slowly but surely, I began to get calls from a number of jurisdictions new to the game. I found myself traveling to the Midwest, Canada, Brazil, Australia, and even China to referee MMA events of all sizes.

In February of 2009, Strikeforce, that local San Jose promotion that had put on only five or six events a year, signed into a multi-year broadcast deal with Showtime to put on three times as many shows. This made them the closest thing the UFC had to a competitor, and Strikeforce CEO Scott Coker began to request me for his events with the commissions. I was grateful for Scott's belief in my talents.

By April, I was refereeing my first Strikeforce bout on Showtime. In November, I officiated the main event at Strikeforce/M-1 Global's "Fedor vs. Rogers" outside Chicago, which broadcasted live on CBS.

This would be my second time refereeing one of Fedor Emelianenko's fights, something I probably wouldn't have been able to do had I stayed aligned with the UFC the way I had until 2007.

I've had the privilege of refereeing many of the greats in MMA. I've admired the way fighters like Randy Couture, Chuck Liddell, Georges St. Pierre, B. J. Penn, and Anderson Silva have handled themselves in and out of the cage. For them, it isn't about anger or ego. It's about competition. No one can go out there and perform well 100 percent of the time, but these guys are all consistent.

Fedor Emelianenko is another fighter I admire. If you're a boxing referee, you want to say you got to do a Muhammad Ali fight. The equivalent in MMA would be Emelianenko.

During my one-year retirement, I'd actually had the opportunity to grapple with Emelianenko as part of a demonstration for National Geographic Channel's *Fight Science* series. Scientists wanted to test the fighter's choking force compared to that of a hungry Burmese python. Before Emelianenko squeezed the test dummy's neck against his forearm, he got to demonstrate the move on *this dummy* for the cameras.

I'd watched Emelianenko establish himself as one of the greatest fighters of the modern era, so I knew there had to be something special about him. With some of the submissions he pulled off, I figured he had to be really strong. And I don't mean in terms of what he could bench-press; I mean brute strength.

We didn't roll hard. When I grabbed him, he went to move his wrist and I felt like I could hold on to it if I wanted to. But it was quickly clear that Emelianenko's advantage wasn't about strength. He's super fast—especially for a heavyweight—and explodes into the movement. Eventually he catches you in a mistake and gets you where he wants you. I'm just glad what we did was for fun, because truly fighting Fedor Emelianenko would've been far from what I'd call enjoyable.

STRIKEFORCE

"Nashville"
April 17, 2010
Bridgestone Arena
Nashville, Tennessee

Bouts I Reffed:
Dan Henderson vs. Jake Shields
Zach Underwood vs. Hunter Worsham
Gegard Mousasi vs. Muhammed Lawal

I knew time had truly flown when I found myself refereeing the son of a fighter I'd officiated for fifteen years prior. It wouldn't be the last time I'd referee for a father and his son, either.

History was doomed to repeat itself when an in-cage altercation broke out between Jason "Mayhem" Miller and Jake Shields' team after the main event on CBS. Miller entered the cage on his own and pushed Shields to try and ignite a rematch, but teammates Nate and Nick Diaz, Gil Melendez, and others jumped in and fists started flying. We managed to break it up, but it came at a price—CBS wouldn't broadcast another Strikeforce event after that.

Because Emelianenko had turned down a UFC contract and fought in the smaller rival Strikeforce promotion instead, I would get to referee three of his fights in the United States. I was inches away when he tapped out to Brazilian jiu-jitsu black belt Fabricio Werdum's armbar-triangle choke combination at Strikeforce "Fedor vs. Werdum," on June 26, 2010, at the HP Pavilion in San Jose, California. It was Emelianenko's first loss in twenty-nine fights and nearly a decade, and he handled it with such professionalism and grace.

I never care which fighter wins. However, I can't help but have a lot of admiration for many of them, Emelianenko included.

That July, I was surprised when I got the call from George Dodd, the new executive officer of the California State Athletic Commission.

After meeting George and seeing where he came from, I knew he was an honest man, and I told him that I'd always be up-front with him. George asked why he was being told that I'd said negative things about the UFC and had a grudge against them. I told him about the interview and encouraged him to listen to it himself and make up his own mind about it.

Shortly after, he gave me an assignment to officiate the UFC's second live event for the Versus channel on August 1, 2010, in San Diego. A few UFCs had come and gone in California since I'd returned to officiating, and I hadn't been assigned to any of them under the previous executive officer's command. I assumed I'd never referee a UFC event in my home state again.

It had been nearly three years since I'd stepped into the Octagon, and some MMA media had made noise about why it had taken so long. After all this time, I tried to think it wasn't a big deal to be returning. However, Elaine's mind raced that this might be a first step toward some kind of reconciliation. I didn't think that would be the case at all. I knew I wasn't wanted by the people who are most important within the Zuffa headquarters: Lorenzo and Dana. I wasn't completely sure about Lorenzo, but one of the best things about Dana is that he has no problem saying how he feels, and he had said enough for me to know I wouldn't be a welcome addition.

At the show, I went about my normal business. It was great to see some of the UFC employees I hadn't spoken to in a while, including event coordinator Burt Watson.

On one of my walks from the locker rooms back to the arena floor, I passed Dana in the hallway. He hadn't spoken kindly of me publicly the last few years, and now he was standing right in front of me. Before he could say anything, I said, "Dana, thank you for everything you've done for the sport and for me in the past. It didn't go unnoticed. I just wanted to tell you that."

I shook his hand as he said, "Thank you," and I continued on my way to sit cageside with the other commission employees.

I can positively say my brief exchange with Dana wasn't planned and was absolutely sincere. Whatever there was between Dana and me didn't change the fact that he, Lorenzo and Frank Fertitta, and Zuffa's dedicated staff had an immense hand in saving MMA from extinction.

Maybe I'd thought this could be the last time I'd speak to Dana, and I wanted him to know I'd never stopped being grateful.

One of the frequently asked questions I get nowadays is "Do you have any hard feelings toward the UFC?"

The truthful answer is I never have. I spent many years trying to get people to understand the UFC and mixed martial arts

STRIKEFORCE

"Henderson vs. Babalu 2"
December 4, 2010
Scottrade Center
St. Louis, Missouri

Bouts I Reffed:
Justin Lawrence vs. Max Martyniouk
Antonio Silva vs. Mike Kyle
Paul Daley vs. Scott Smith
Renato "Babalu" Sobral vs. Dan Henderson

It was a night of devastation—the last three main card bouts ended with first-round knockouts, something rare for a big event.

In the main event, Henderson connected with his big right hand. Sobral shot for a takedown on the two-time Olympic wrestler. When that failed, Sobral pulled Henderson into his guard. When Henderson landed another big punch, Sobral was struggling to stay in it, but I knew he was done. It was one of those fights I wanted to stop right then, but I had to let it play out. Henderson landed another punch, and it was all over.

for the competition it is. When everyone said the UFC was going to die, I fought to keep interest alive. When everyone told me to leave the organization I believed in, I stayed.

I never owned any part of the UFC, but I always felt like I was a part of it. Eventually that feeling kind of went away. Was that my own fault? Maybe.

I made the decision to leave on my own. Zuffa stayed loyal to me the whole time, though back then I thought Lorenzo and Dana wouldn't be able to back me up forever.

I read the crystal ball wrong. I made the wrong call.

Sometimes you have to gamble big to understand the game. My big payoff out of all of this was wisdom, and you know what? That's okay. I figured out what really counts.

What makes life great is the experiences you have. Usually they involve other people, and the memories can never be taken away. I always say if you can count your real friends on one hand, you're doing pretty good.

When you're young, everything is about what you have. When you get older and realize what's important, everything is about what you do and how you do it.

There was a time when I did everything in my power to be at every UFC because I thought it was that important. I can admit now that sometimes my priorities were screwed up.

I missed many things I should have been at. I left my family in the middle of a vacation because I was asked to be at a commission meeting to help get MMA regulated. I missed my son's high school graduation because I felt like I needed to be at a UFC. I felt like I owed the UFC, Zuffa, and Dana.

I used to think the greatest compliment I could receive was from the fighters when they'd say, "I've waited my whole career to have you referee my fight," or when they specifically requested me as their referee. But more than any affirmations I could get from any fighter, more than any rules I wrote or any historic bouts I got to officiate, the greatest accomplishment in my life is my family.

I'm overjoyed that my sons, Ron and Johnny, are the honorable people they are and that my daughter is trying to do good things with her life in the military. I have a wonderful wife who cares about me—not about what we have or where we're going next. She just wants to be together. That's what counts.

In the last few years, Zuffa has taken the UFC to heights I wouldn't have dreamed possible. In March of 2011, they purchased their closest rival, Strikeforce, uniting 90 percent of the world's greatest MMA talent under one roof. As they predicted they would, they have truly become the league of the sport.

In the last couple years, I've refereed over 1,000 fights, twice as many as I had from the beginning of my career in 1994 until I retired in 2007. I don't officiate every big fight anymore, but I've gotten to see something better in a way. I've observed the sport's grassroots movement firsthand, and I know MMA is not only going to survive; it's going to flourish, expand, and become one of the biggest sports in the world.

Dear Mr. McCarthy,

    My name is Adam _____. I am 11 years old. I am a second degree black belt in Kempo Karate. The UFC is my favorite sport. I watch it every chance I can. I hope to one day become an MMA fighter in the UFC. Reffing must be tough. I am happy that we have good refs for the UFC. You are my favorite referee and I would be so happy if I could have your autograph. It would be the coolest thing ever. Unfortunately, I have nothing to send to you but this index card, but I am still happy.

                Sincerely,

               Adam

Fan letters like this always put a smile on my face.

It's a great thing to see a promotion providing a positive environment for new fighters and putting out a strong product for the fans. It's also exciting to see kids that I know will make it.

On the other hand, I've watched a referee make a bad call or seen judges give a win to the wrong guy, breaking the spirit of a kid who should have won but will never fight again. That's the kind of thing I'm trying to keep from happening.

When commissions asked me to come and teach other referees back in 2004, I resisted, thinking, *Why would I teach your guys to take my job?*

I quickly realized I was being shortsighted. They weren't going to take my job, and if I didn't referee every big fight, it wasn't the end of the world. It was right to share what I'd been privileged enough to learn along the way.

My three-day COMMAND courses have evolved so much over the last few years. At first, I know I crammed too much information in for anyone to retain it all, but I learned to manage time and focus on the crucial information. In turn, I know I'm now a better referee than I ever was before, because I'm drilling the important information into my students, which also drills it into me. I'm proud of the fact that many of my students have gone on to work major MMA shows, including for the UFC, Strikeforce, WEC, and others.

Now I'm working at having instructors available to teach classes all over the world. My main goal is to have the same information being communicated to every MMA official everywhere. Every time I teach now, I bring along another instructor, Jerin Valel, who completed both my referee and judging courses by March of 2009.

Valel, a Brazilian jiu-jitsu brown belt, had already been licensed as a referee in the Canadian province Manitoba with over 100 bouts under his belt, but he sought out the courses to improve. I could tell Valel was an exceptional student because of the questions he asked in class, so when he called me a few months later to ask how he could become a certified instructor, I listened.

Valel spent the next sixteen months traveling from Manitoba to Valencia on his own dime and earned the teaching certification in August of 2010. He referees in his province and has made it onto some of the bigger shows throughout Canada. He's a phenomenal representative for COMMAND and also for the future of officiating in MMA.

It would be easy to say my life would have been easier if I hadn't left refereeing and essentially the UFC, but I know I would have missed other opportunities. COMMAND continues to grow, and our gym has expanded to 28,500 square feet, which makes it one of the largest mixed martial arts facilities in the country.

My eldest son, Ron, became a judge for California's growing

amateur MMA program in 2009. In 2011, we sat side by side to officiate a Strikeforce event together.

I'm closer to my father and mother than I've ever been in my life. And I'll become a grandfather myself this October.

In life, I've taken chances, then faced what happens next. I do sort of live by the words I preach: Let's get it on. Opportunities abound if you're open enough to notice and go for them.

PHOTO BY PATRICK SEAN KENNEDY

Officiating a fight with my eldest son, Ron, at a Strikeforce event (January 2011)

It's been a long journey since the beginning. I have many things I'm proud of and some things I wish I could change, but that's exactly what life is all about. We have highs, and we have lows. I've told everyone over the last eighteen years that I'm a lucky man, and I couldn't have had a more exciting or fulfilling life thus far.

The one thing I want everyone to remember in the end is that all the things I've shared with you in this book involved people who were brave enough to take a chance.

When I talk with people about certain fighters or other figures in the sport, I'm sometimes taken aback by statements that someone should have done something better or differently. I always remember that hindsight is twenty-twenty. You will always have a clearer picture of how something should have been done once you have the entire story, but that's not the way life works.

PHOTO BY LORETTA HUNT

Life is about experiences and family: at my daughter Brit's graduation with Elaine, my father, and his wife, Sandra

I always give credit to the doers of this world, the people who took a chance and strove for greatness. Sometimes it's a fighter, but many times it's just the average person who simply believes and takes that first step toward something greater. Everyone has it inside of them; you just have to believe it.

For this book's last call, I give you my favorite quote of all time. This is for everyone who's taken a chance, faced both victory and defeat, and continued to move forward—because you will never know until you try.

It is not the critic who counts; not the man who points out how the strong man stumbles, or where the doer of deeds could have done them better. The credit belongs to the man who is actually in the arena, whose face is marred by dust and sweat and blood; who strives valiantly; who errs, who comes short again and again, because there is no effort without error and shortcoming; but who does actually strive to do the deeds; who knows great enthusiasms, the great devotions; who spends himself in a worthy cause; who at the best knows in the end the triumph of high achievement, and who at the worst, if he fails, at least fails while daring greatly, so that his place shall never be with those cold and timid souls who know neither victory nor defeat.

—Theodore Roosevelt

ACKNOWLEDGMENTS

I would like to acknowledge the following people:

Scott Massey, for being passionate and believing in a rockhead who thought he was smarter than you back then. You were a great coach, person, and friend, and I am sorry I didn't say this to you when I should have.

Jeff Blatnick, who came into our sport with an open mind and was always willing to learn and help. You did much more than most people realize, and you will always be someone I respect and am proud to call my friend.

Chris and Denise, the best of what has come into the second part of my life. Chris, you can accomplish anything, and you have already proved it. Denise, thank you for being a savior. You are relied upon, and you come through every day.

Brian, Felicia, Mike, Majeed, Lou, and all my instructors. Thank you for making BJMUTA what it is, a special place with special people who work hard to make other people's lives better.

—"Big" John McCarthy

●

The authors would also like to express our gratitude to Rose Gracie, the team at Medallion Press, including Adam Mock, Heather Musick, Paul Ohlson, Jim Tampa, Brigitte Shepard, and Michal Wlos, as well as Jen Wisnowski from Independent Publishers Group. A special thank-you goes to our editor Emily Steele, whose commitment and gentle touch were appreciated every step of the way. Thank you all for giving us the freedom to make our vision a reality.

And to our agent Margaret O'Connor, who found this book its perfect home and supported us through the process to the finish line.

●

John, thank you for your trust, patience, bravery and willingness to share history with the world.

For Joe Hall, Brian Knapp, and Mike Fridley, who made all the difference.

For my husband, Shane, my Irish saint. You are my one and only.

—Loretta Hunt

MEDALLION
P R E S S

Be in the know on the latest
Medallion Press news by becoming a
Medallion Press Insider!

As an Insider you'll receive:

· Our FREE expanded monthly newsletter, giving you more insight
into Medallion Press

· Advanced press releases and breaking news

· Greater access to all your favorite Medallion authors

Joining is easy. Just visit our website at
www.medallionpress.com and click on the Medallion Press
Insider tab.

medallionpress.com

MEDALLION